Flash™ 5

- In an Instant -

by Michael Toot and Sherry Willard Kinkoph

Visual™

From
maranGraphics®

&

Hungry Minds™

Best-Selling Books • Digital Downloads • e-Books • Answer Networks •
e-Newsletters • Branded Web Sites • e-Learning

New York, NY • Cleveland, OH • Indianapolis, IN

Flash™ 5 In an Instant

Published by
Hungry Minds, Inc.
909 Third Avenue
New York, NY 10022
www.hungryminds.com

maranGraphics, Inc.
5755 Coopers Avenue
Mississauga, Ontario, Canada L4Z 1R9
Library of Congress Control Number: 2001091864
ISBN: 0-7645-3624-9
Printed in the United States of America
10 9 8 7 6 5 4 3 2 1
1B/TQ/QX/QR/IN
Distributed in the United States by Hungry Minds, Inc.

Distributed by CDG Books Canada Inc. for Canada; by Transworld Publishers Limited in the United Kingdom; by IDG Norge Books for Norway; by IDG Sweden Books for Sweden; by IDG Books Australia Publishing Corporation Pty. Ltd. for Australia and New Zealand; by TransQuest Publishers Pte Ltd. for Singapore, Malaysia, Thailand, Indonesia, and Hong Kong; by Gotop Information Inc. for Taiwan; by ICG Muse, Inc. for Japan; by Intersoft for South Africa; by Eyrolles for France; by International Thomson Publishing for Germany, Austria, and Switzerland; by Distribuidora Cuspide for Argentina; by LR International for Brazil; by Galileo Libros for Chile; by Ediciones ZETA S.C.R. Ltda. for Peru; by WS Computer Publishing Corporation, Inc., for the Philippines; by Contemporanea de Ediciones for Venezuela; by Express Computer Distributors for the Caribbean and West Indies; by Micronesia Media Distributor, Inc., for Micronesia; by Chips Computadoras S.A. de C.V. for Mexico; by Editorial Norma de Panama S.A. for Panama; by American Bookshops for Finland.

For corporate orders, please call maranGraphics at 800-469-6616 or fax 905-890-9434.

For general information on Hungry Minds' products and services, please contact our Customer Care Department within the U.S. at 800-762-2974, outside the U.S. at 317-572-3993, or fax 317-572-4002.

For sales inquiries and reseller information, including discounts, premium and bulk quantity sales, and foreign-language translations, please contact our Customer Care Department at 800-434-3422, fax 317-572-4002, or write to Hungry Minds, Inc., Attn: Customer Care Department, 10475 Crosspoint Boulevard, Indianapolis, IN 46256.
For information on licensing foreign or domestic rights, please contact our Sub-Rights Customer Care Department at 212-884-5000.
For information on using Hungry Minds' products and services in the classroom or for ordering examination copies, please contact our Educational Sales Department at 800-434-2086 or fax 317-572-4005.
For press review copies, author interviews, or other publicity information, please contact our Public Relations department at 317-572-3168 or fax 317-572-4168.

For authorization to photocopy items for corporate, personal, or educational use, please contact Copyright Clearance Center, 222 Rosewood Drive, Danvers, MA 01923, or fax 978-750-4470. Screen shots displayed in this book are based on pre-released software and are subject to change.

Trademark Acknowledgments

Permissions

Hungry Minds™ is a trademark of Hungry Minds, Inc.

U.S. Corporate Sales	U.S. Trade Sales
Contact maranGraphics at (800) 469-6616 or fax (905) 890-9434.	Contact Hungry Minds at (800) 434-3422 or fax (317) 572-4002.

Some comments from our readers...

"I have to praise you and your company on the fine products you turn out. I have twelve of the *Teach Yourself VISUALLY* and *Simplified* books in my house. They were instrumental in helping me pass a difficult computer course. Thank you for creating books that are easy to follow."

–Gordon Justin (Brielle, NJ)

"I commend your efforts and your success. I teach in an outreach program for the Dr. Eugene Clark Library in Lockhart, TX. Your *Teach Yourself VISUALLY* books are incredible and I use them in my computer classes. All my students love them!"

–Michele Schalin (Lockhart, TX)

"Thank you so much for helping people like me learn about computers. The Maran family is just what the doctor ordered. Thank you, thank you, thank you."

–Carol Moten (New Kensington, PA)

"I would like to take this time to compliment maranGraphics on creating such great books. Thank you for making it clear. Keep up the good work."

–Kirk Santoro (Burbank, CA)

"I write to extend my thanks and appreciation for your books. They are clear, easy to follow, and straight to the point. Keep up the good work!"

–Seward Kollie (Dakar, Senegal)

"What fantastic teaching books you have produced! Congratulations to you and your staff. You deserve the Nobel prize in Education in the Software category. Thanks for helping me to understand computers."

–Bruno Tonon (Melbourne, Australia)

"Over time, I have bought a number of your 'Read Less, Learn More' books. For me, they are THE way to learn anything easily."

–José A. Mazón (Cuba, NY)

"I was introduced to maranGraphics about four years ago and YOU ARE THE GREATEST THING THAT EVER HAPPENED TO INTRODUCTORY COMPUTER BOOKS!"

–Glenn Nettleton (Huntsville, AL)

"Compliments To The Chef!! Your books are extraordinary! Or, simply put, Extra-Ordinary, meaning way above the rest! THANK YOU THANK YOU THANK YOU! for creating these."

–Christine J. Manfrin (Castle Rock, CO)

"I'm a grandma who was pushed by an 11-year-old grandson to join the computer age. I found myself hopelessly confused and frustrated until I discovered the Visual series. I'm no expert by any means now, but I'm a lot further along than I would have been otherwise. Thank you!"

–Carol Louthain (Logansport, IN)

"Thank you, thank you, thank you...for making it so easy for me to break into this high-tech world. I now own four of your books. I recommend them to anyone who is a beginner like myself. Now... if you could just do one for programming VCRs, it would make my day!"

–Gay O'Donnell (Calgary, Alberta, Canada)

"You're marvelous! I am greatly in your debt."

–Patrick Baird (Lacey, WA)

maranGraphics is a family-run business
located near Toronto, Canada.

At *maranGraphics*, we believe in producing great computer books — one book at a time.

Each maranGraphics book uses the award-winning communication process that we have been developing over the last 25 years. Using this process, we organize screen shots and text in a way that makes it easy for you to learn new concepts and tasks.

We spend hours deciding the best way to perform each task, so you don't have to!

Our clear, easy-to-follow screen shots and instructions walk you through each task from beginning to end.

We want to thank you for purchasing what we feel are the best computer books money can buy. We hope you enjoy using this book as much as we enjoyed creating it!

Sincerely,

The Maran Family

Please visit us on the Web at:
www.maran.com

CREDITS

Major Contributors
Michael Toot,
Sherry Willard Kinkoph

Project Editor
Dana Rhodes Lesh

Acquisitions Editor
Jen Dorsey

Product Developmental Supervisor
Lindsay Sandman

Copy Editors
Tim Borek
Paula Lowell

Technical Editor
Kyle Bowen

Editorial Manager
Rev Mengle

Editorial Assistant
Amanda Foxworth

Book Design
maranGraphics®

Production Coordinator
Dale White

Layout
Joyce Haughey
LeAndra Johnson
Barry Offringa
Kendra Span
Erin Zeltner

Screen Artists
Ronda David-Burroughs
David E. Gregory
Mark Harris
Jill A. Proll

Proofreaders
David Faust
Mary Lagu

Indexer
Sharon Hilgenberg

Special Help
Maureen Spears

ACKNOWLEDGMENTS

Hungry Minds, Inc.: John Kilcullen, CEO; Bill Barry, President and COO; John Ball, Executive VP, Operations & Administration; John Harris, Executive VP and CFO

Hungry Minds Technology Publishing Group: Richard Swadley, Senior Vice President and Publisher; Mary Bednarek, Vice President and Publisher; Walter R. Bruce III, Vice President and Publisher; Joseph Wikert, Vice President and Publisher; Mary C. Corder, Editorial Director; Andy Cummings, Publishing Director, General User Group; Barry Pruett, Publishing Director, Visual Group

Hungry Minds Manufacturing: Ivor Parker, Vice President, Manufacturing

Hungry Minds Marketing: John Helmus, Assistant Vice President, Director of Marketing

Hungry Minds Production for Branded Press: Debbie Stailey, Production Director

Hungry Minds Sales: Michael Violano, Vice President, International Sales and Sub Rights

The publisher would like to give special thanks to Patrick J. McGovern, without whom this book would not have been possible.

TABLE OF CONTENTS

TABLE OF CONTENTS

OPEN A FLASH FILE

Flash files are called *documents* or *movies*. After you save a file, you can open it and work on it again. Use the Open dialog box to access Flash files you have saved.

OPEN A FLASH FILE

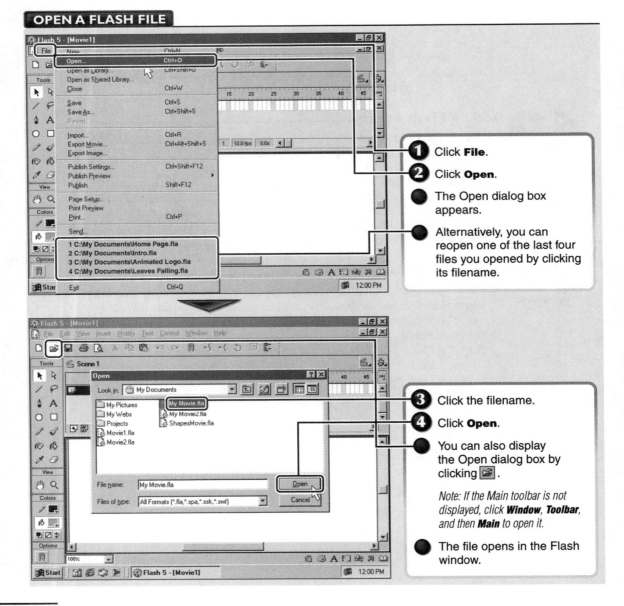

① Click **File**.

② Click **Open**.

● The Open dialog box appears.

● Alternatively, you can reopen one of the last four files you opened by clicking its filename.

③ Click the filename.

④ Click **Open**.

● You can also display the Open dialog box by clicking ⊞.

*Note: If the Main toolbar is not displayed, click **Window**, **Toolbar**, and then **Main** to open it.*

● The file opens in the Flash window.

START A NEW FLASH FILE

You can start a new Flash file at any time, even if you are currently working on another file.

START A NEW FLASH FILE

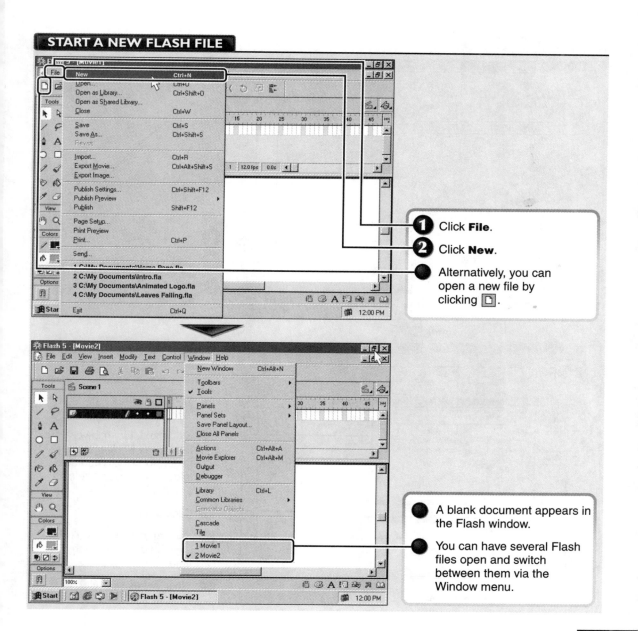

1 Click **File**.

2 Click **New**.

● Alternatively, you can open a new file by clicking 🗋.

● A blank document appears in the Flash window.

● You can have several Flash files open and switch between them via the Window menu.

3

SAVE A FLASH FILE

As you create movies in Flash, you
need to save them in order to work
on them again. FLA is the default file
format for Flash movies.

SAVE A FLASH FILE

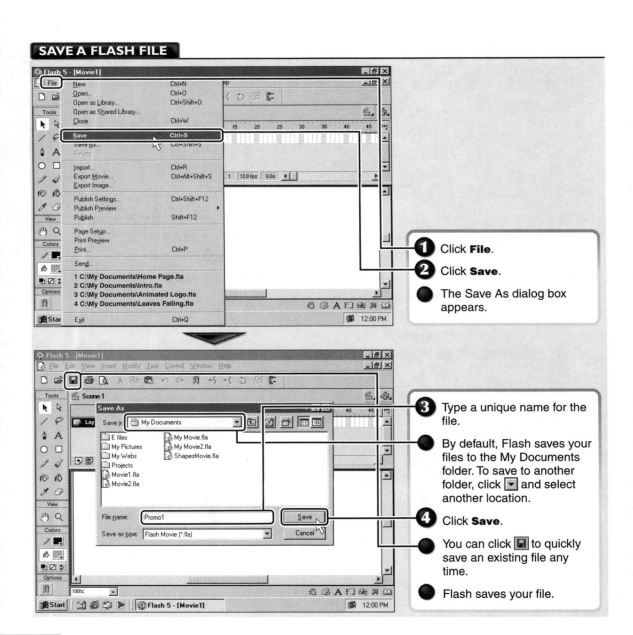

1 Click **File**.

2 Click **Save**.

● The Save As dialog box
appears.

3 Type a unique name for the
file.

● By default, Flash saves your
files to the My Documents
folder. To save to another
folder, click ▼ and select
another location.

4 Click **Save**.

● You can click 🔲 to quickly
save an existing file any
time.

● Flash saves your file.

CLOSE A FLASH FILE

You can close Flash files that you are no longer using to free up memory on your computer. Be sure to save your changes before closing a file.

CLOSE A FLASH FILE

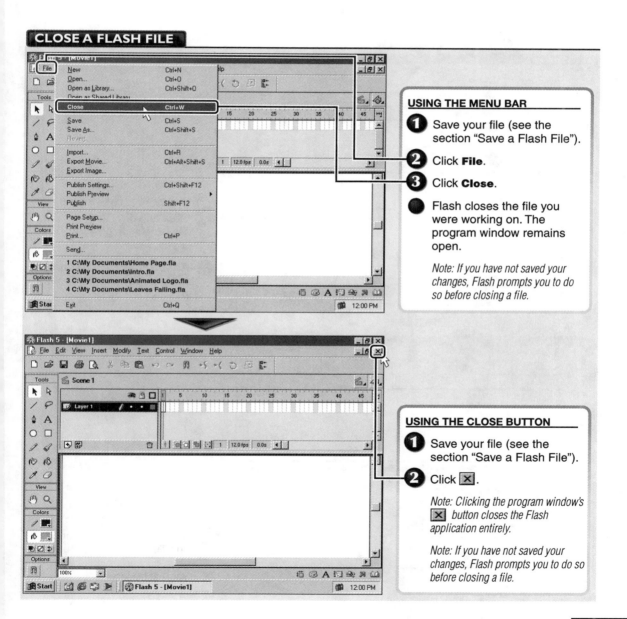

USING THE MENU BAR

1 Save your file (see the section "Save a Flash File").

2 Click **File**.

3 Click **Close**.

● Flash closes the file you were working on. The program window remains open.

Note: If you have not saved your changes, Flash prompts you to do so before closing a file.

USING THE CLOSE BUTTON

1 Save your file (see the section "Save a Flash File").

2 Click ☒.

Note: Clicking the program window's ☒ button closes the Flash application entirely.

Note: If you have not saved your changes, Flash prompts you to do so before closing a file.

MOVE AND DOCK THE TIMELINE WINDOW

You can move the Flash Timeline around
within the program window, or you can
dock it to any side of the window.

MOVE THE TIMELINE WINDOW

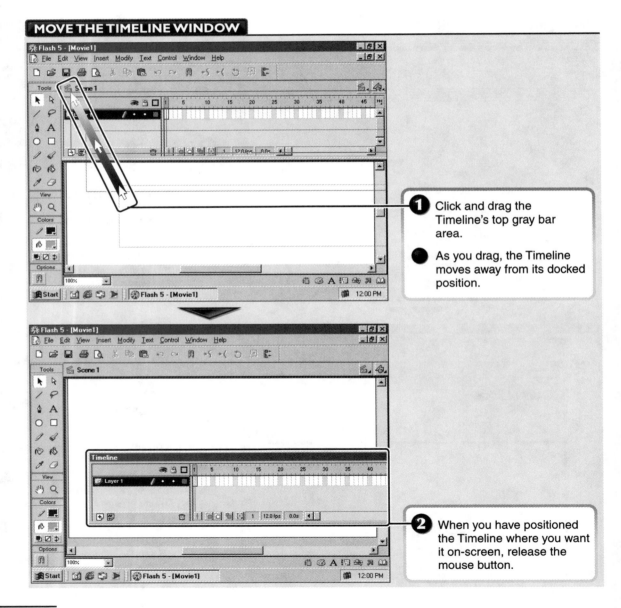

1 Click and drag the
Timeline's top gray bar
area.

● As you drag, the Timeline
moves away from its docked
position.

2 When you have positioned
the Timeline where you want
it on-screen, release the
mouse button.

in an *instant*

DOCK THE TIMELINE WINDOW

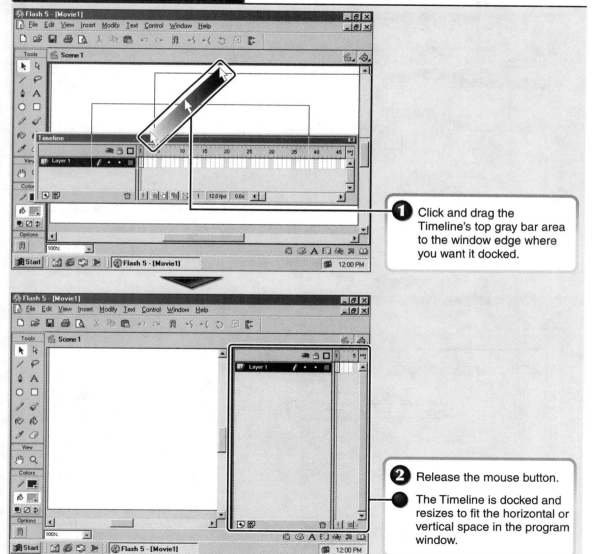

1 Click and drag the Timeline's top gray bar area to the window edge where you want it docked.

2 Release the mouse button.

The Timeline is docked and resizes to fit the horizontal or vertical space in the program window.

SET THE FLASH STAGE SIZE

The Stage is the on-screen area where you can view the contents of a frame and draw graphic objects. You can control the size and appearance of the Stage.

SET THE FLASH STAGE SIZE

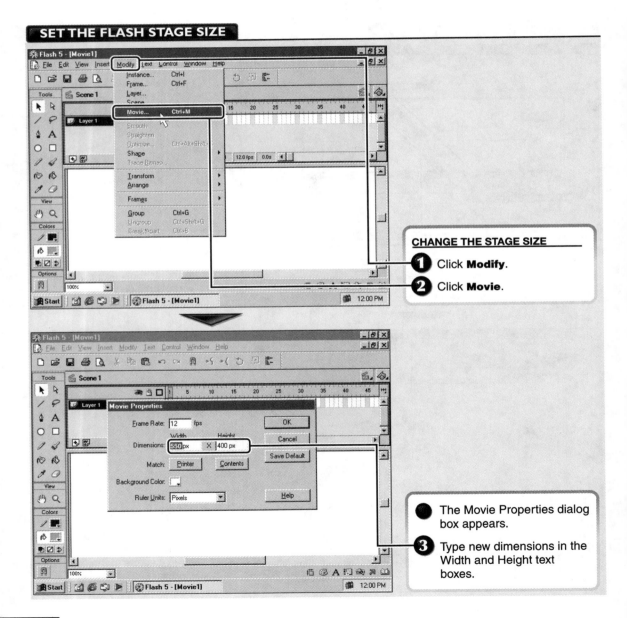

CHANGE THE STAGE SIZE

1 Click **Modify**.

2 Click **Movie**.

● The Movie Properties dialog box appears.

3 Type new dimensions in the Width and Height text boxes.

in an

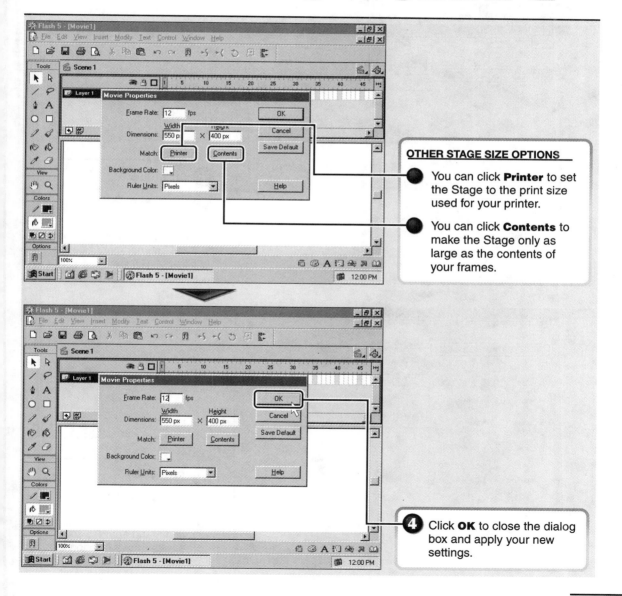

OTHER STAGE SIZE OPTIONS

● You can click **Printer** to set the Stage to the print size used for your printer.

● You can click **Contents** to make the Stage only as large as the contents of your frames.

4 Click **OK** to close the dialog box and apply your new settings.

9

ZOOM OUT OR IN

When working with various elements on the
Stage, you can zoom in or out for a better view.

ZOOM OUT OR IN

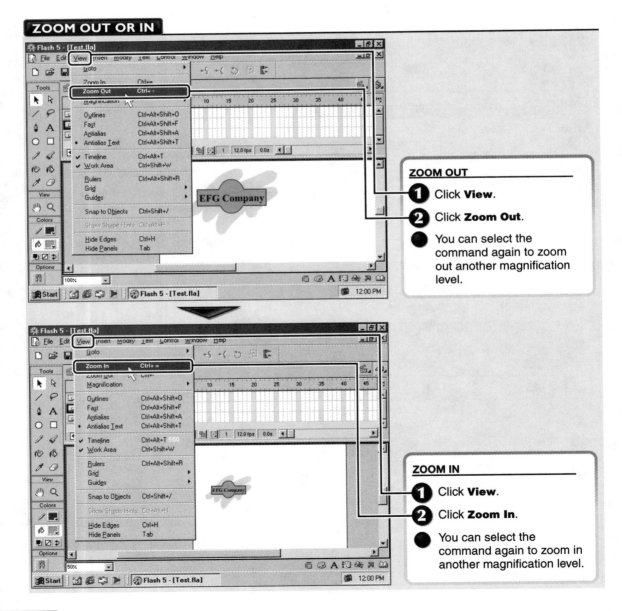

ZOOM OUT

1. Click **View**.

2. Click **Zoom Out**.

● You can select the command again to zoom out another magnification level.

ZOOM IN

1. Click **View**.

2. Click **Zoom In**.

● You can select the command again to zoom in another magnification level.

in an *instant*

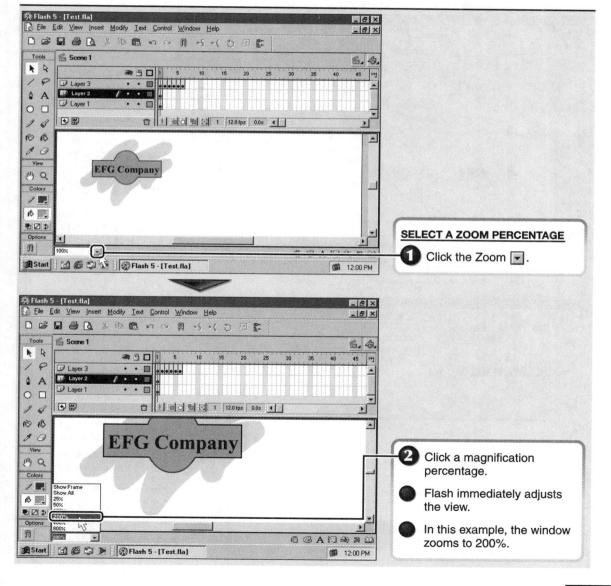

SELECT A ZOOM PERCENTAGE

1 Click the Zoom ▼.

2 Click a magnification percentage.

● Flash immediately adjusts the view.

● In this example, the window zooms to 200%.

11

WORK WITH FLASH TOOLBARS

The Flash toolbars have buttons for frequently used commands and features. You can hide or display toolbars as you need them, and they can be docked to one side of the screen or float as separate windows.

WORK WITH FLASH TOOLBARS

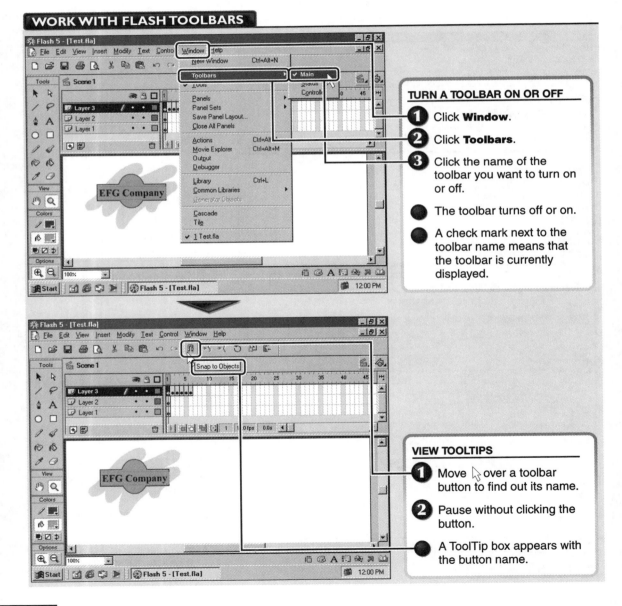

TURN A TOOLBAR ON OR OFF

1. Click **Window**.

2. Click **Toolbars**.

3. Click the name of the toolbar you want to turn on or off.

● The toolbar turns off or on.

● A check mark next to the toolbar name means that the toolbar is currently displayed.

VIEW TOOLTIPS

1. Move ▷ over a toolbar button to find out its name.

2. Pause without clicking the button.

● A ToolTip box appears with the button name.

in an instant

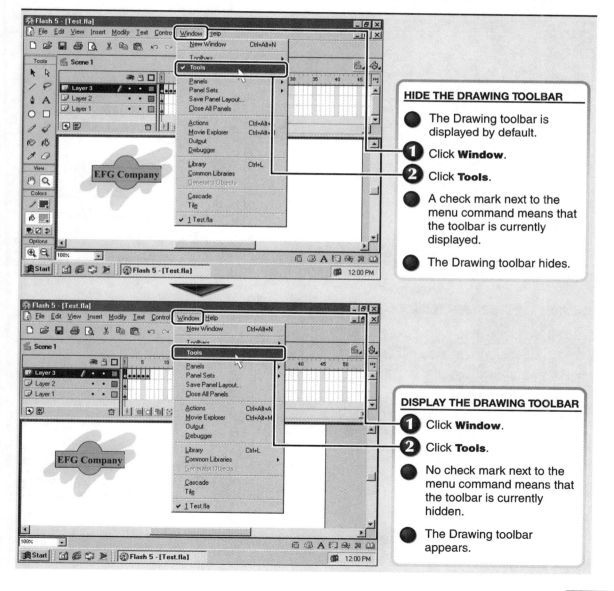

HIDE THE DRAWING TOOLBAR

- The Drawing toolbar is displayed by default.

1 Click **Window**.

2 Click **Tools**.

- A check mark next to the menu command means that the toolbar is currently displayed.

- The Drawing toolbar hides.

DISPLAY THE DRAWING TOOLBAR

1 Click **Window**.

2 Click **Tools**.

- No check mark next to the menu command means that the toolbar is currently hidden.

- The Drawing toolbar appears.

USING RULERS AND GRIDS

To help you draw with more precision, turn on
the Flash Rulers and grid lines. Both tools can
help you position objects on the Stage.

USING RULERS AND GRIDS

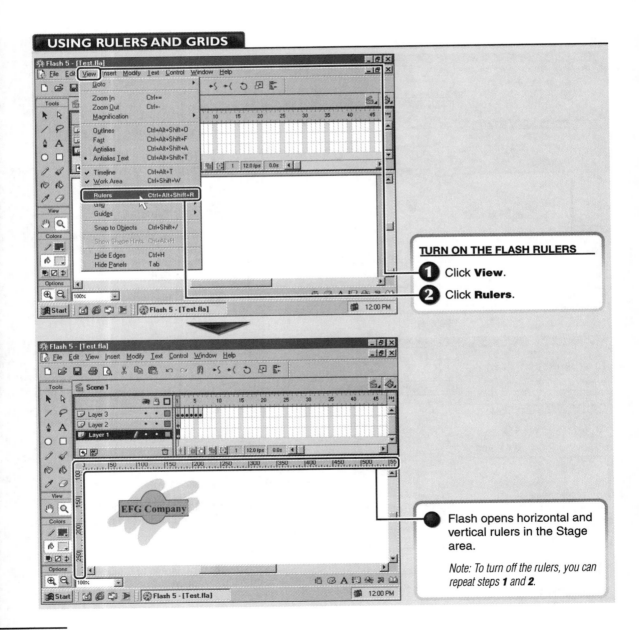

TURN ON THE FLASH RULERS

1 Click **View**.

2 Click **Rulers**.

● Flash opens horizontal and
vertical rulers in the Stage
area.

*Note: To turn off the rulers, you can
repeat steps 1 and 2.*

in an *instant*

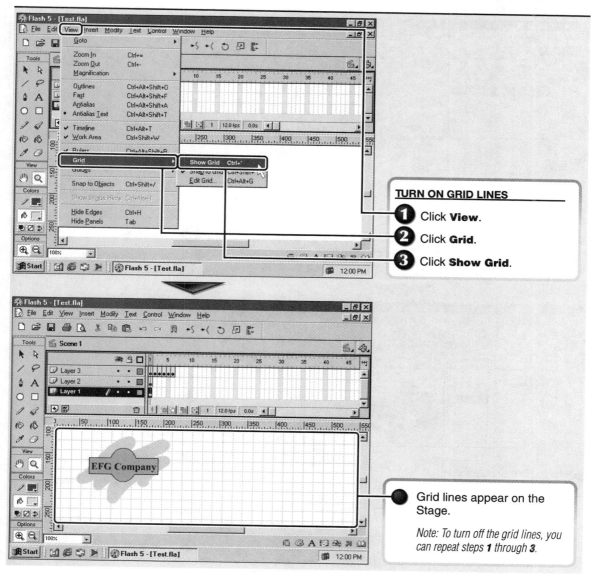

TURN ON GRID LINES

1 Click **View**.

2 Click **Grid**.

3 Click **Show Grid**.

● Grid lines appear on the Stage.

Note: To turn off the grid lines, you can repeat steps 1 through 3.

GET HELP

Flash comes with extensive Help resources, including lessons to help you better understand Flash capabilities and sample Flash movies to study.

GET HELP

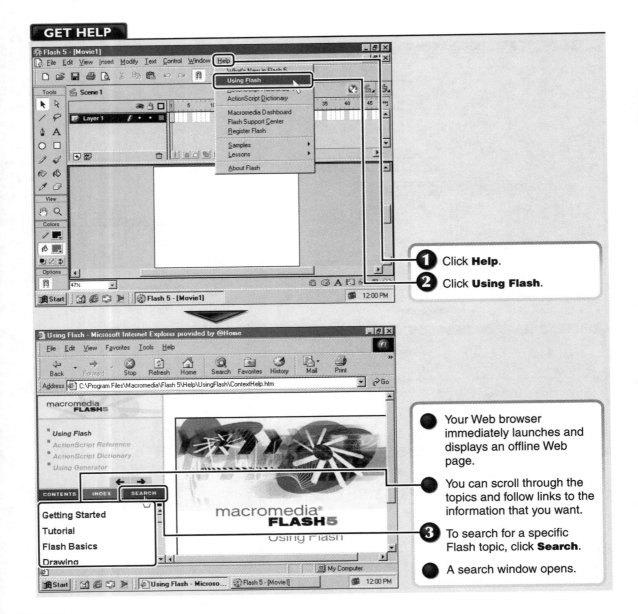

1 Click **Help**.

2 Click **Using Flash**.

● Your Web browser immediately launches and displays an offline Web page.

● You can scroll through the topics and follow links to the information that you want.

3 To search for a specific Flash topic, click **Search**.

● A search window opens.

in an *instant*

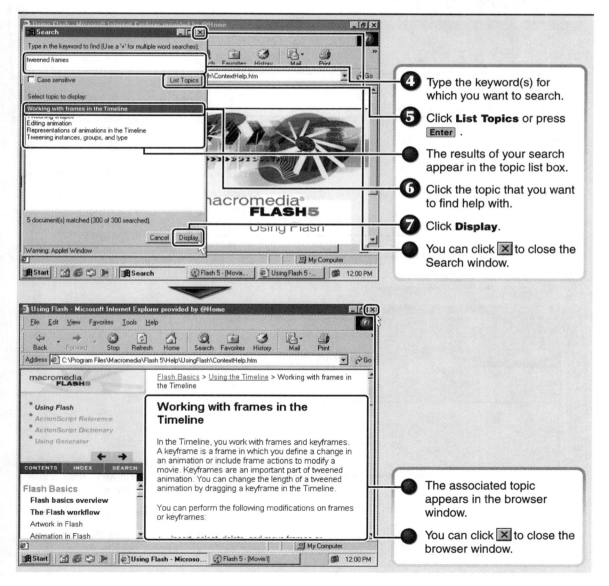

4 Type the keyword(s) for which you want to search.

5 Click **List Topics** or press `Enter`.

The results of your search appear in the topic list box.

6 Click the topic that you want to find help with.

7 Click **Display**.

You can click ☒ to close the Search window.

The associated topic appears in the browser window.

You can click ☒ to close the browser window.

DRAW LINE SEGMENTS

You can draw all sorts of objects with lines, which are also called *strokes* in Flash. The easiest way to draw straight lines in Flash is to use the Line tool. To draw a freeform line, use the Pencil tool.

DRAW LINE SEGMENTS

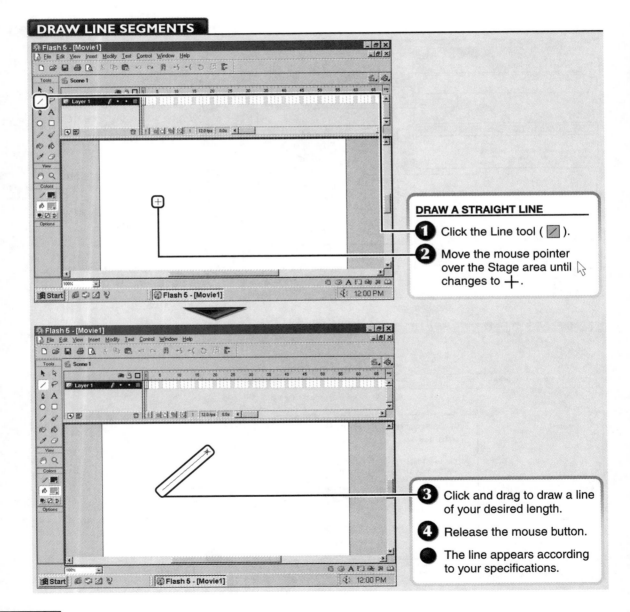

DRAW A STRAIGHT LINE

1 Click the Line tool ( ).

2 Move the mouse pointer over the Stage area until changes to +.

3 Click and drag to draw a line of your desired length.

4 Release the mouse button.

● The line appears according to your specifications.

in an instant

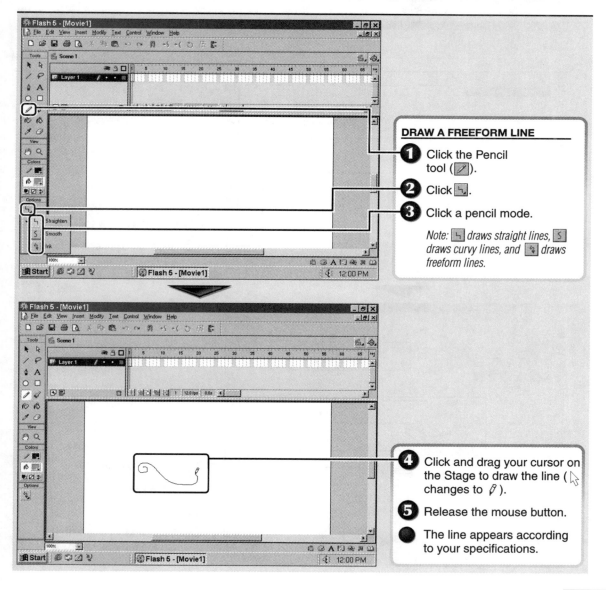

DRAW A FREEFORM LINE

1 Click the Pencil tool (⟋).

2 Click ⤵.

3 Click a pencil mode.

Note: ⤵ draws straight lines, 〜 draws curvy lines, and ⟿ draws freeform lines.

4 Click and drag your cursor on the Stage to draw the line (⬉ changes to ⟡).

5 Release the mouse button.

● The line appears according to your specifications.

19

FORMAT LINE SEGMENTS

By default, lines you draw on the Stage are solid black lines, 1-point thick. You can control a line's thickness, style, and color by using the formatting controls found in the panel window.

FORMAT LINE SEGMENTS

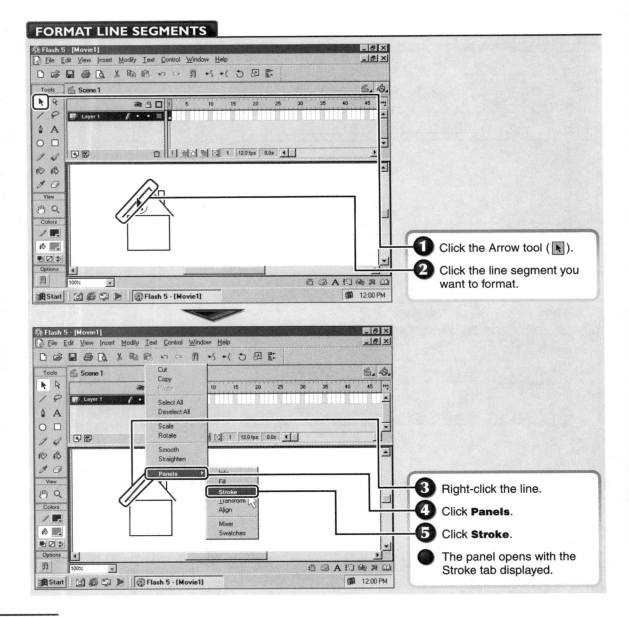

1 Click the Arrow tool (![arrow]).

2 Click the line segment you want to format.

3 Right-click the line.

4 Click **Panels**.

5 Click **Stroke**.

● The panel opens with the Stroke tab displayed.

in an *instant*

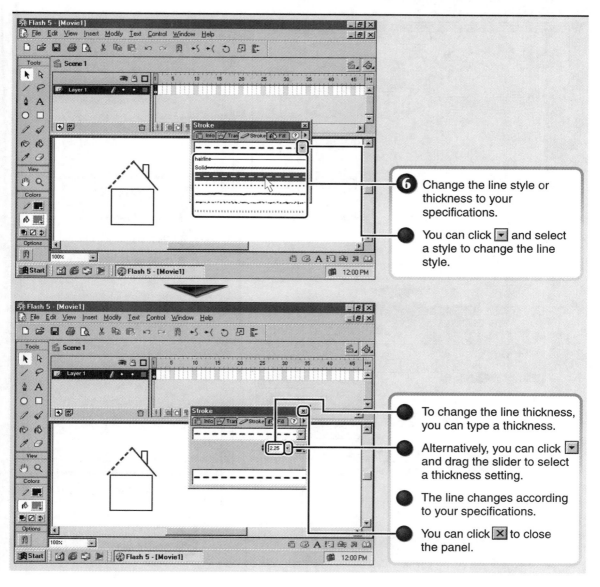

6 Change the line style or thickness to your specifications.

● You can click [▼] and select a style to change the line style.

● To change the line thickness, you can type a thickness.

● Alternatively, you can click [▼] and drag the slider to select a thickness setting.

● The line changes according to your specifications.

● You can click [X] to close the panel.

DRAW A CUSTOM LINE

You can customize a line style by using the options in the Line Style dialog box. For example, you may want a dotted line with the dots spaced far apart or very close together.

DRAW A CUSTOM LINE

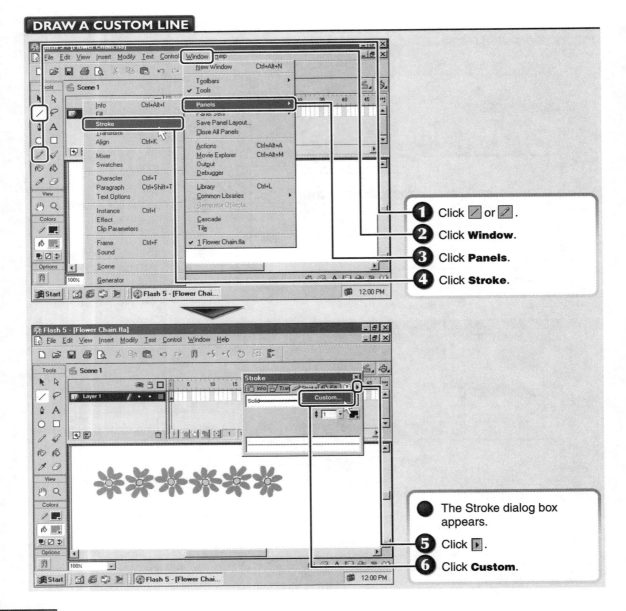

1 Click ▱ or ▱ .

2 Click **Window**.

3 Click **Panels**.

4 Click **Stroke**.

● The Stroke dialog box appears.

5 Click ▶ .

6 Click **Custom**.

in an instant

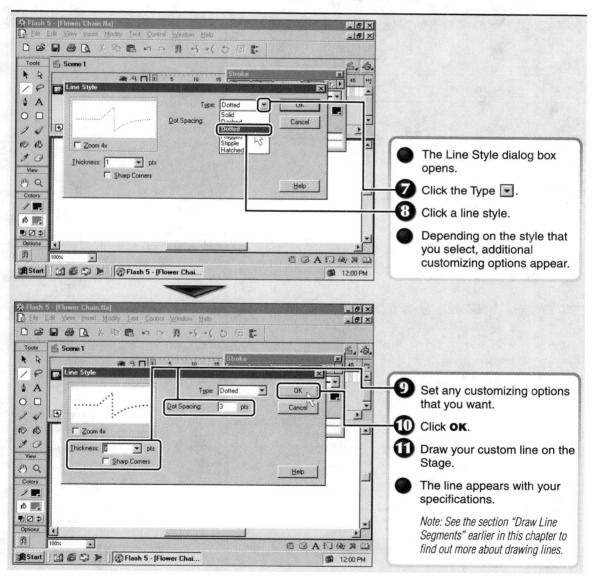

The Line Style dialog box opens.

7 Click the Type ▾.

8 Click a line style.

Depending on the style that you select, additional customizing options appear.

9 Set any customizing options that you want.

10 Click **OK**.

11 Draw your custom line on the Stage.

The line appears with your specifications.

Note: See the section "Draw Line Segments" earlier in this chapter to find out more about drawing lines.

DRAW CURVES WITH THE PEN TOOL

You can draw precise curves by using the Pen tool. Using this tool takes some getting used to, but with a little practice, you will be able to draw curves easily.

DRAW CURVES WITH THE PEN TOOL

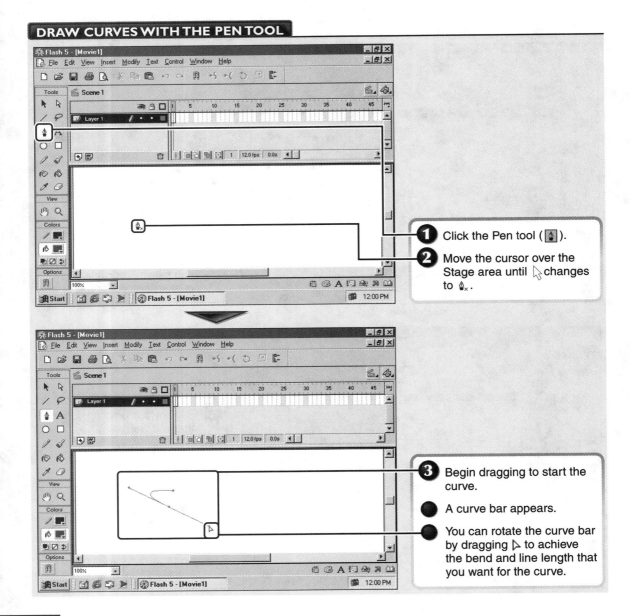

1 Click the Pen tool ( ).

2 Move the cursor over the Stage area until changes to .

3 Begin dragging to start the curve.

● A curve bar appears.

● You can rotate the curve bar by dragging to achieve the bend and line length that you want for the curve.

in an instant

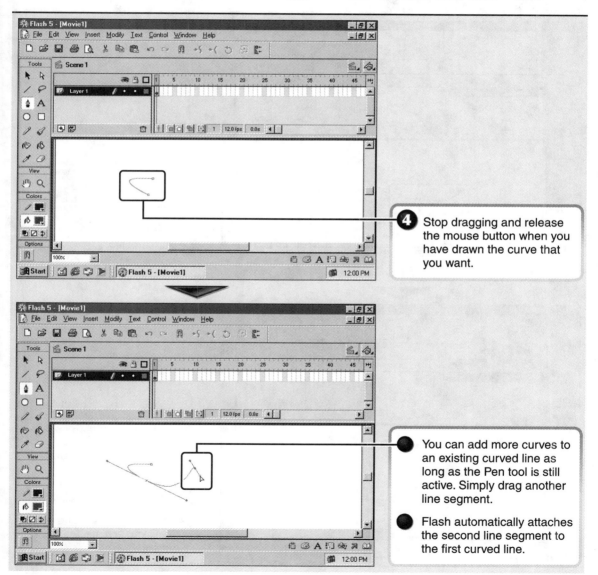

4 Stop dragging and release the mouse button when you have drawn the curve that you want.

● You can add more curves to an existing curved line as long as the Pen tool is still active. Simply drag another line segment.

● Flash automatically attaches the second line segment to the first curved line.

Flash has two controls for modifying the appearance of lines that you draw: Smooth and Straighten. These controls enable you to smooth or straighten lines to create subtle or dramatic changes to your drawing.

SMOOTH A LINE SEGMENT

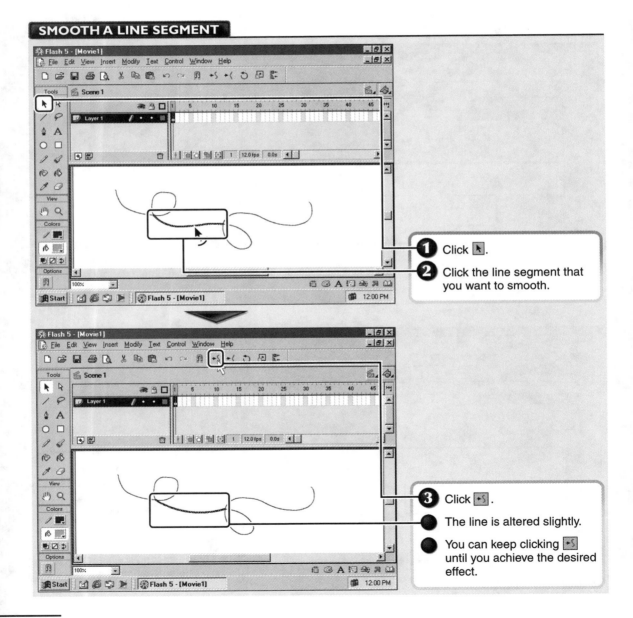

1 Click ▶.

2 Click the line segment that you want to smooth.

3 Click ⦁S .

■ The line is altered slightly.

■ You can keep clicking ⦁S until you achieve the desired effect.

in an *instant*

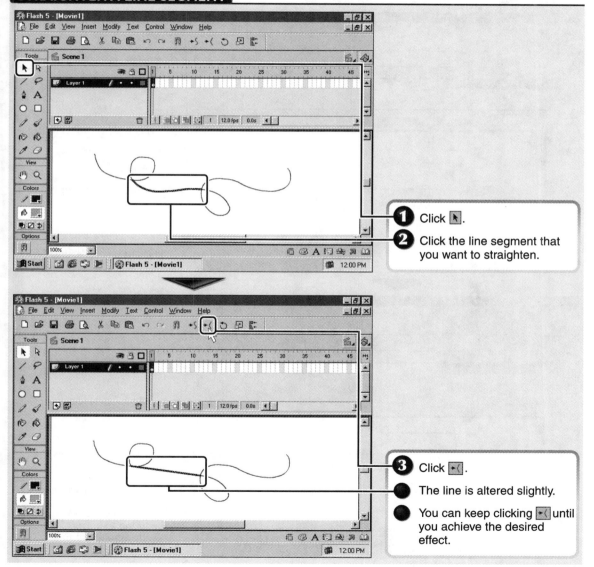

1 Click 🔖.

2 Click the line segment that you want to straighten.

3 Click 📐.

● The line is altered slightly.

● You can keep clicking 📐 until you achieve the desired effect.

DRAW OVAL AND RECTANGLE SHAPES

You can create simple shapes in Flash and then fill them with a color or pattern or use them as part of a drawing.

DRAW OVAL AND RECTANGLE SHAPES

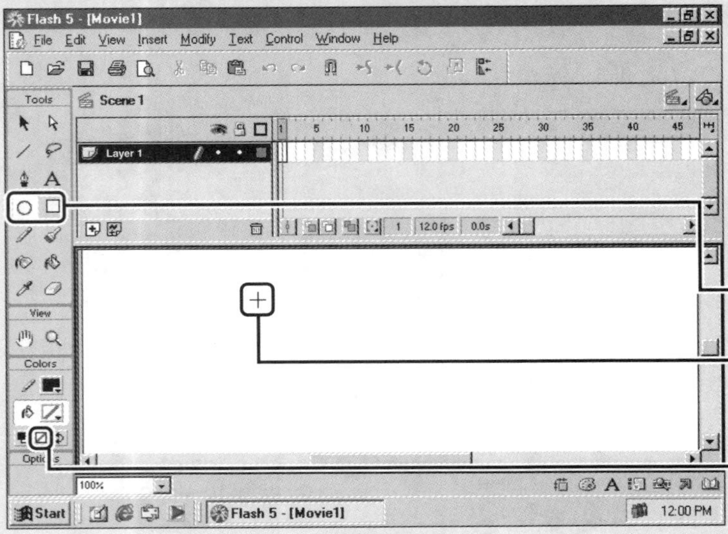

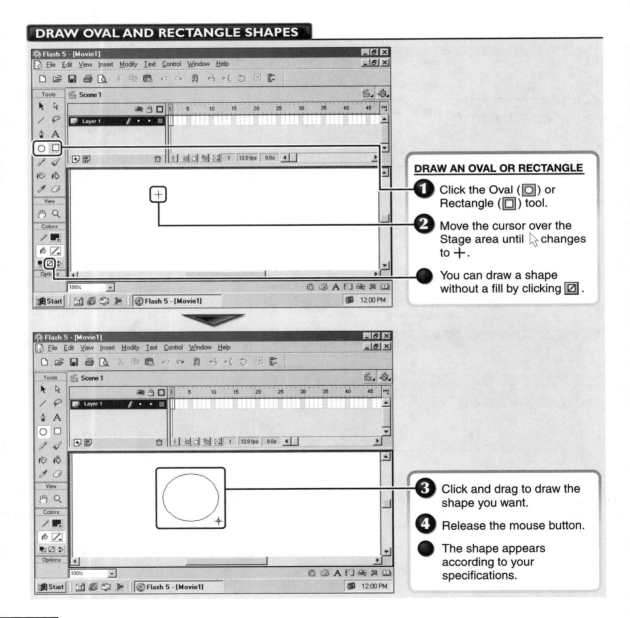

DRAW AN OVAL OR RECTANGLE

1. Click the Oval (○) or Rectangle (□) tool.
2. Move the cursor over the Stage area until ↖ changes to +.

- You can draw a shape without a fill by clicking ⊘.

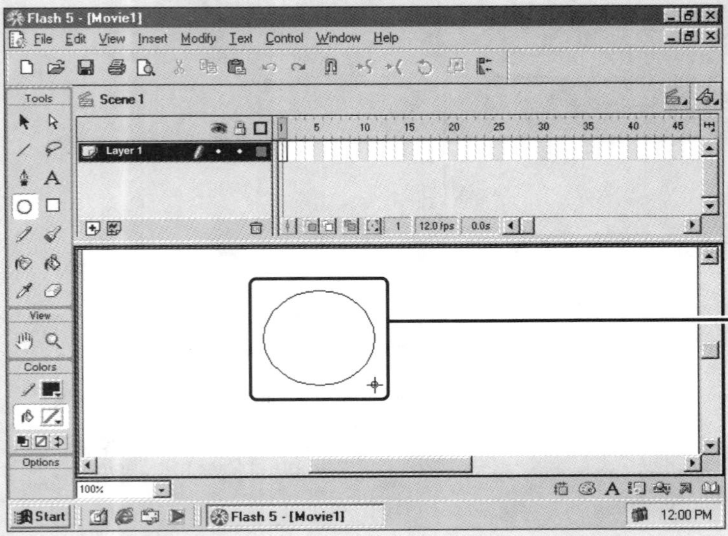

3. Click and drag to draw the shape you want.
4. Release the mouse button.

- The shape appears according to your specifications.

in an instant

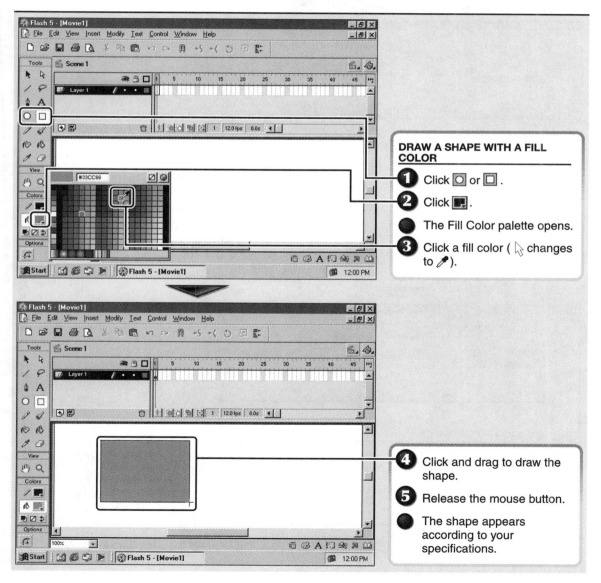

DRAW A SHAPE WITH A FILL COLOR

1 Click ☐ or ☐ .

2 Click ■ .

● The Fill Color palette opens.

3 Click a fill color (⬚ changes to ✎).

4 Click and drag to draw the shape.

5 Release the mouse button.

● The shape appears according to your specifications.

DRAW OBJECTS WITH THE BRUSH TOOL

You can use the Brush tool to draw with brush strokes, much like a paintbrush. You can control the size and shape of the brush as well as how the brush strokes appear on the Stage.

DRAW OBJECTS WITH THE BRUSH TOOL

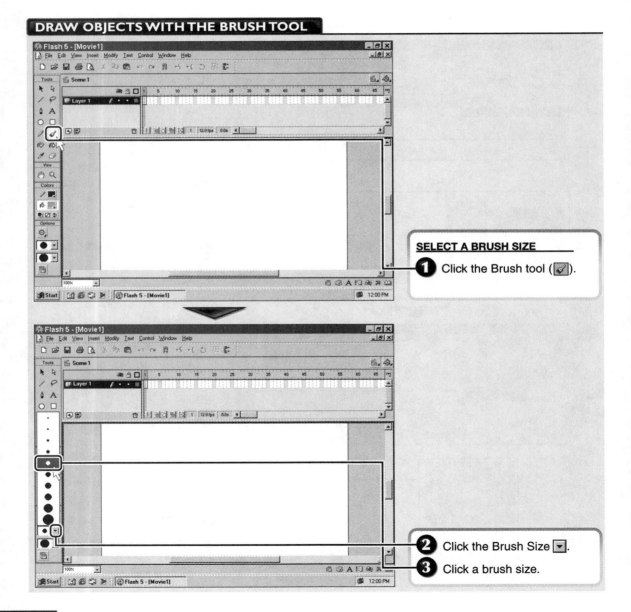

SELECT A BRUSH SIZE

1 Click the Brush tool (🖌).

2 Click the Brush Size 🔽.

3 Click a brush size.

in an *instant*

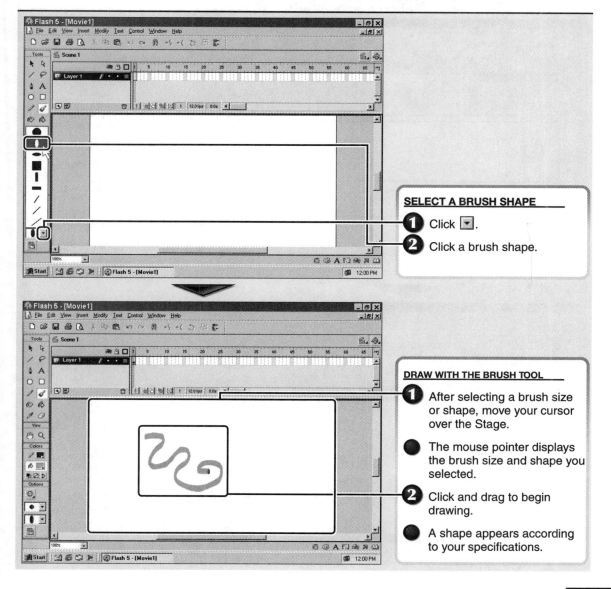

SELECT A BRUSH SHAPE

1 Click ▣.

2 Click a brush shape.

DRAW WITH THE BRUSH TOOL

1 After selecting a brush size or shape, move your cursor over the Stage.

● The mouse pointer displays the brush size and shape you selected.

2 Click and drag to begin drawing.

● A shape appears according to your specifications.

You can use the Paint Bucket tool to fill objects with a color, a gradient effect, or even a picture. The color palette comes with numerous colors and shades, as well as several pre-made gradient effects.

FILL OBJECTS WITH THE PAINT BUCKET TOOL

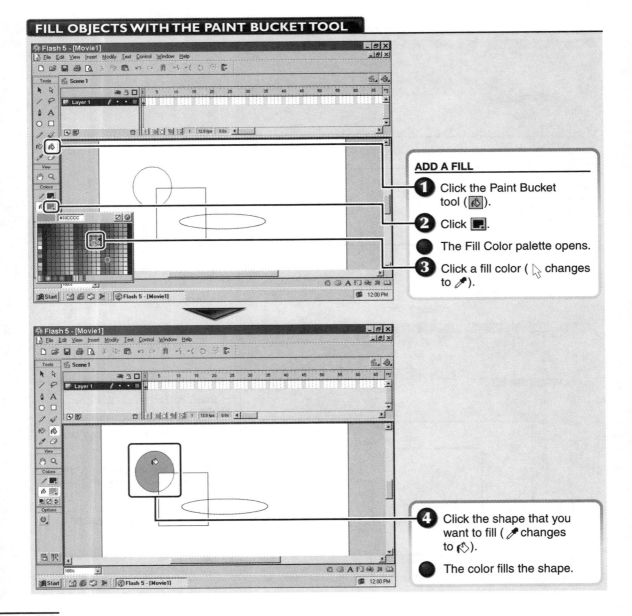

ADD A FILL

1 Click the Paint Bucket tool ( ).

2 Click .

■ The Fill Color palette opens.

3 Click a fill color (changes to).

4 Click the shape that you want to fill (changes to).

■ The color fills the shape.

in an *instant*

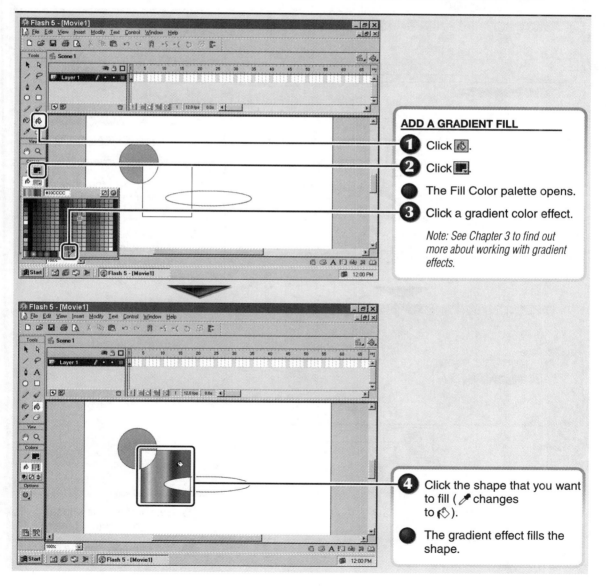

ADD A GRADIENT FILL

1 Click 🖐.

2 Click 🔲.

● The Fill Color palette opens.

3 Click a gradient color effect.

Note: See Chapter 3 to find out more about working with gradient effects.

4 Click the shape that you want to fill (🖊 changes to 🖐).

● The gradient effect fills the shape.

SELECT OBJECTS

To work with objects that you draw or place on the Flash Stage, you must first select them. The more lines and shapes that are on the Stage, the trickier it is to select only the ones you want. Flash offers you several different ways to select objects: by clicking, dragging, or lassoing them.

SELECT OBJECTS

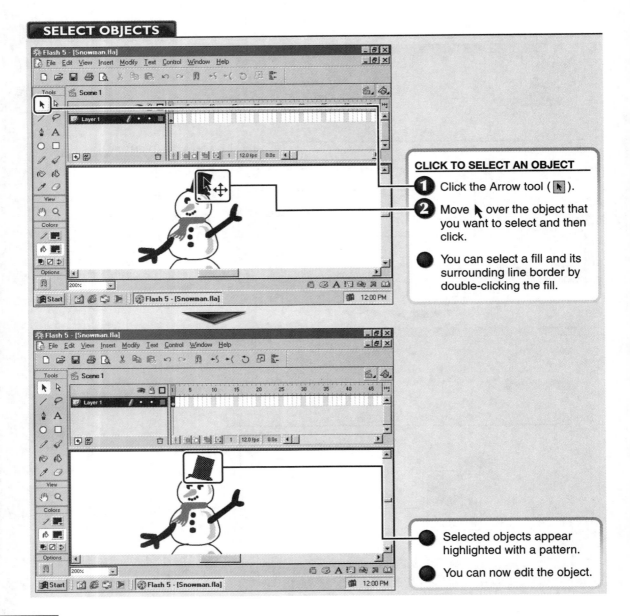

CLICK TO SELECT AN OBJECT

1 Click the Arrow tool ( ).

2 Move ↖ over the object that you want to select and then click.

● You can select a fill and its surrounding line border by double-clicking the fill.

● Selected objects appear highlighted with a pattern.

● You can now edit the object.

in an *instant*

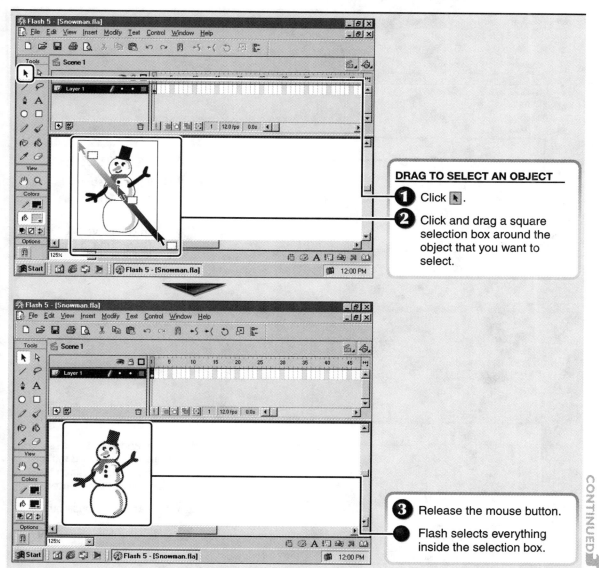

DRAG TO SELECT AN OBJECT

1 Click 🔖.

2 Click and drag a square selection box around the object that you want to select.

3 Release the mouse button.

● Flash selects everything inside the selection box.

CONTINUED

SELECT OBJECTS

You can use the Lasso tool to select irregular objects. The Lasso tool draws a freehand "rope" around the item that you want to select. This allows you to select an oddly shaped object or just a small portion of an object.

SELECT OBJECTS (CONTINUED)

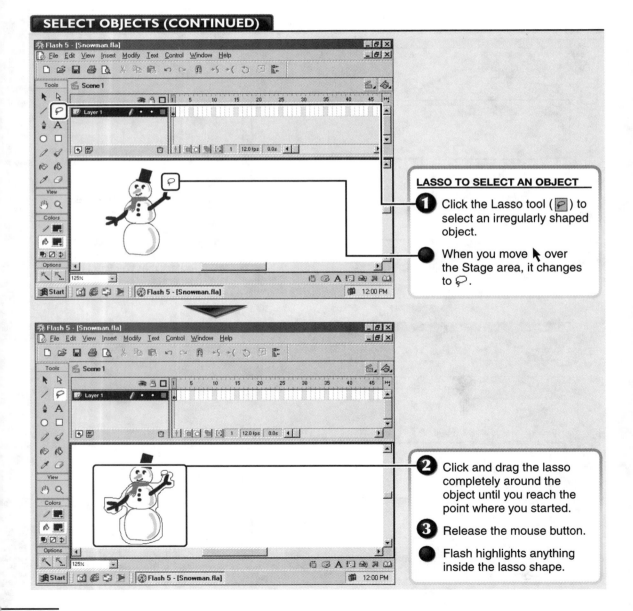

LASSO TO SELECT AN OBJECT

1 Click the Lasso tool (🔗) to select an irregularly shaped object.

● When you move ▶ over the Stage area, it changes to 🔗.

2 Click and drag the lasso completely around the object until you reach the point where you started.

3 Release the mouse button.

● Flash highlights anything inside the lasso shape.

in an *instant*

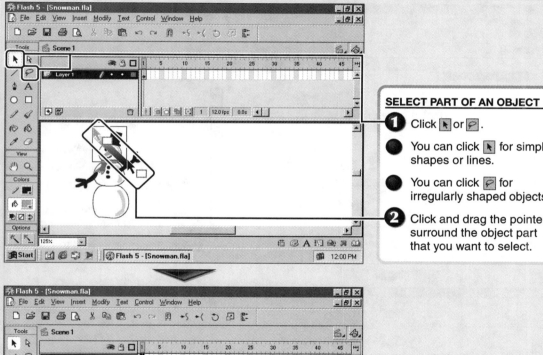

SELECT PART OF AN OBJECT

1 Click ⬆ or ✎.

● You can click ⬆ for simple shapes or lines.

● You can click ✎ for irregularly shaped objects.

2 Click and drag the pointer to surround the object part that you want to select.

3 Release the mouse button.

● Everything inside the area that you dragged over is selected.

MOVE AND COPY OBJECTS

You can easily reposition objects on the Flash stage. Flash lets you quickly move an object from one area to another or make copies of the original object.

MOVE AN OBJECT

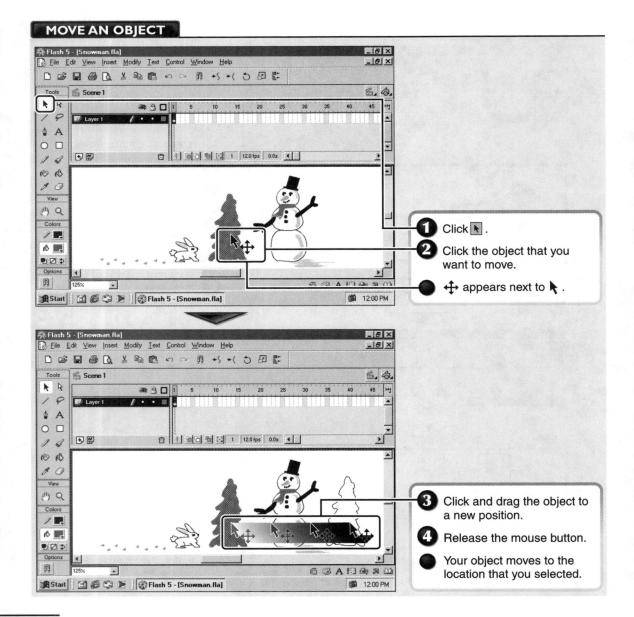

1 Click ↖ .

2 Click the object that you want to move.

● ✛ appears next to ↖ .

3 Click and drag the object to a new position.

4 Release the mouse button.

● Your object moves to the location that you selected.

in an *instant*

COPY AN OBJECT

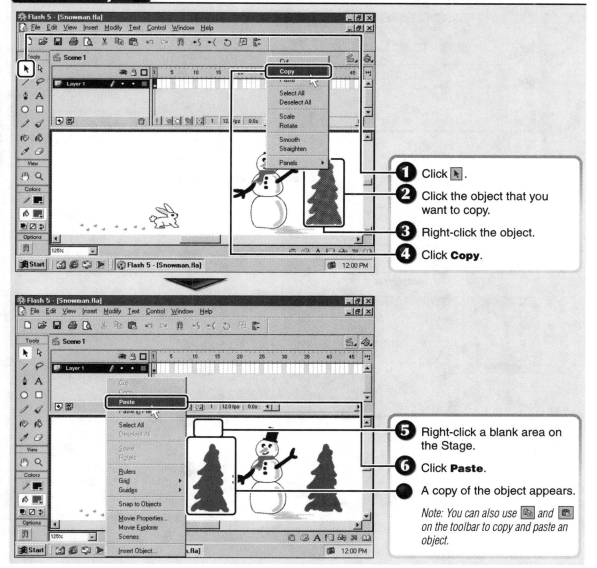

1 Click ▶.

2 Click the object that you want to copy.

3 Right-click the object.

4 Click **Copy**.

5 Right-click a blank area on the Stage.

6 Click **Paste**.

● A copy of the object appears.

Note: You can also use 🖹 and 🖺 on the toolbar to copy and paste an object.

EDIT LINE SEGMENTS

You can change a line by adjusting its length or reshaping its curve. You can change a line's angle, extend a curved line to make it appear longer, or just simply make a curve more curvy.

EDIT LINE SEGMENTS

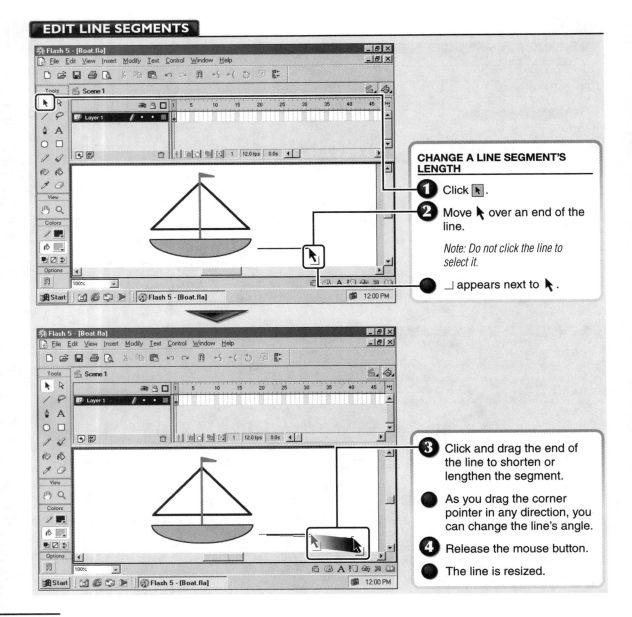

CHANGE A LINE SEGMENT'S LENGTH

1 Click ▶.

2 Move ▶ over an end of the line.

Note: Do not click the line to select it.

⌐ appears next to ▶.

3 Click and drag the end of the line to shorten or lengthen the segment.

● As you drag the corner pointer in any direction, you can change the line's angle.

4 Release the mouse button.

● The line is resized.

40

in an *instant*

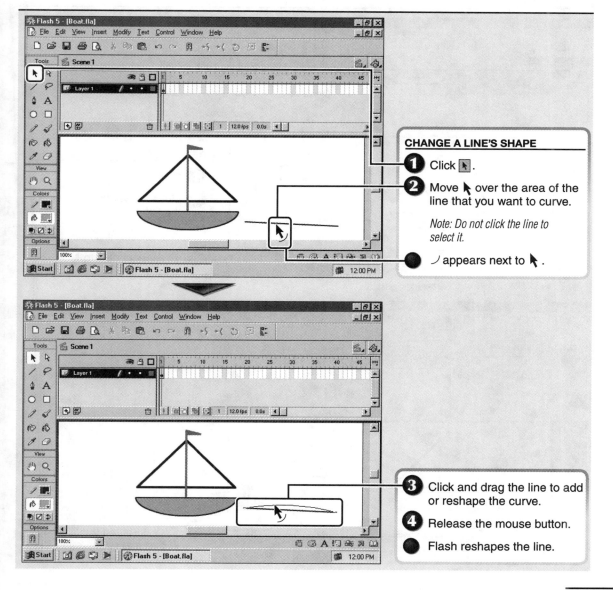

CHANGE A LINE'S SHAPE

1 Click ▶.

2 Move ▶ over the area of the line that you want to curve.

Note: Do not click the line to select it.

◢ appears next to ▶.

3 Click and drag the line to add or reshape the curve.

4 Release the mouse button.

● Flash reshapes the line.

EDIT FILLS

You can edit fills just as you can edit line segments. For example, you can change a fill shape by adjusting the sides of the fill, and you can change the fill color at any time.

EDIT FILLS

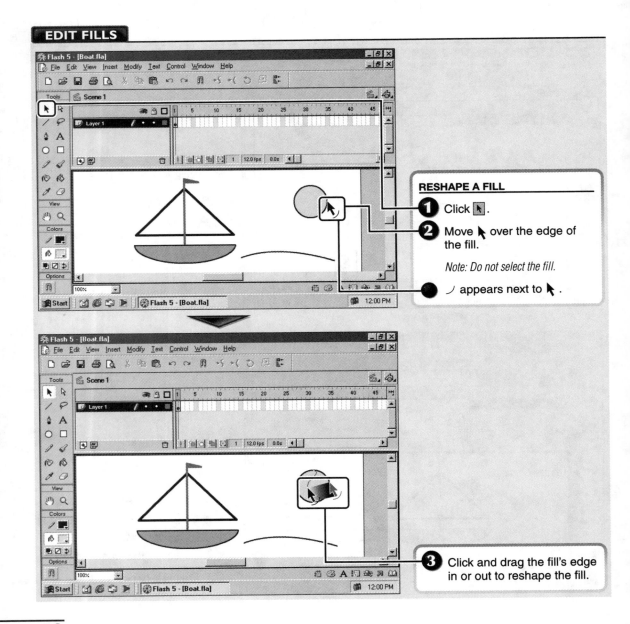

RESHAPE A FILL

1 Click ▶.

2 Move ▶ over the edge of the fill.

Note: Do not select the fill.

● ⌒ appears next to ▶.

3 Click and drag the fill's edge in or out to reshape the fill.

in an *instant*

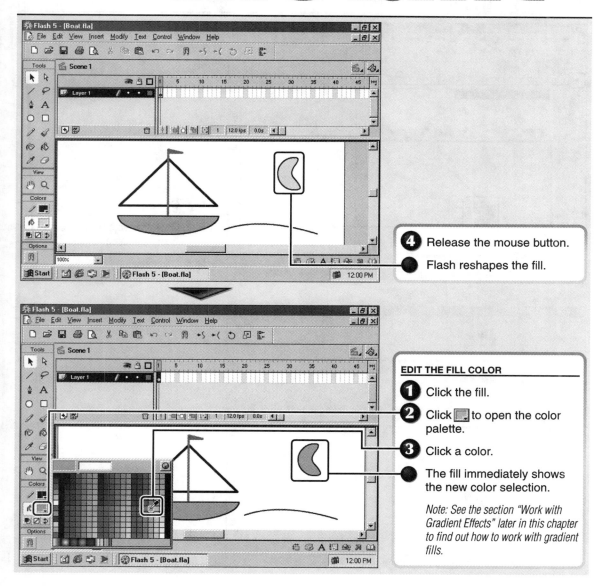

4 Release the mouse button.

Flash reshapes the fill.

EDIT THE FILL COLOR

1 Click the fill.

2 Click ▢ to open the color palette.

3 Click a color.

The fill immediately shows the new color selection.

Note: See the section "Work with Gradient Effects" later in this chapter to find out how to work with gradient fills.

RESIZE OBJECTS

You can scale objects in Flash to change their sizes without changing their shapes.

RESIZE OBJECTS

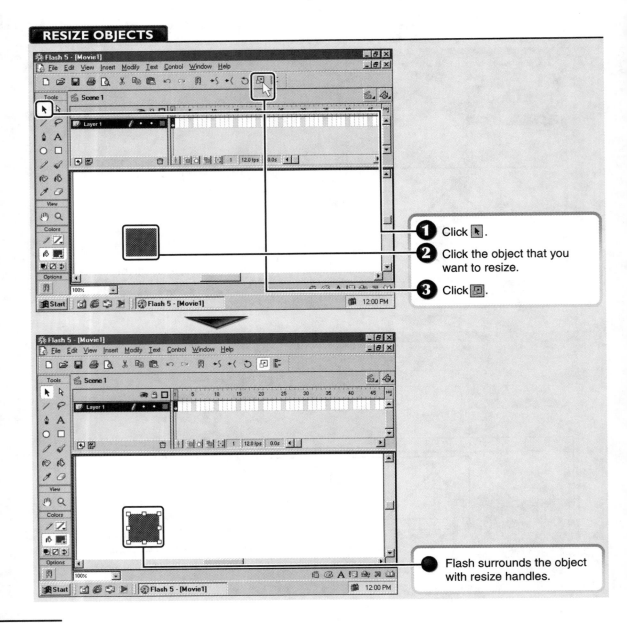

1 Click ▶.

2 Click the object that you want to resize.

3 Click 🔲.

● Flash surrounds the object with resize handles.

in an *instant*

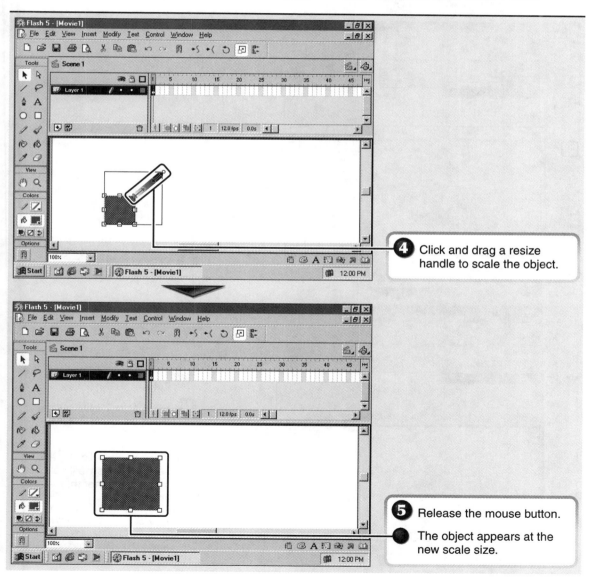

4 Click and drag a resize handle to scale the object.

5 Release the mouse button.

● The object appears at the new scale size.

ADD STROKES TO SHAPES

The Ink Bottle tool adds outlines to fills or changes existing outline strokes. You can control the stroke's thickness and color and even add inside and outside strokes at the same time.

ADD STROKES TO SHAPES

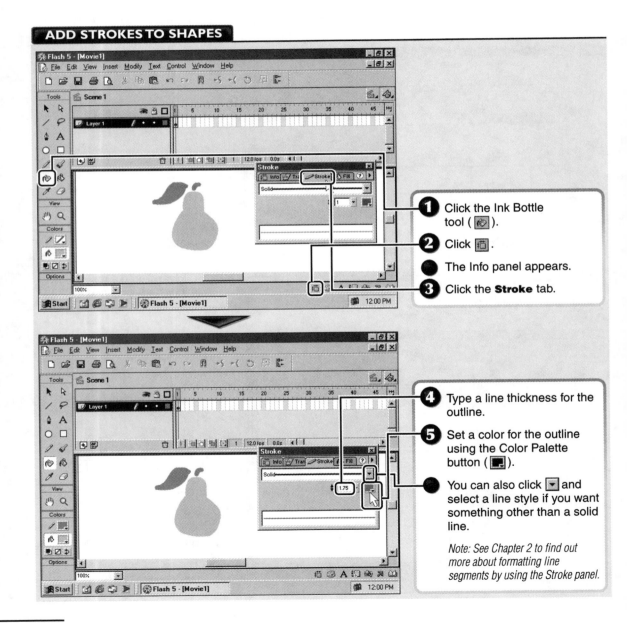

1 Click the Ink Bottle tool ( ).

2 Click .

■ The Info panel appears.

3 Click the **Stroke** tab.

4 Type a line thickness for the outline.

5 Set a color for the outline using the Color Palette button ( ).

■ You can also click and select a line style if you want something other than a solid line.

Note: See Chapter 2 to find out more about formatting line segments by using the Stroke panel.

in an *instant*

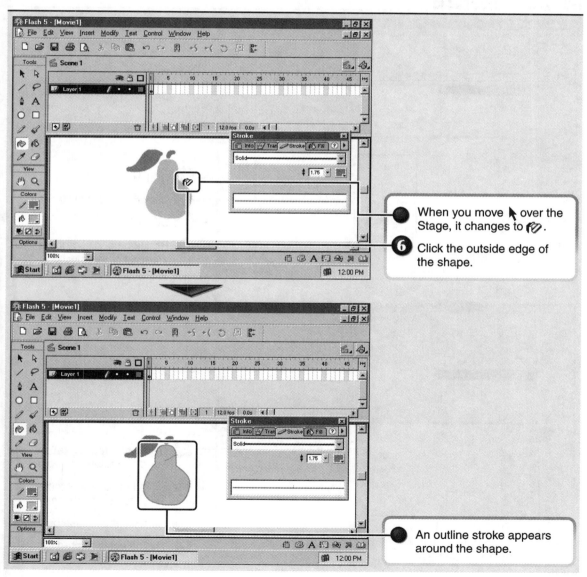

When you move ▶ over the Stage, it changes to 🖎.

6 Click the outside edge of the shape.

An outline stroke appears around the shape.

ROTATE AND FLIP OBJECTS

You can rotate an object based on its center point, or you can flip an object vertically or horizontally. These actions enable you to quickly change an object's alignment in a frame.

ROTATE AN OBJECT

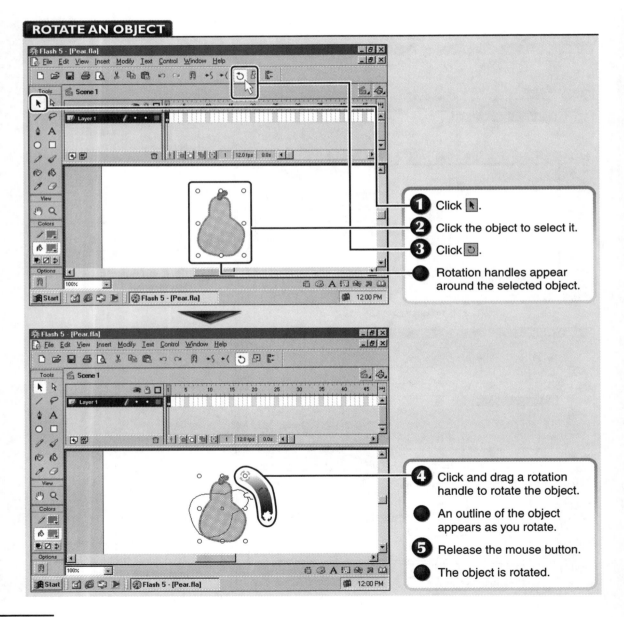

① Click ▶.

② Click the object to select it.

③ Click ↺.

● Rotation handles appear around the selected object.

④ Click and drag a rotation handle to rotate the object.

● An outline of the object appears as you rotate.

⑤ Release the mouse button.

● The object is rotated.

48

in an *instant*

FLIP AN OBJECT

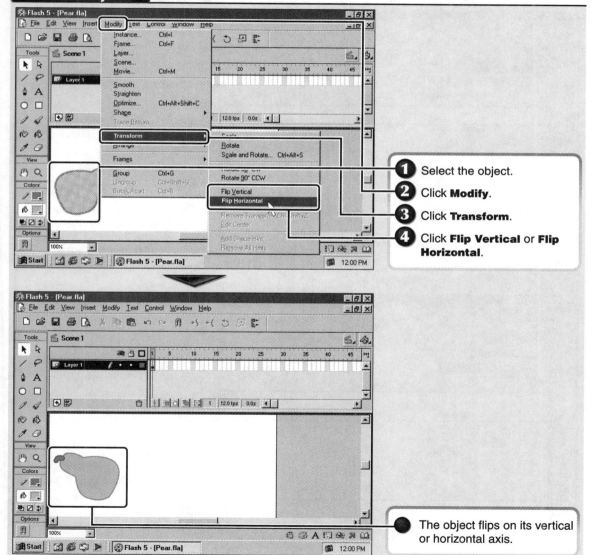

1 Select the object.

2 Click **Modify**.

3 Click **Transform**.

4 Click **Flip Vertical** or **Flip Horizontal**.

● The object flips on its vertical or horizontal axis.

USING THE ERASER TOOL

You can use the Eraser tool to erase parts of a drawing or object, or you can use it to create new shapes within an object. The Eraser tool has several modifiers that you can use to control how it works.

USING THE ERASER TOOL

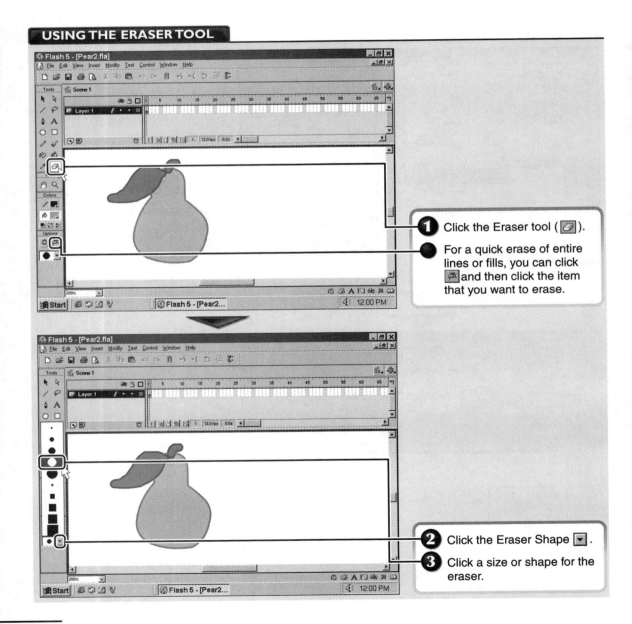

1 Click the Eraser tool ( ).

For a quick erase of entire lines or fills, you can click and then click the item that you want to erase.

2 Click the Eraser Shape .

3 Click a size or shape for the eraser.

in an instant

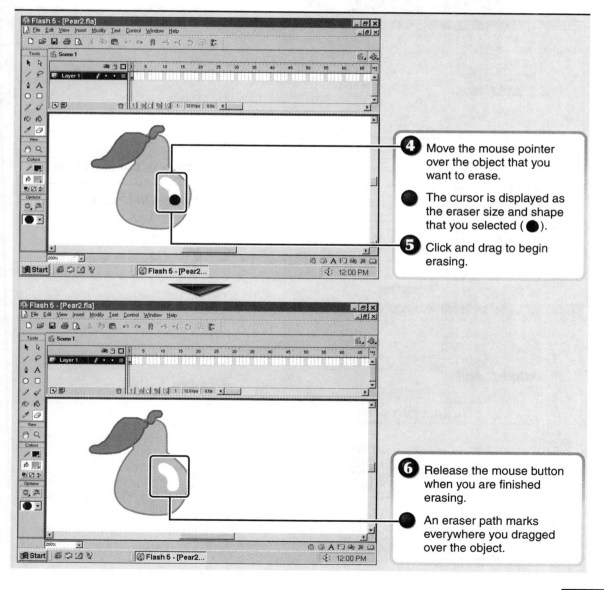

4 Move the mouse pointer over the object that you want to erase.

● The cursor is displayed as the eraser size and shape that you selected (●).

5 Click and drag to begin erasing.

6 Release the mouse button when you are finished erasing.

● An eraser path marks everywhere you dragged over the object.

51

WORK WITH GRADIENT EFFECTS

A *gradient effect* is a band of blended color or shading. Gradient effects can add depth and dimension to your Flash drawings. By default, the Fill Color palette offers several gradient effects that you can use, or you can create your own.

USING EXISTING GRADIENT EFFECTS

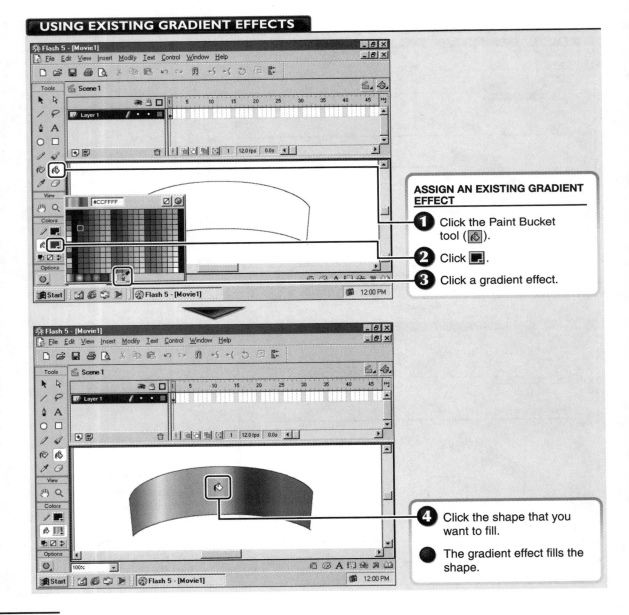

ASSIGN AN EXISTING GRADIENT EFFECT

1 Click the Paint Bucket tool ( ).

2 Click .

3 Click a gradient effect.

4 Click the shape that you want to fill.

● The gradient effect fills the shape.

52

in an *instant*

CREATE A NEW GRADIENT

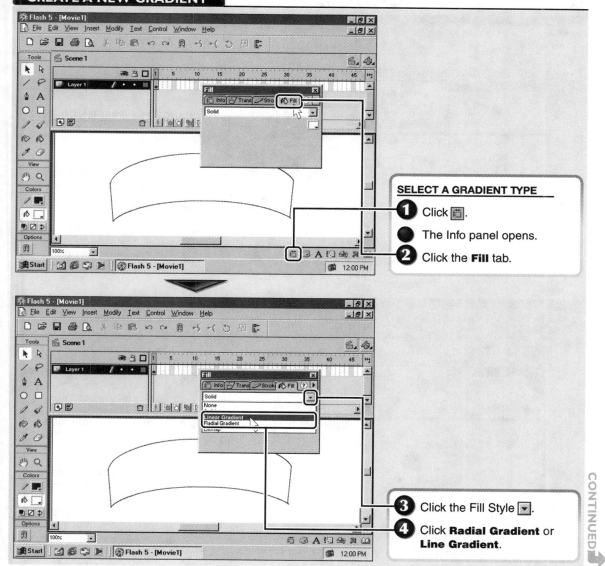

SELECT A GRADIENT TYPE

1 Click 🏛.

● The Info panel opens.

2 Click the **Fill** tab.

3 Click the Fill Style ▾.

4 Click **Radial Gradient** or **Line Gradient**.

CONTINUED ➡

WORK WITH GRADIENT EFFECTS

You can change the properties of the gradient you create by adjusting different colors, color markers, or color intensity bandwidths. After you create the gradient just the way you want it, you can save it to reuse again in other Flash projects.

CREATE A NEW GRADIENT (CONTINUED)

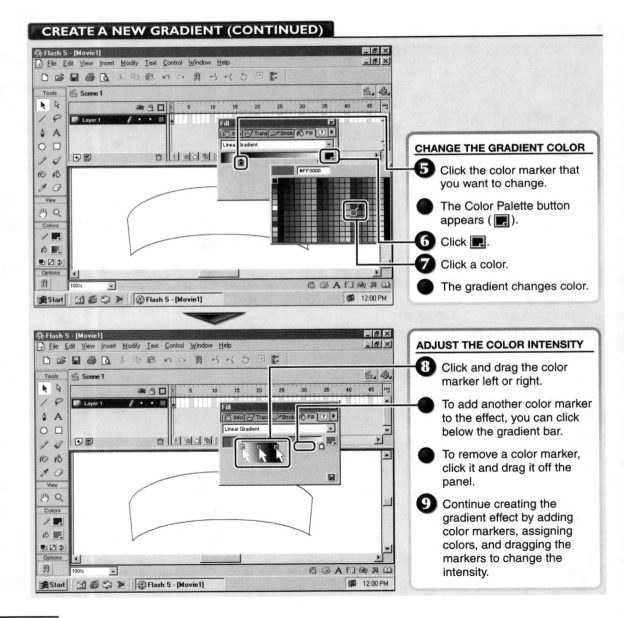

CHANGE THE GRADIENT COLOR

5 Click the color marker that you want to change.

● The Color Palette button appears (▣).

6 Click ▣.

7 Click a color.

● The gradient changes color.

ADJUST THE COLOR INTENSITY

8 Click and drag the color marker left or right.

● To add another color marker to the effect, you can click below the gradient bar.

● To remove a color marker, click it and drag it off the panel.

9 Continue creating the gradient effect by adding color markers, assigning colors, and dragging the markers to change the intensity.

in an *instant*

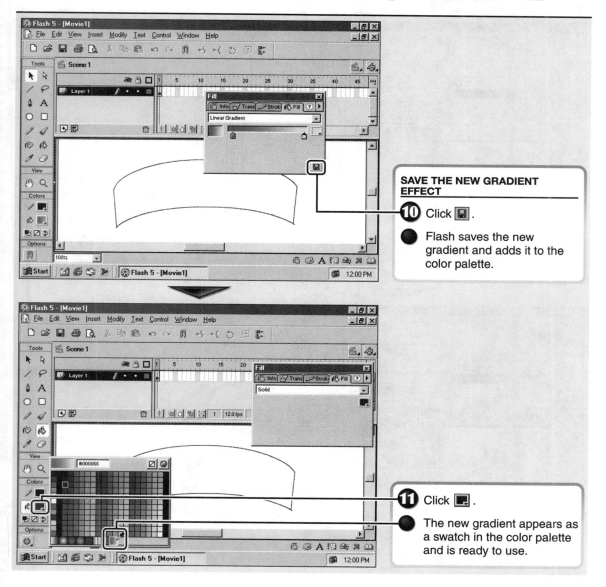

SAVE THE NEW GRADIENT EFFECT

10 Click 🖫 .

● Flash saves the new gradient and adds it to the color palette.

11 Click 🔳 .

● The new gradient appears as a swatch in the color palette and is ready to use.

EDIT A COLOR SET

You can make new color sets based on Flash's default color set by removing colors that you do not need for a particular project. You can then save the edited color set for use in other Flash projects. Color sets are saved with the **.clr** file extension.

EDIT A COLOR SET

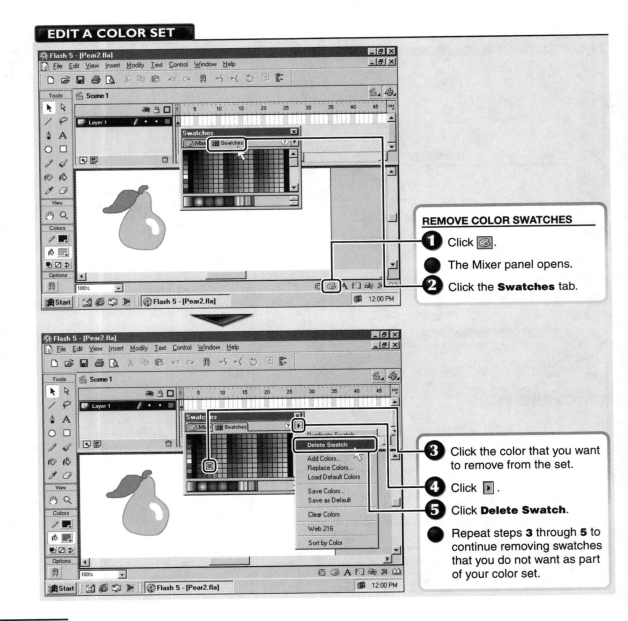

REMOVE COLOR SWATCHES

1 Click 🎨.

● The Mixer panel opens.

2 Click the **Swatches** tab.

3 Click the color that you want to remove from the set.

4 Click ▶.

5 Click **Delete Swatch**.

● Repeat steps **3** through **5** to continue removing swatches that you do not want as part of your color set.

in an instant

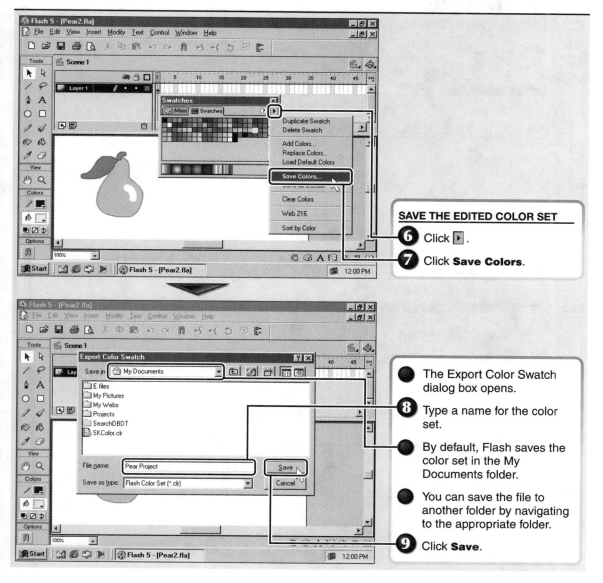

SAVE THE EDITED COLOR SET

6 Click ▶ .

7 Click **Save Colors**.

● The Export Color Swatch dialog box opens.

8 Type a name for the color set.

● By default, Flash saves the color set in the My Documents folder.

● You can save the file to another folder by navigating to the appropriate folder.

9 Click **Save**.

COPY LINE ATTRIBUTES

You can use the Dropper tool to quickly copy line attributes from one line segment to another.

COPY LINE ATTRIBUTES

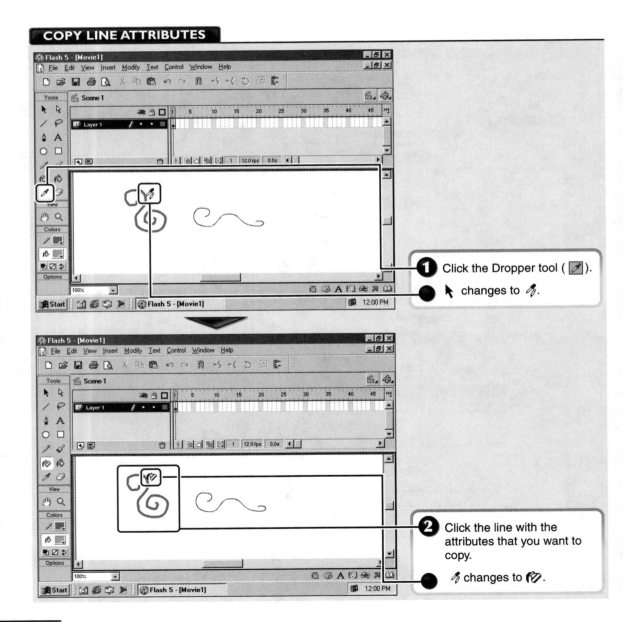

1 Click the Dropper tool ( ).

➤ changes to .

2 Click the line with the attributes that you want to copy.

changes to .

in an *instant*

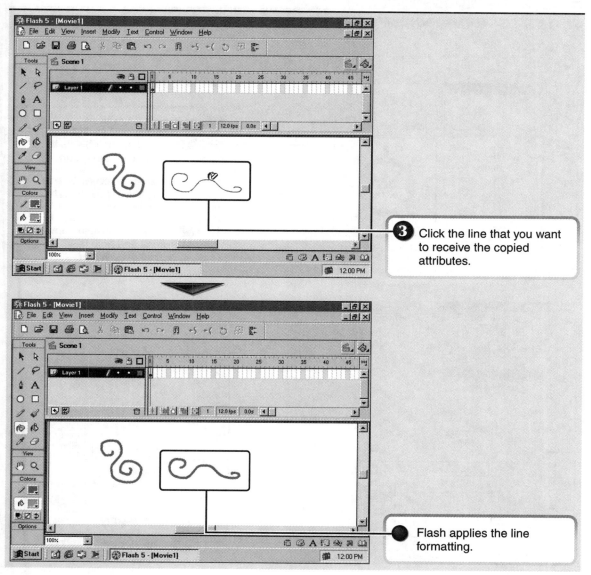

3 Click the line that you want to receive the copied attributes.

Flash applies the line formatting.

WORK WITH GROUPED OBJECTS

You can work on multiple items at the same time by placing them in a group. A group enables you to treat the items as a single unit. Any edits you make affect all the items in the group.

WORK WITH GROUPED OBJECTS

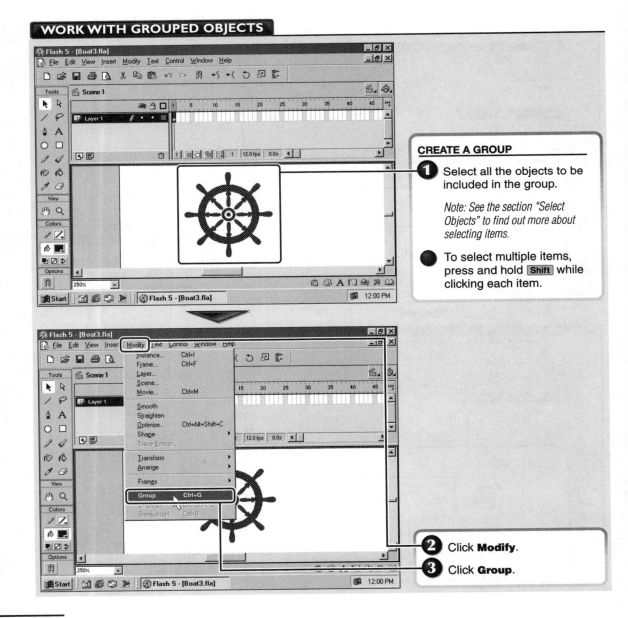

CREATE A GROUP

1 Select all the objects to be included in the group.

Note: See the section "Select Objects" to find out more about selecting items.

● To select multiple items, press and hold **Shift** while clicking each item.

2 Click **Modify**.

3 Click **Group**.

in an *instant*

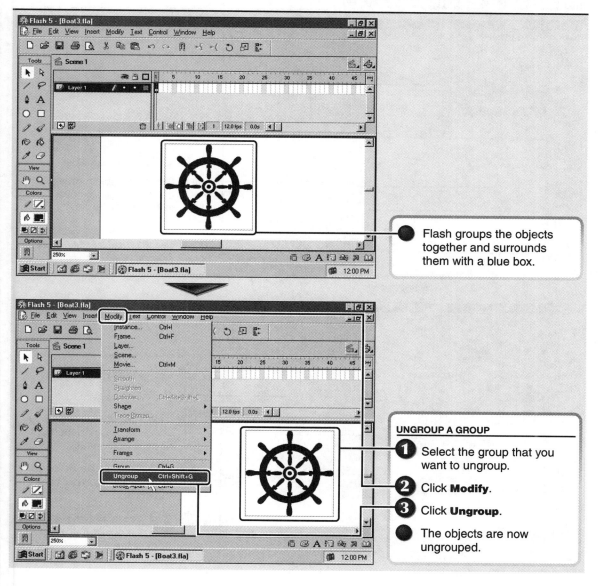

Flash groups the objects
together and surrounds
them with a blue box.

UNGROUP A GROUP

1 Select the group that you
want to ungroup.

2 Click **Modify**.

3 Click **Ungroup**.

The objects are now
ungrouped.

WORK WITH STACKED OBJECTS

You can move objects on top of other objects, or *stack* them, in Flash. You can control exactly where an object appears in a stack. You can place an object at the very back of a stack, at the very front, or somewhere in between.

WORK WITH STACKED OBJECTS

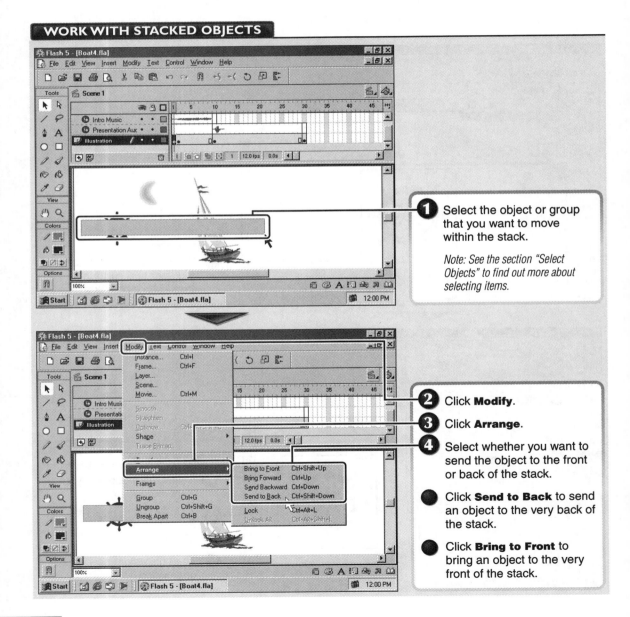

1 Select the object or group that you want to move within the stack.

Note: See the section "Select Objects" to find out more about selecting items.

2 Click **Modify**.

3 Click **Arrange**.

4 Select whether you want to send the object to the front or back of the stack.

● Click **Send to Back** to send an object to the very back of the stack.

● Click **Bring to Front** to bring an object to the very front of the stack.

in an instant

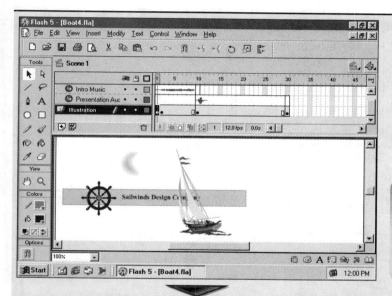

● The object appears in the stacking order as directed.

● In this example, the blue bar moved to the back of the stack.

● In this example, the text block moves in front of the sailboat.

ALIGN OBJECTS

The Align panel has tools for controlling precisely where an object sits on the Stage. You can align objects vertically and horizontally by their edges or center. You can align objects with other objects or with the edges of the Stage, and you can control the amount of space between objects.

ALIGN OBJECTS

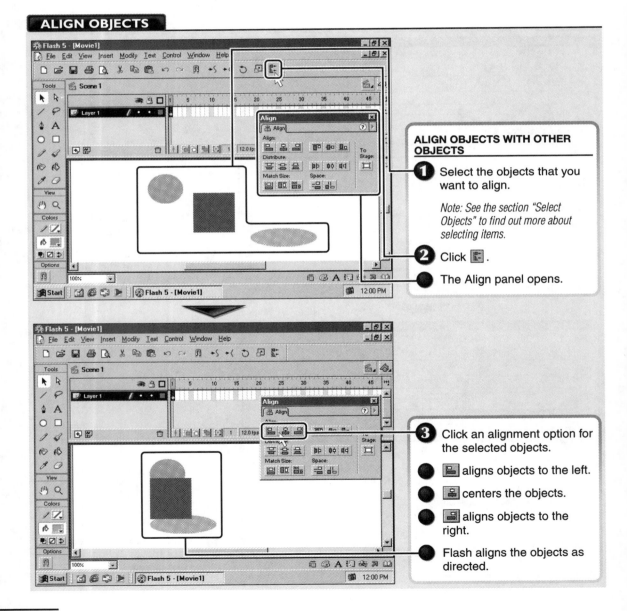

ALIGN OBJECTS WITH OTHER OBJECTS

1 Select the objects that you want to align.

Note: See the section "Select Objects" to find out more about selecting items.

2 Click 🗐.

● The Align panel opens.

3 Click an alignment option for the selected objects.

● 🗐 aligns objects to the left.

● 🗐 centers the objects.

● 🗐 aligns objects to the right.

● Flash aligns the objects as directed.

in an *instant*

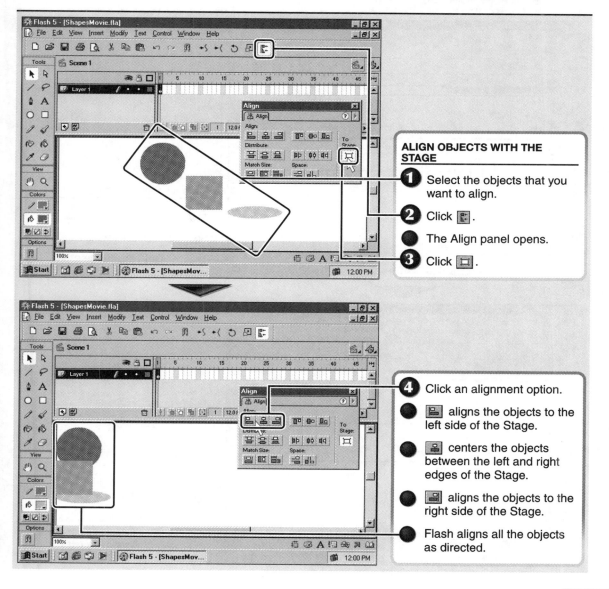

ALIGN OBJECTS WITH THE STAGE

① Select the objects that you want to align.

② Click 🗃.

● The Align panel opens.

③ Click ▢.

④ Click an alignment option.

● ▣ aligns the objects to the left side of the Stage.

● ▣ centers the objects between the left and right edges of the Stage.

● ▣ aligns the objects to the right side of the Stage.

● Flash aligns all the objects as directed.

ADD TEXT WITH THE TEXT TOOL

You can use the Text tool to add text to a movie or graphic. You can insert label or block text boxes on the Stage area. With a label text box, you can click where you want the text to appear and start typing. With block text, you define the box size first.

ADD TEXT WITH THE TEXT TOOL

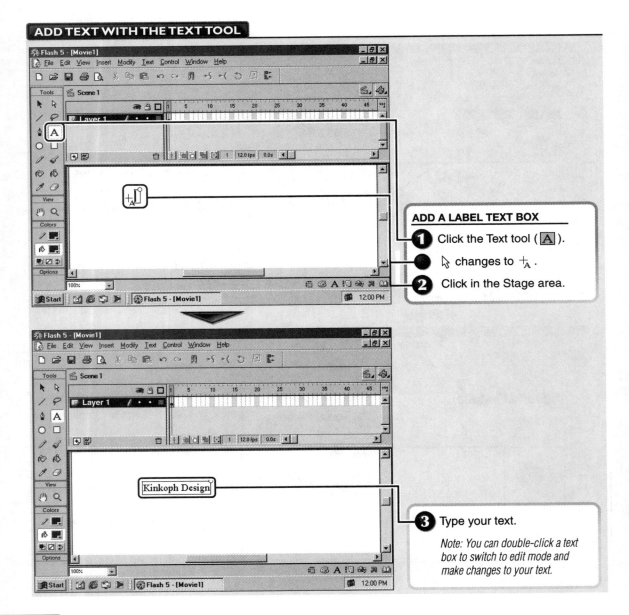

ADD A LABEL TEXT BOX

1 Click the Text tool (A).

■ changes to +A.

2 Click in the Stage area.

3 Type your text.

Note: You can double-click a text box to switch to edit mode and make changes to your text.

in an *instant*

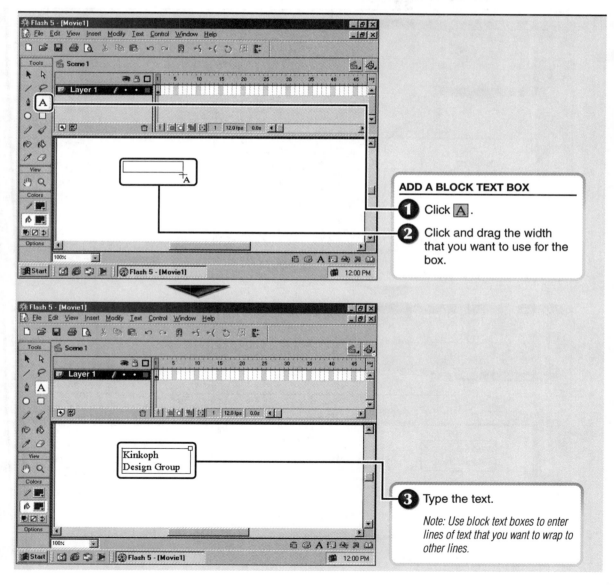

ADD A BLOCK TEXT BOX

1 Click A.

2 Click and drag the width that you want to use for the box.

3 Type the text.

Note: Use block text boxes to enter lines of text that you want to wrap to other lines.

67

FORMAT TEXT

You can easily format text by using the Character panel. It has all the controls for formatting text located in one convenient window.

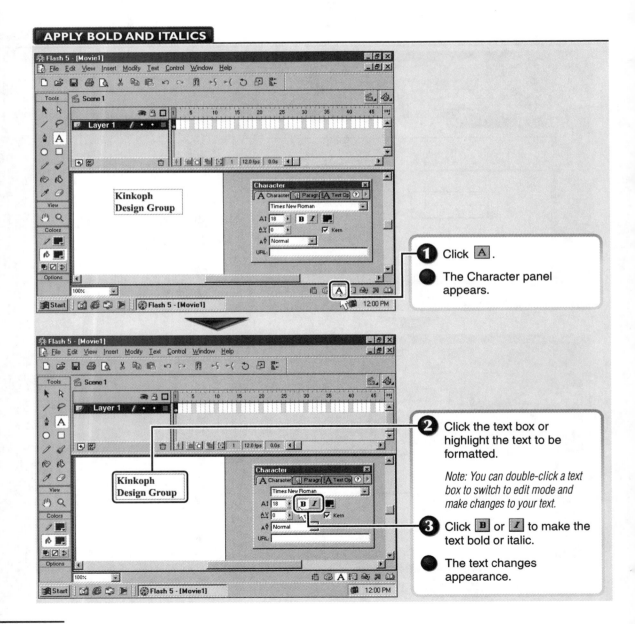

1 Click A.

■ The Character panel appears.

2 Click the text box or highlight the text to be formatted.

Note: You can double-click a text box to switch to edit mode and make changes to your text.

3 Click B or I to make the text bold or italic.

■ The text changes appearance.

in an *instant*

CHANGE THE FONT AND SIZE

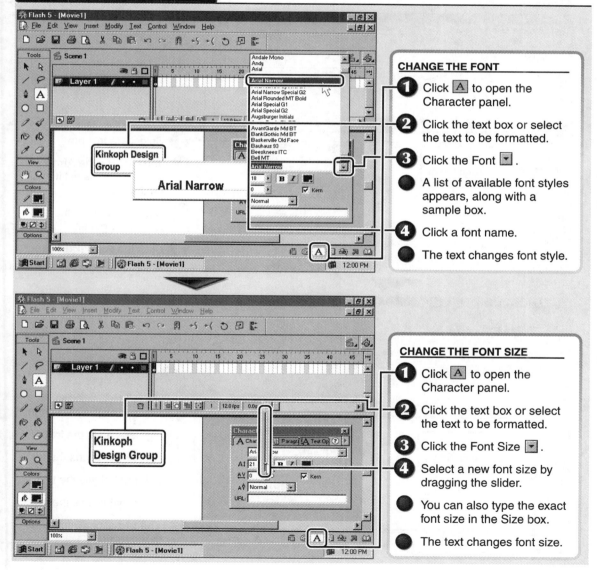

CHANGE THE FONT

1 Click A to open the Character panel.

2 Click the text box or select the text to be formatted.

3 Click the Font ▼.

● A list of available font styles appears, along with a sample box.

4 Click a font name.

● The text changes font style.

CHANGE THE FONT SIZE

1 Click A to open the Character panel.

2 Click the text box or select the text to be formatted.

3 Click the Font Size ▼.

4 Select a new font size by dragging the slider.

● You can also type the exact font size in the Size box.

● The text changes font size.

You can change the way text is aligned within a text box by using the options found in the Paragraph panel. You can also *kern* the text, which means that you adjust the amount of space between individual letters.

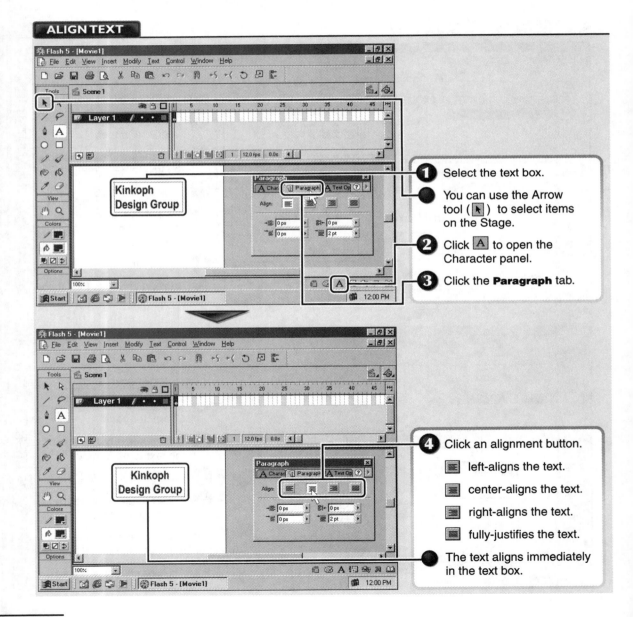

1 Select the text box.

● You can use the Arrow tool (▮) to select items on the Stage.

2 Click **A** to open the Character panel.

3 Click the **Paragraph** tab.

4 Click an alignment button.

▤ left-aligns the text.

▤ center-aligns the text.

▤ right-aligns the text.

▤ fully-justifies the text.

● The text aligns immediately in the text box.

in an *instant*

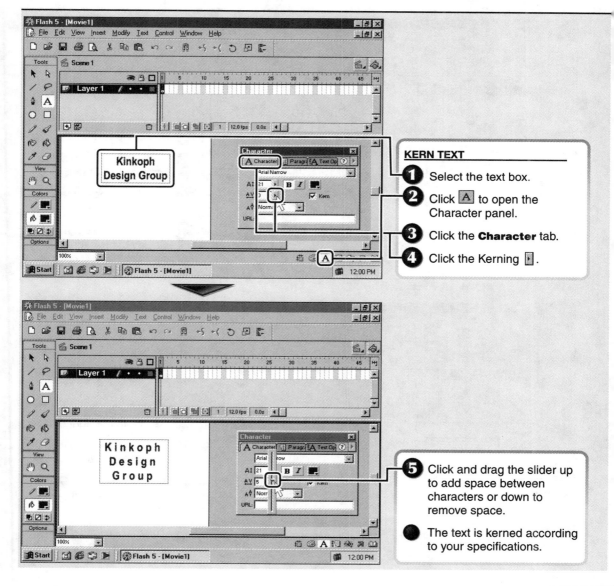

KERN TEXT

1 Select the text box.

2 Click **A** to open the Character panel.

3 Click the **Character** tab.

4 Click the Kerning ▶.

5 Click and drag the slider up to add space between characters or down to remove space.

● The text is kerned according to your specifications.

SET TEXT BOX MARGINS AND LINE INDENTS

You can set margins and indents within text boxes for greater control of text positioning. You can find margin and indent commands in the Paragraph panel.

SET MARGINS

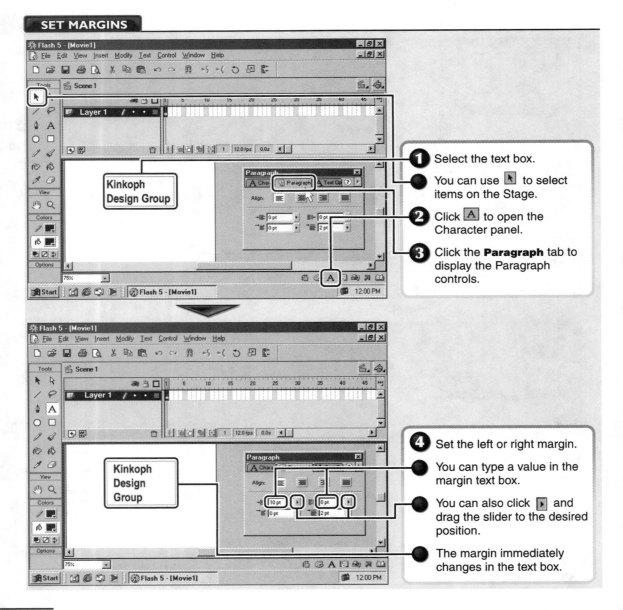

1. Select the text box.

   You can use ![cursor] to select items on the Stage.

2. Click ![A] to open the Character panel.

3. Click the **Paragraph** tab to display the Paragraph controls.

4. Set the left or right margin.

   You can type a value in the margin text box.

   You can also click ![slider] and drag the slider to the desired position.

   The margin immediately changes in the text box.

in an

SET LINE INDENTS

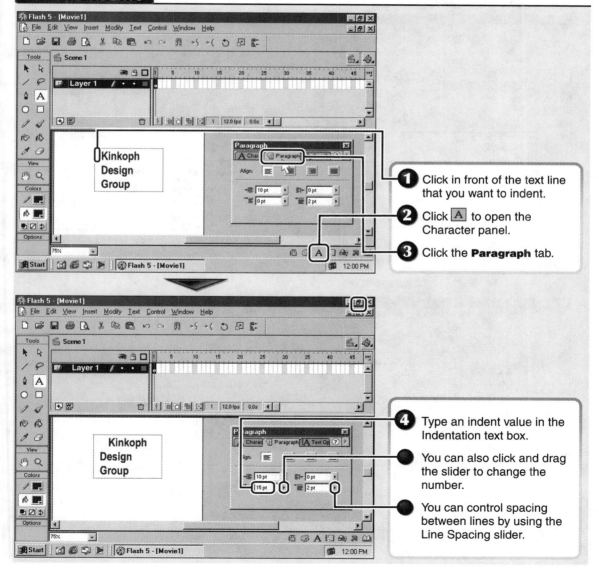

1 Click in front of the text line that you want to indent.

2 Click A to open the Character panel.

3 Click the **Paragraph** tab.

4 Type an indent value in the Indentation text box.

● You can also click and drag the slider to change the number.

● You can control spacing between lines by using the Line Spacing slider.

MOVE AND RESIZE TEXT BOXES

You can move text boxes around on the
Flash Stage or resize them as needed.

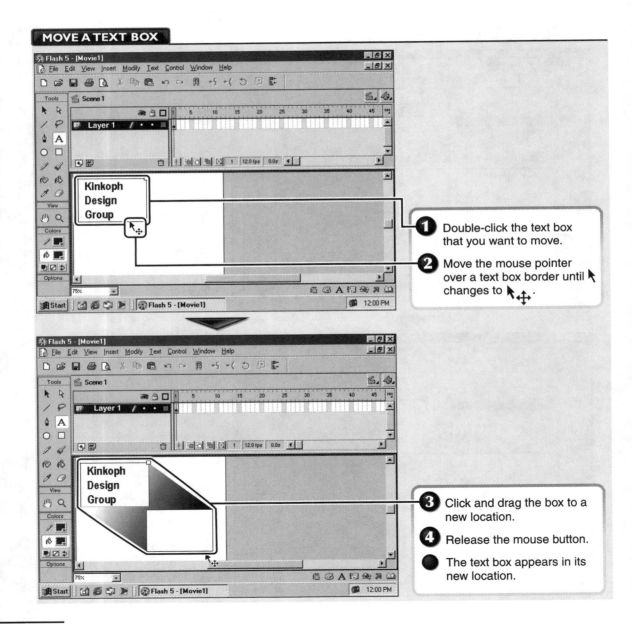

MOVE A TEXT BOX

1 Double-click the text box
that you want to move.

2 Move the mouse pointer
over a text box border until
changes to.

3 Click and drag the box to a
new location.

4 Release the mouse button.

● The text box appears in its
new location.

in an *instant*

RESIZE A TEXT BOX

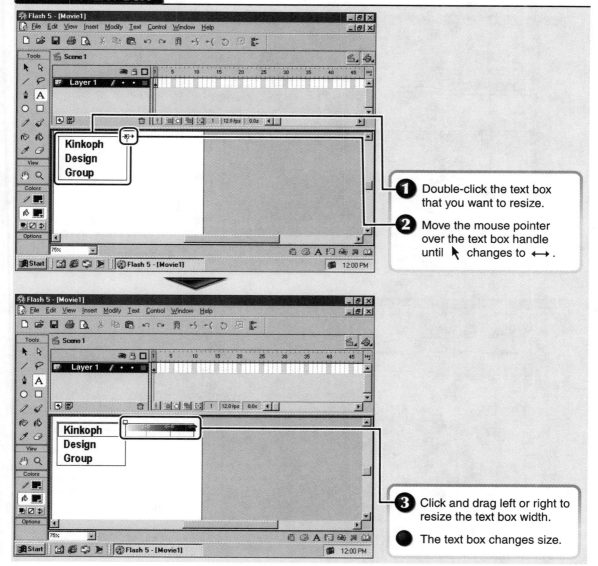

1 Double-click the text box that you want to resize.

2 Move the mouse pointer over the text box handle until ▶ changes to ←→.

3 Click and drag left or right to resize the text box width.

● The text box changes size.

ADD AND DELETE LAYERS

When you create a new movie or scene, Flash starts you out with a single layer and a Timeline. You can add layers to the Timeline or delete layers that you no longer need. Additional layers do not affect the file size, so you can add and delete as many layers as your project requires.

ADD A LAYER

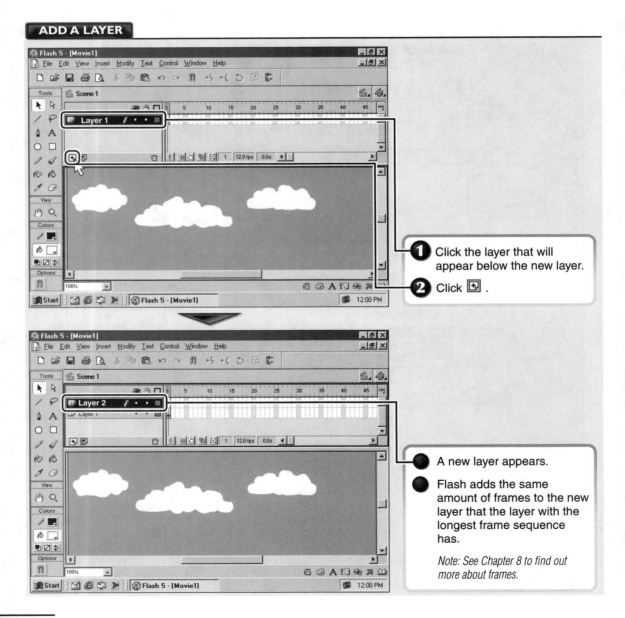

1 Click the layer that will appear below the new layer.

2 Click 🔁 .

● A new layer appears.

● Flash adds the same amount of frames to the new layer that the layer with the longest frame sequence has.

Note: See Chapter 8 to find out more about frames.

in an *instant*

DELETE A LAYER

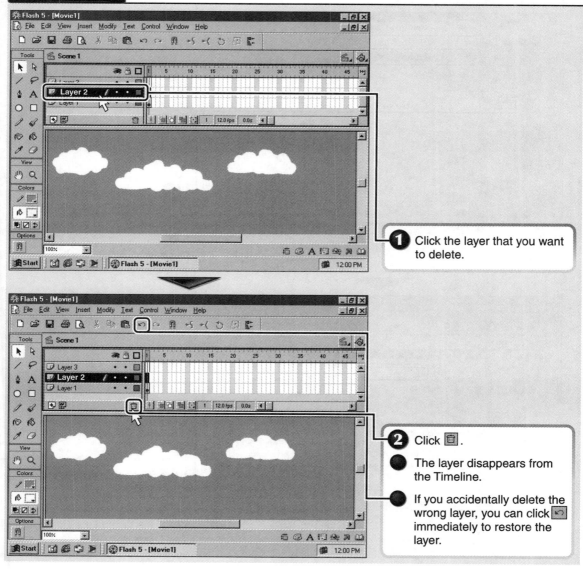

1 Click the layer that you want to delete.

2 Click 🗑.

● The layer disappears from the Timeline.

● If you accidentally delete the wrong layer, you can click ↩ immediately to restore the layer.

SET LAYER PROPERTIES

You can change any aspect of a layer in the
Layer Properties dialog box, a one-stop shop
for controlling a layer's name, function, and
appearance.

SET LAYER PROPERTIES

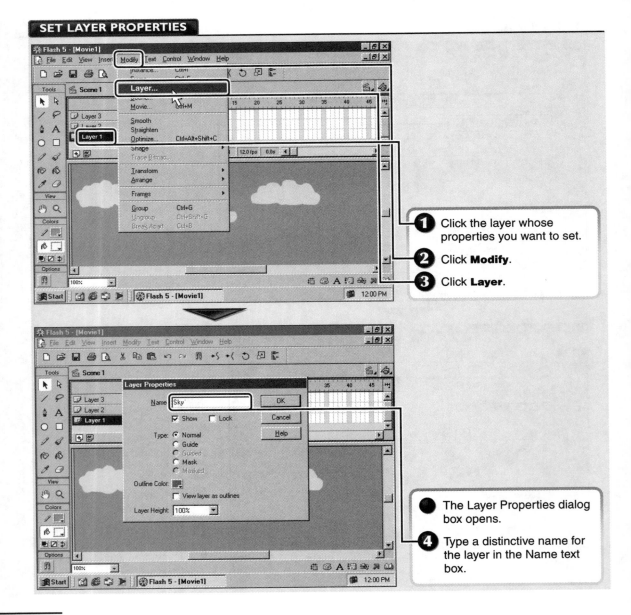

1 Click the layer whose
properties you want to set.

2 Click **Modify**.

3 Click **Layer**.

● The Layer Properties dialog
box opens.

4 Type a distinctive name for
the layer in the Name text
box.

in an *instant*

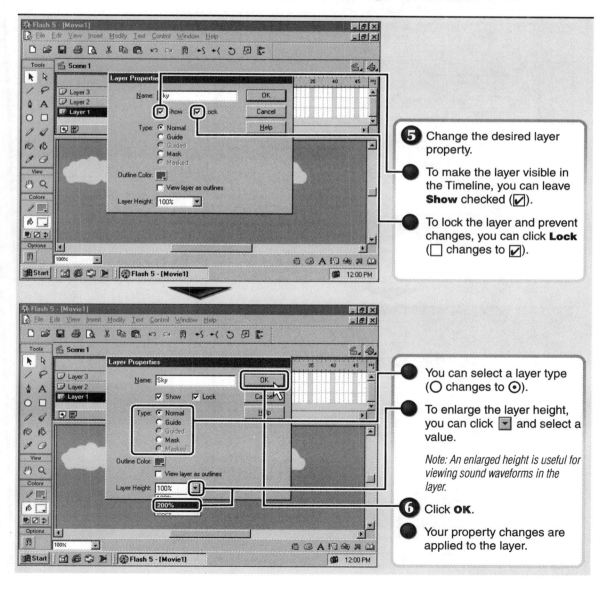

5 Change the desired layer property.

To make the layer visible in the Timeline, you can leave **Show** checked (✓).

To lock the layer and prevent changes, you can click **Lock** (☐ changes to ✓).

You can select a layer type (○ changes to ⊙).

To enlarge the layer height, you can click ▼ and select a value.

Note: An enlarged height is useful for viewing sound waveforms in the layer.

6 Click **OK**.

Your property changes are applied to the layer.

WORK WITH LAYERS IN THE TIMELINE

Flash makes it easy to control layers in the Timeline. You can quickly rename a layer, hide a layer, or lock a layer to prevent changes.

WORK WITH LAYERS IN THE TIMELINE

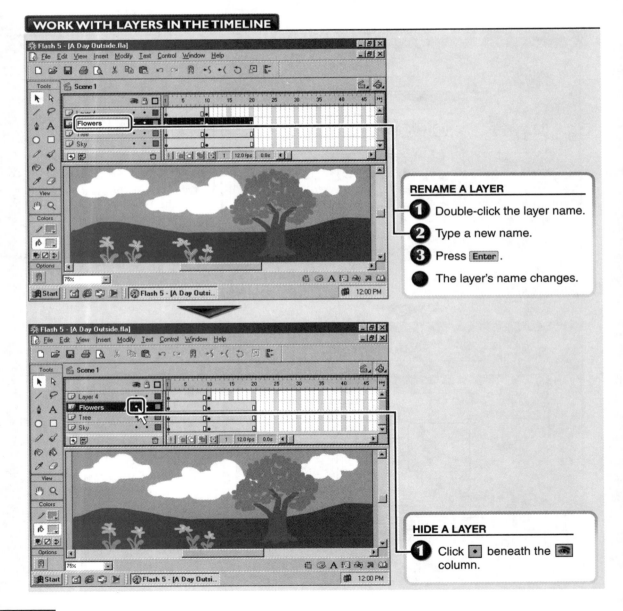

RENAME A LAYER

1 Double-click the layer name.

2 Type a new name.

3 Press [Enter].

● The layer's name changes.

HIDE A LAYER

1 Click ● beneath the 👁 column.

80

in an instant

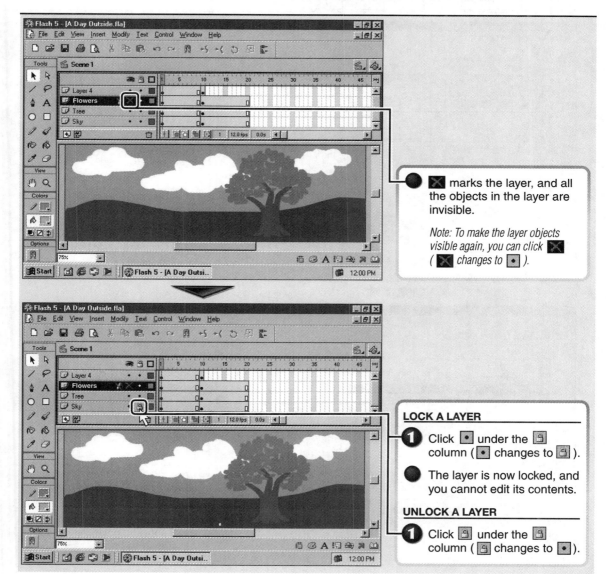

marks the layer, and all the objects in the layer are invisible.

Note: To make the layer objects visible again, you can click ✖ (✖ changes to ●).

LOCK A LAYER

1 Click ● under the 🔒 column (● changes to 🔒).

● The layer is now locked, and you cannot edit its contents.

UNLOCK A LAYER

1 Click 🔒 under the 🔒 column (🔒 changes to ●).

CHANGE THE LAYER STACKING ORDER

To rearrange how objects appear in a Flash movie, you can stack layers in a manner similar to how you stack objects in a drawing. For example, if you have a layer containing background elements, you can move the layer to the back of the layer stack.

CHANGE THE LAYER STACKING ORDER

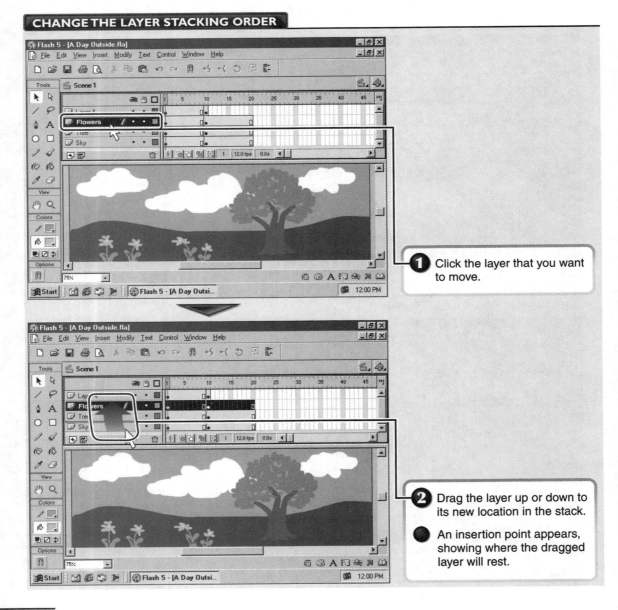

1 Click the layer that you want to move.

2 Drag the layer up or down to its new location in the stack.

● An insertion point appears, showing where the dragged layer will rest.

82

in an *instant*

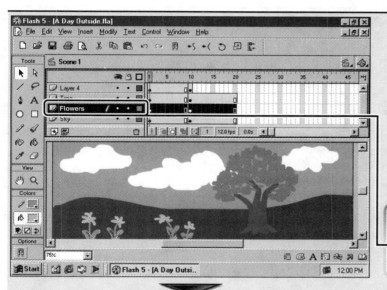

3 Release the mouse button.

■ The layer assumes its new position.

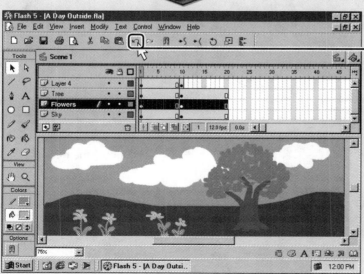

■ You can click ⟲ to move the layer back to its original position.

ADD GUIDE LAYERS

There are two types of guide layers in Flash: *plain* and *motion*. A plain guide layer can help you position objects on the Stage. A motion guide layer contains an animation path that links to an object on another layer. Neither guide layer appears in your final movie.

ADD GUIDE LAYERS

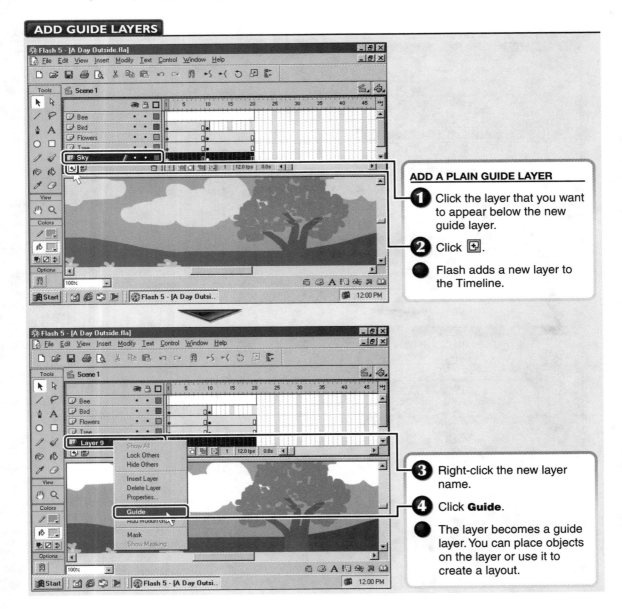

ADD A PLAIN GUIDE LAYER

1 Click the layer that you want to appear below the new guide layer.

2 Click 🔁.

● Flash adds a new layer to the Timeline.

3 Right-click the new layer name.

4 Click **Guide**.

● The layer becomes a guide layer. You can place objects on the layer or use it to create a layout.

in an *instant*

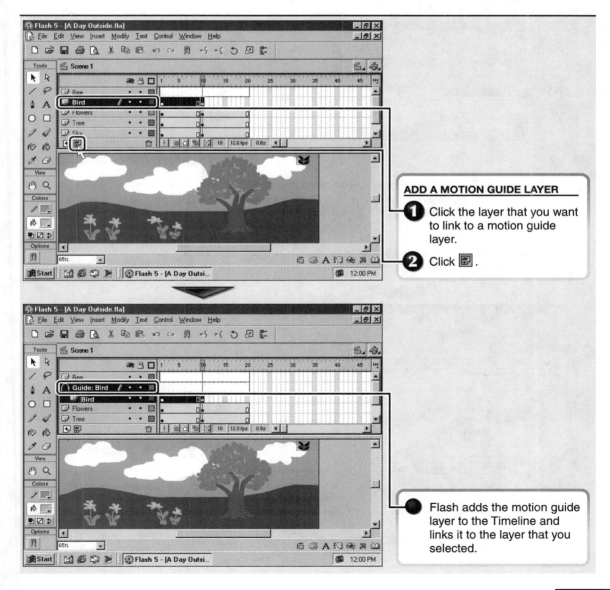

1 Click the layer that you want to link to a motion guide layer.

2 Click 🖼️.

● Flash adds the motion guide layer to the Timeline and links it to the layer that you selected.

CREATE MASK LAYERS

You can use mask layers to hide various elements on underlying layers. A mask is much like a stencil you tape to a wall: only certain portions of the underlying layer appear through the mask design, while other parts of the layer are hidden, or *masked*. Masked layers are linked to layers and are exported in the final movie file.

CREATE MASK LAYERS

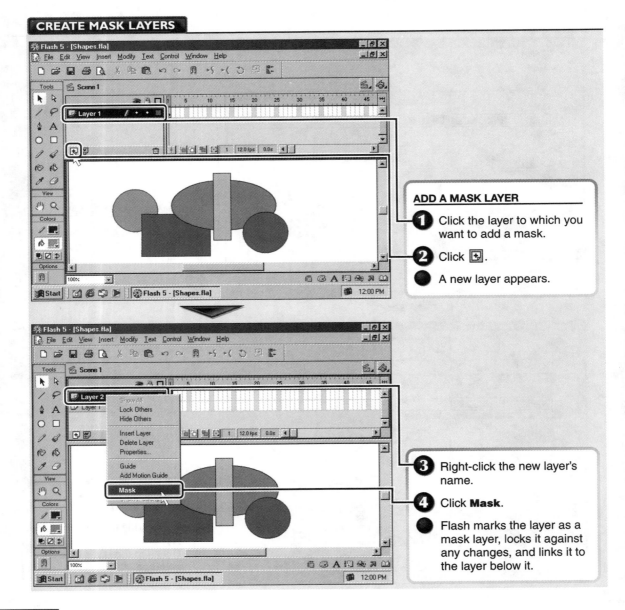

ADD A MASK LAYER

1 Click the layer to which you want to add a mask.

2 Click ⊞.

● A new layer appears.

3 Right-click the new layer's name.

4 Click **Mask**.

● Flash marks the layer as a mask layer, locks it against any changes, and links it to the layer below it.

in an

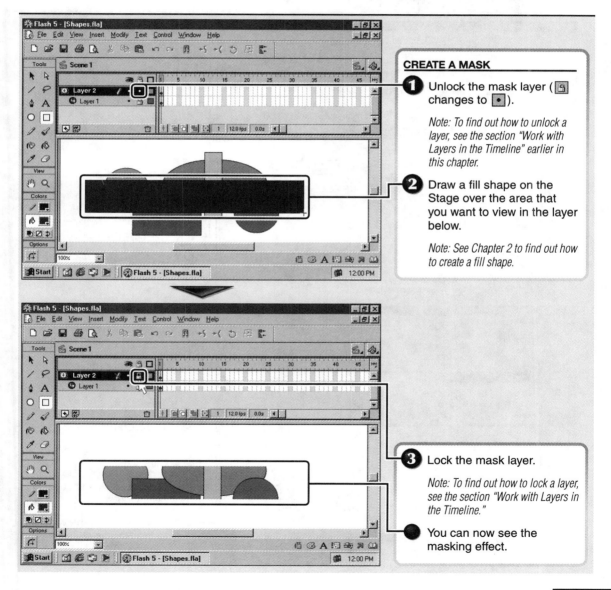

CREATE A MASK

1 Unlock the mask layer (changes to).

Note: To find out how to unlock a layer, see the section "Work with Layers in the Timeline" earlier in this chapter.

2 Draw a fill shape on the Stage over the area that you want to view in the layer below.

Note: See Chapter 2 to find out how to create a fill shape.

3 Lock the mask layer.

Note: To find out how to lock a layer, see the section "Work with Layers in the Timeline."

● You can now see the masking effect.

USING THE FLASH LIBRARY

A Flash project may contain hundreds of graphics, sounds, interactive buttons, and movie clips. The Flash Library helps you organize these elements. You can store related symbols in the same folder, create new folders, or delete folders and symbols that you no longer need for your projects.

OPEN THE LIBRARY WINDOW

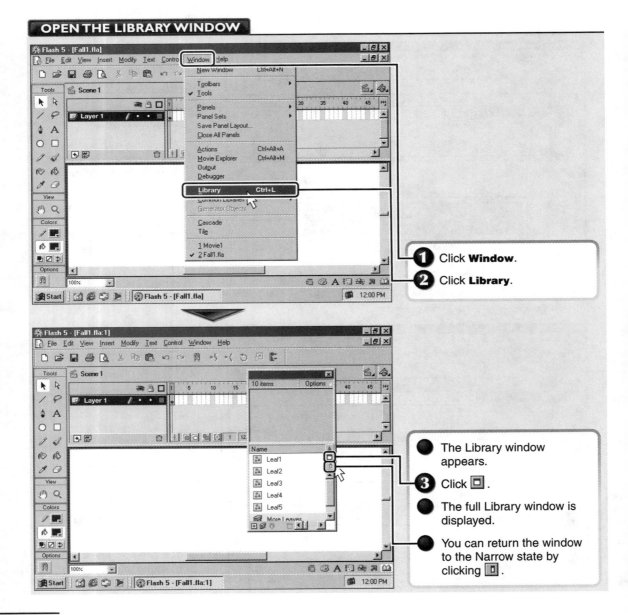

① Click **Window**.

② Click **Library**.

● The Library window appears.

③ Click 🔲 .

● The full Library window is displayed.

● You can return the window to the Narrow state by clicking 🔲 .

in an *instant*

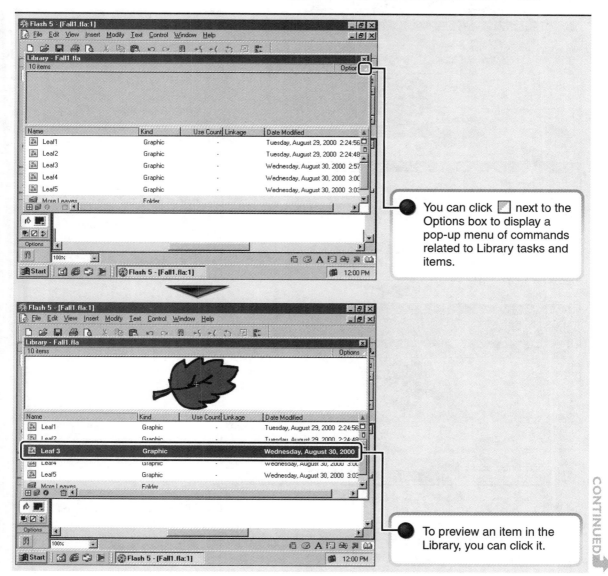

You can click [ ] next to the Options box to display a pop-up menu of commands related to Library tasks and items.

To preview an item in the Library, you can click it.

You can use the folders in the Library window to help you organize symbols for your projects. You can add and delete folders and move symbols from one folder to another.

ORGANIZE SYMBOLS WITH FOLDERS

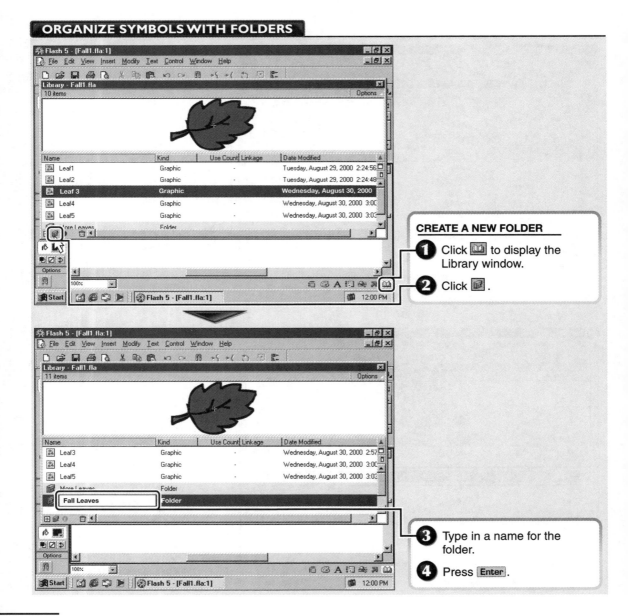

CREATE A NEW FOLDER

1 Click 📖 to display the Library window.

2 Click 📁 .

3 Type in a name for the folder.

4 Press Enter .

in an *instant*

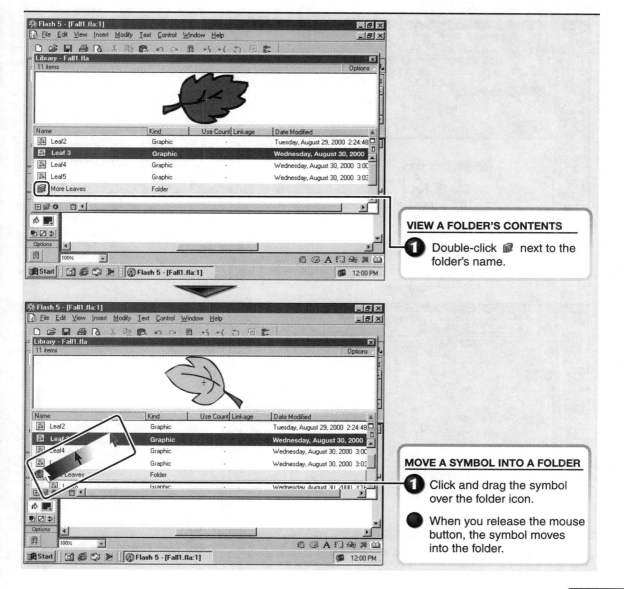

VIEW A FOLDER'S CONTENTS

1 Double-click 📁 next to the folder's name.

MOVE A SYMBOL INTO A FOLDER

1 Click and drag the symbol over the folder icon.

● When you release the mouse button, the symbol moves into the folder.

CREATE SYMBOLS

You can easily turn any object you draw on the Flash Stage into a symbol that you can reuse throughout your project.

CREATE SYMBOLS

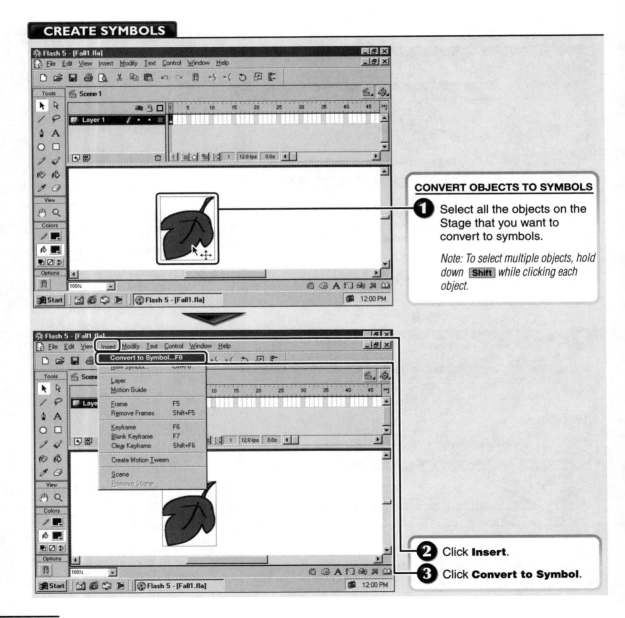

CONVERT OBJECTS TO SYMBOLS

① Select all the objects on the Stage that you want to convert to symbols.

Note: To select multiple objects, hold down **Shift** *while clicking each object.*

② Click **Insert**.

③ Click **Convert to Symbol**.

in an *instant*

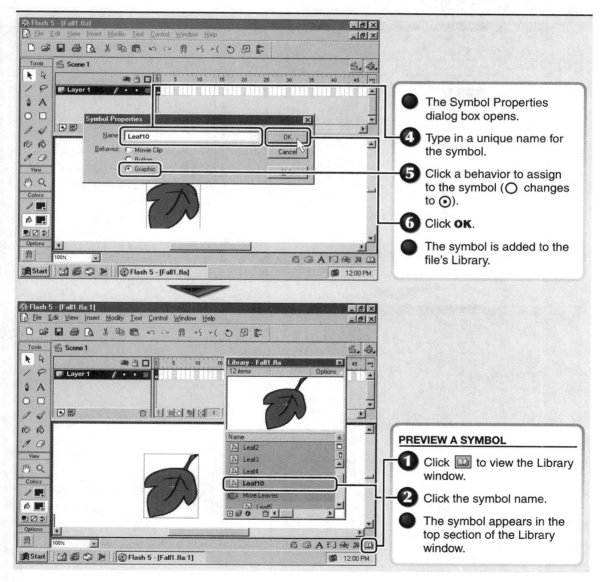

The Symbol Properties dialog box opens.

4 Type in a unique name for the symbol.

5 Click a behavior to assign to the symbol (○ changes to ⊙).

6 Click **OK**.

The symbol is added to the file's Library.

PREVIEW A SYMBOL

1 Click 📖 to view the Library window.

2 Click the symbol name.

The symbol appears in the top section of the Library window.

INSERT A SYMBOL INSTANCE

To reuse a symbol in your Flash project, you can place an instance of it on the Stage. An *instance* is a copy of the original symbol. An instance references the original instead of duplicating it all over again, which decreases the movie's file size.

INSERT A SYMBOL INSTANCE

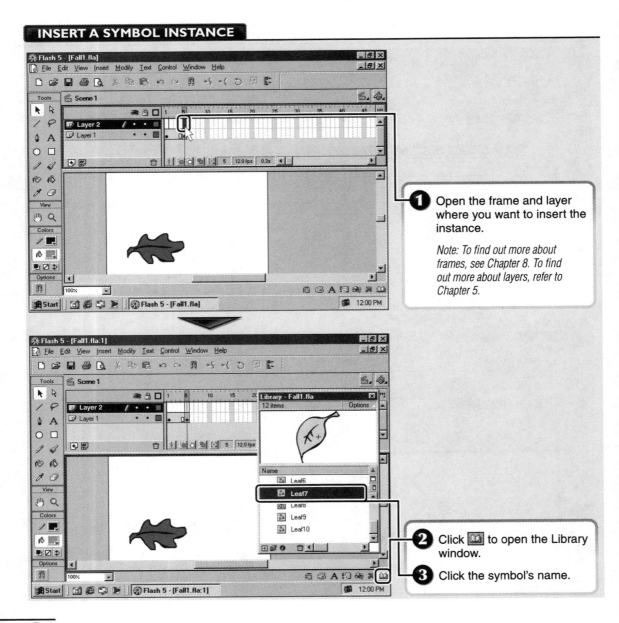

1 Open the frame and layer where you want to insert the instance.

Note: To find out more about frames, see Chapter 8. To find out more about layers, refer to Chapter 5.

2 Click 📖 to open the Library window.

3 Click the symbol's name.

in an *instant*

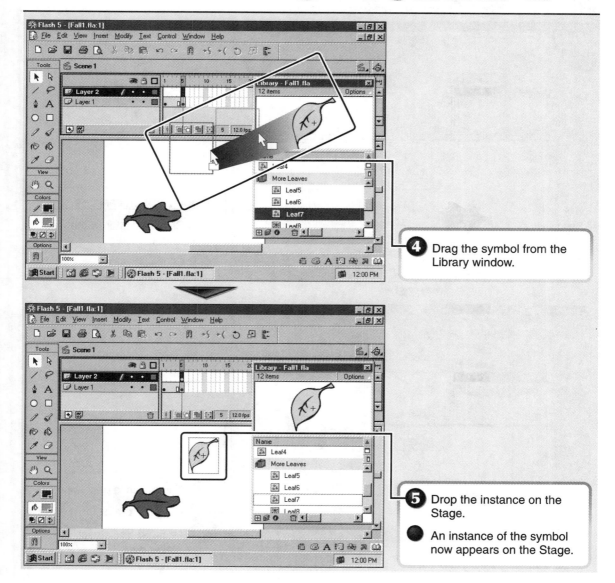

4 Drag the symbol from the Library window.

5 Drop the instance on the Stage.

● An instance of the symbol now appears on the Stage.

MODIFY A SYMBOL INSTANCE

You can change the way a symbol instance appears without
changing the original symbol. For example, you can change its
color or make it appear transparent.

MODIFY A SYMBOL INSTANCE

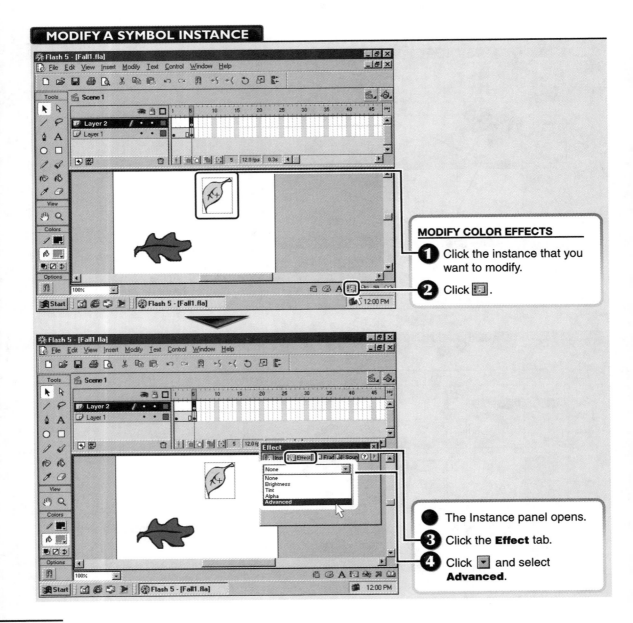

MODIFY COLOR EFFECTS

1 Click the instance that you want to modify.

2 Click ▦.

● The Instance panel opens.

3 Click the **Effect** tab.

4 Click ▾ and select **Advanced**.

in an *instant*

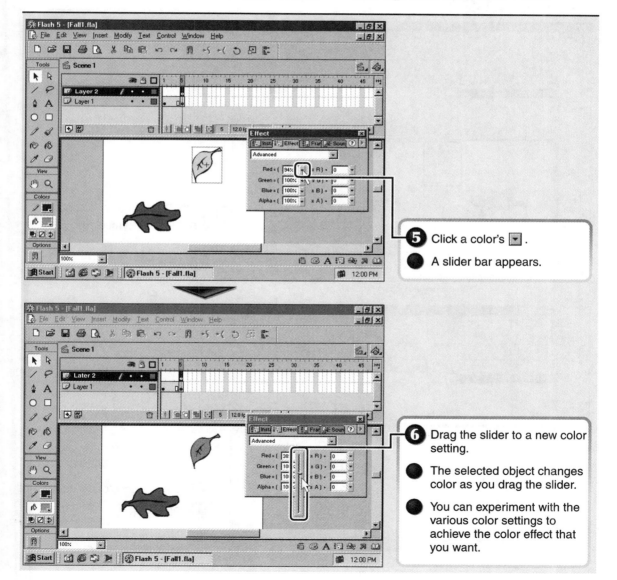

5 Click a color's ▼.

● A slider bar appears.

6 Drag the slider to a new color setting.

● The selected object changes color as you drag the slider.

● You can experiment with the various color settings to achieve the color effect that you want.

EDIT SYMBOLS

You can make changes to an original symbol, and Flash will automatically update all instances of that symbol in your movie.

EDIT SYMBOLS

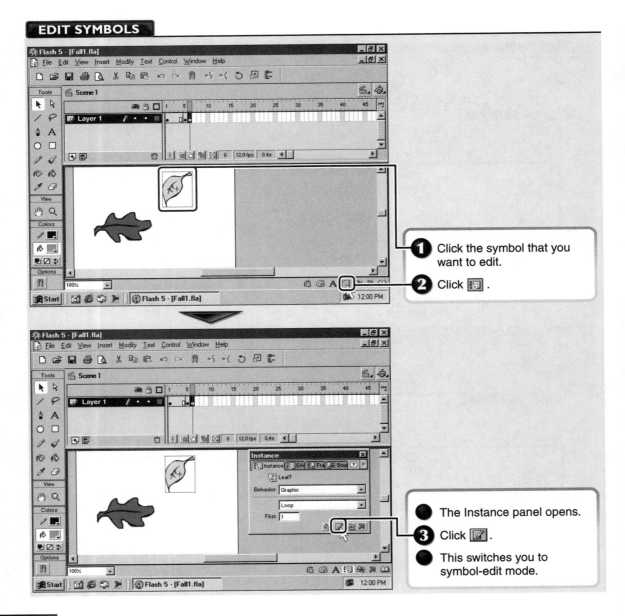

1 Click the symbol that you want to edit.

2 Click [button].

■ The Instance panel opens.

3 Click [button].

■ This switches you to symbol-edit mode.

in an *instant*

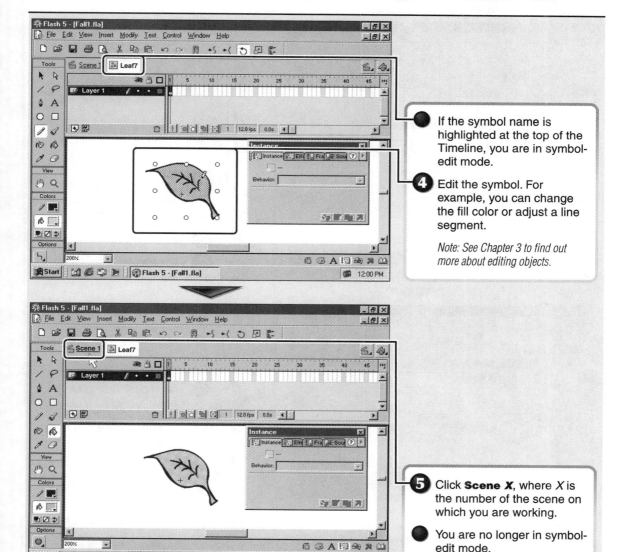

If the symbol name is highlighted at the top of the Timeline, you are in symbol-edit mode.

④ Edit the symbol. For example, you can change the fill color or adjust a line segment.

Note: See Chapter 3 to find out more about editing objects.

⑤ Click **Scene X**, where *X* is the number of the scene on which you are working.

● You are no longer in symbol-edit mode.

IMPORT GRAPHICS

You can import graphics from other sources
to use in your Flash animations.

IMPORT GRAPHICS

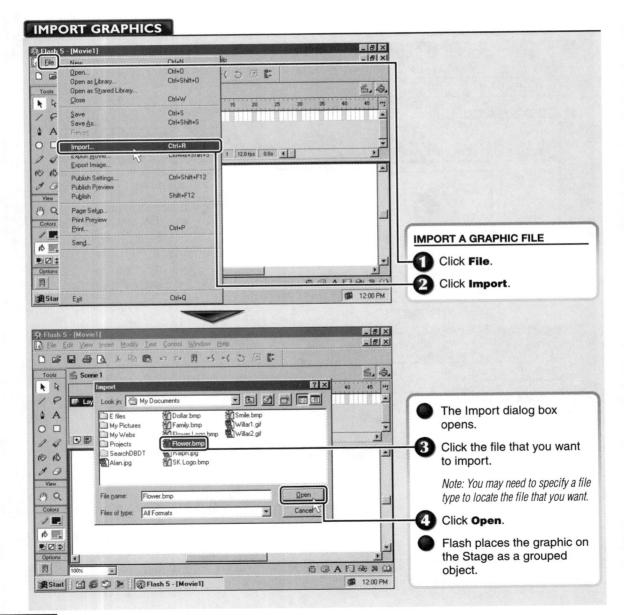

IMPORT A GRAPHIC FILE

1. Click **File**.

2. Click **Import**.

● The Import dialog box
opens.

3. Click the file that you want
to import.

*Note: You may need to specify a file
type to locate the file that you want.*

4. Click **Open**.

● Flash places the graphic on
the Stage as a grouped
object.

in an *instant*

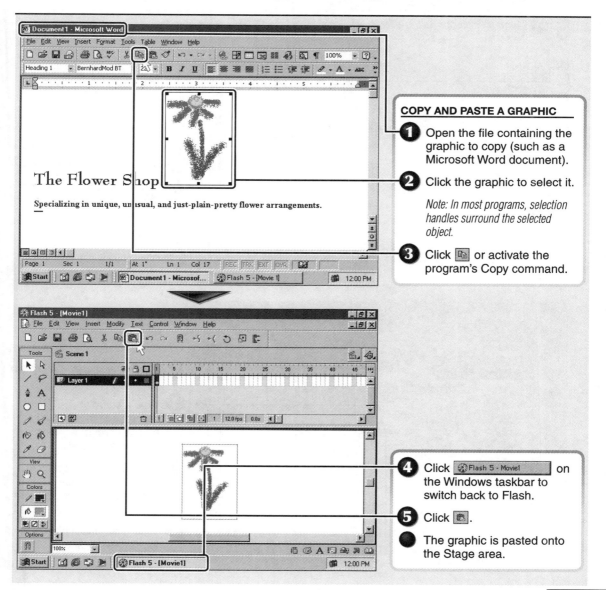

COPY AND PASTE A GRAPHIC

1 Open the file containing the graphic to copy (such as a Microsoft Word document).

2 Click the graphic to select it.

Note: In most programs, selection handles surround the selected object.

3 Click 🗐 or activate the program's Copy command.

4 Click 🦋 Flash 5 - Movie1 on the Windows taskbar to switch back to Flash.

5 Click 🗐.

● The graphic is pasted onto the Stage area.

CONVERT BITMAPS TO VECTOR GRAPHICS

Turning a bitmap graphic into a vector graphic can minimize the file size and enable you to manipulate the graphic using Flash tools. Bitmap graphics are made up of pixels and often have large file sizes; vector graphics use mathematical equations instead of pixels to define the shape, color, position, and size and are easily scaled.

CONVERT BITMAPS TO VECTOR GRAPHICS

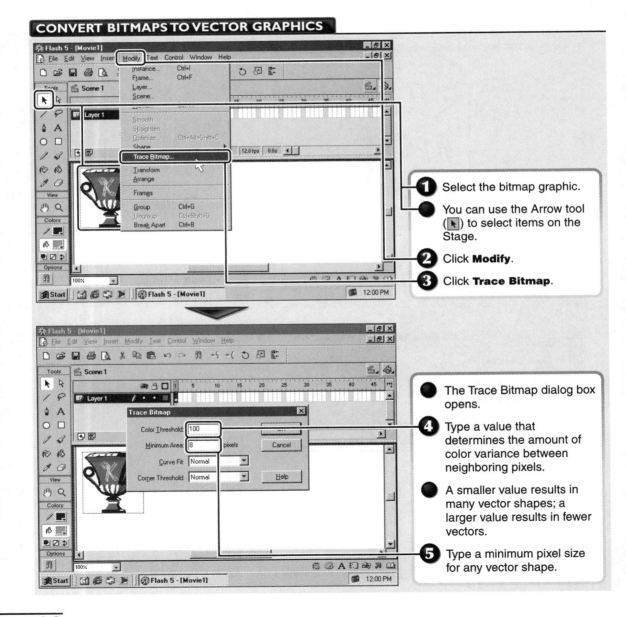

1 Select the bitmap graphic.

■ You can use the Arrow tool (▸) to select items on the Stage.

2 Click **Modify**.

3 Click **Trace Bitmap**.

■ The Trace Bitmap dialog box opens.

4 Type a value that determines the amount of color variance between neighboring pixels.

■ A smaller value results in many vector shapes; a larger value results in fewer vectors.

5 Type a minimum pixel size for any vector shape.

in an *instant*

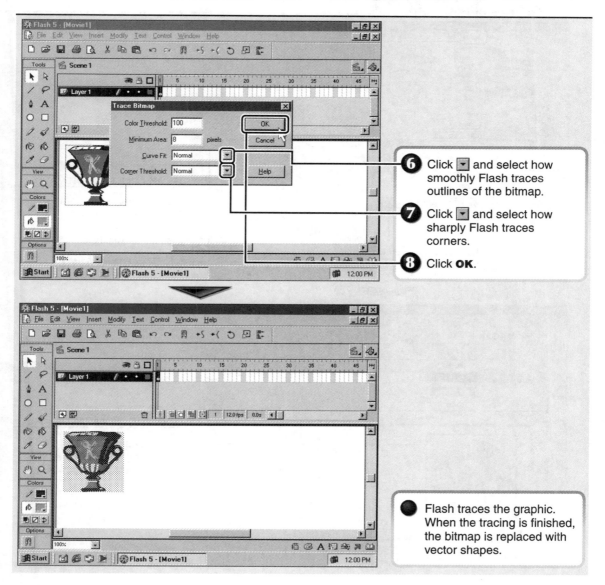

6 Click ▼ and select how smoothly Flash traces outlines of the bitmap.

7 Click ▼ and select how sharply Flash traces corners.

8 Click **OK**.

● Flash traces the graphic. When the tracing is finished, the bitmap is replaced with vector shapes.

TURN BITMAPS INTO FILLS

You can turn a bitmap image into a fill so that you can
use it with the Flash drawing tools that use fills, such as
the Oval, Rectangle, or Brush.

TURN BITMAPS INTO FILLS

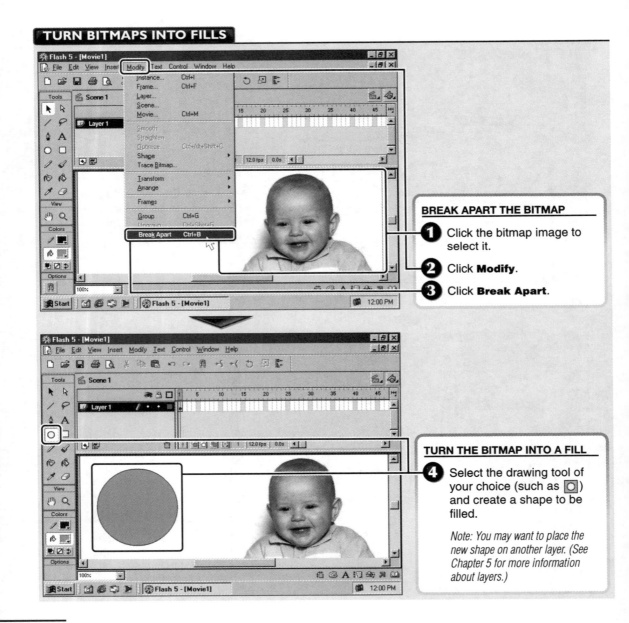

BREAK APART THE BITMAP

1 Click the bitmap image to
select it.

2 Click **Modify**.

3 Click **Break Apart**.

TURN THE BITMAP INTO A FILL

4 Select the drawing tool of
your choice (such as ◯)
and create a shape to be
filled.

*Note: You may want to place the
new shape on another layer. (See
Chapter 5 for more information
about layers.)*

in an *instant*

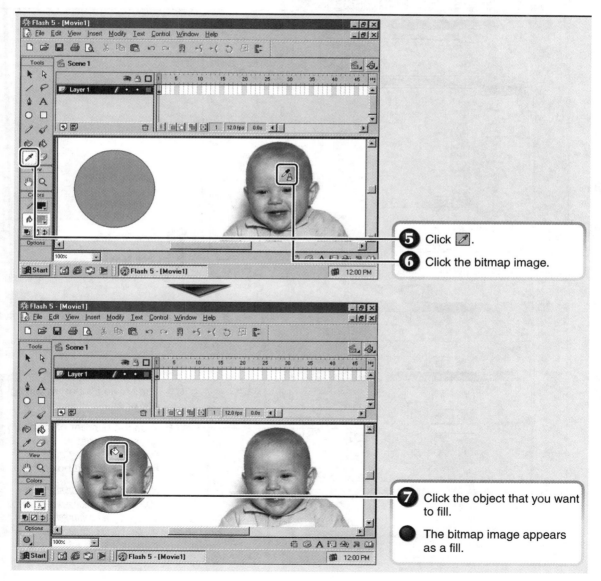

5 Click 🖋.

6 Click the bitmap image.

7 Click the object that you want to fill.

● The bitmap image appears as a fill.

SET MOVIE DIMENSIONS AND SPEED

A movie's *dimensions* refer to its vertical and horizontal size on the Stage. The movie's play speed determines the number of frames per second, or *fps,* for the animation. Take time to set up the size of your movie and the speed at which you want it to play. Planning out your project in advance saves you time and headaches later.

SET MOVIE DIMENSIONS AND SPEED

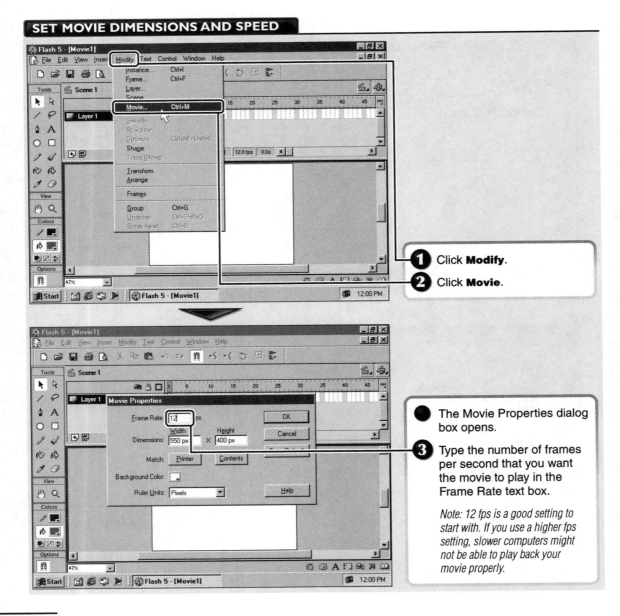

1 Click **Modify**.

2 Click **Movie**.

● The Movie Properties dialog box opens.

3 Type the number of frames per second that you want the movie to play in the Frame Rate text box.

Note: 12 fps is a good setting to start with. If you use a higher fps setting, slower computers might not be able to play back your movie properly.

106

in an instant

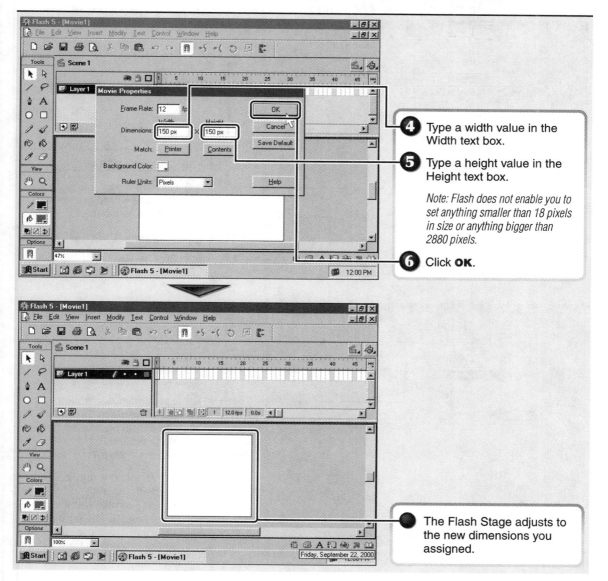

4 Type a width value in the Width text box.

5 Type a height value in the Height text box.

Note: Flash does not enable you to set anything smaller than 18 pixels in size or anything bigger than 2880 pixels.

6 Click **OK**.

● The Flash Stage adjusts to the new dimensions you assigned.

107

ADD REGULAR FRAMES OR KEYFRAMES

When you add a new layer or start a new file, Flash starts you out with one keyframe in the Timeline and lots of placeholder frames. To add content to your movie, you must add frames to the Timeline: either regular frames to repeat keyframe content or keyframes to define changes in the animation's appearance.

ADD REGULAR FRAMES OR KEYFRAMES

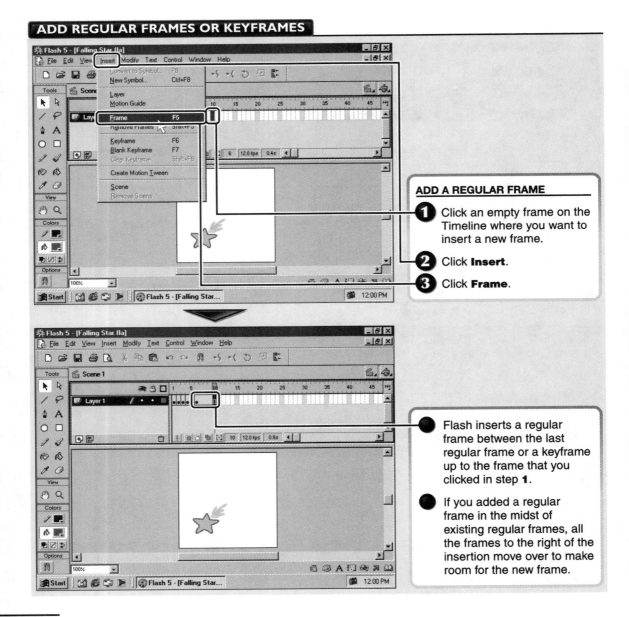

ADD A REGULAR FRAME

1 Click an empty frame on the Timeline where you want to insert a new frame.

2 Click **Insert**.

3 Click **Frame**.

● Flash inserts a regular frame between the last regular frame or a keyframe up to the frame that you clicked in step **1**.

● If you added a regular frame in the midst of existing regular frames, all the frames to the right of the insertion move over to make room for the new frame.

in an instant

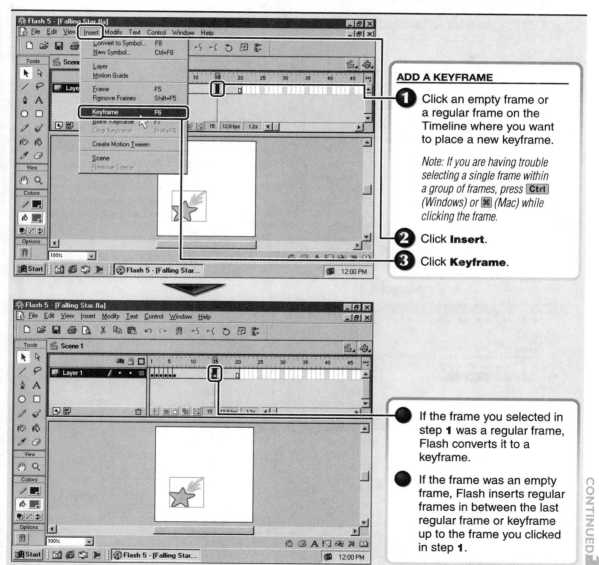

ADD A KEYFRAME

1 Click an empty frame or a regular frame on the Timeline where you want to place a new keyframe.

Note: If you are having trouble selecting a single frame within a group of frames, press Ctrl (Windows) or ⌘ (Mac) while clicking the frame.

2 Click **Insert**.

3 Click **Keyframe**.

● If the frame you selected in step **1** was a regular frame, Flash converts it to a keyframe.

● If the frame was an empty frame, Flash inserts regular frames in between the last regular frame or keyframe up to the frame you clicked in step **1**.

CONTINUED

ADD REGULAR FRAMES OR KEYFRAMES

You can add a default keyframe or add a blank keyframe. If you add a default keyframe, Flash copies the previous keyframe, and you can quickly edit its contents on the Stage. If you add a blank keyframe, the frame is completely empty and ready for new content.

ADD REGULAR FRAMES OR KEYFRAMES (CONTINUED)

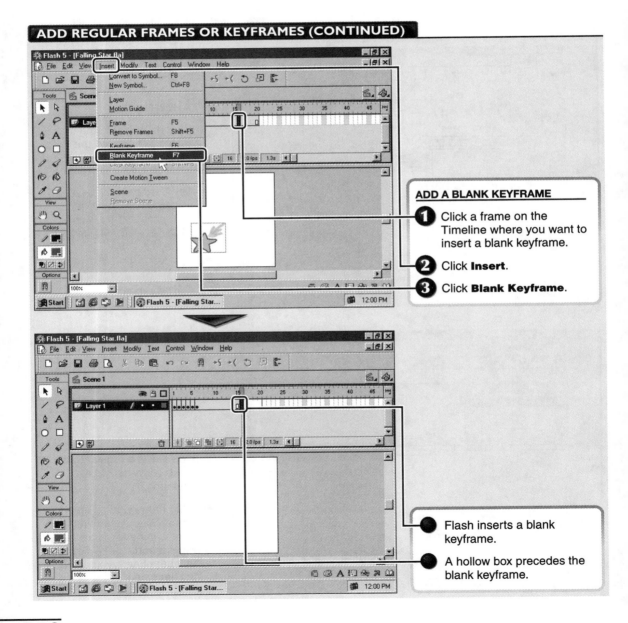

ADD A BLANK KEYFRAME

1 Click a frame on the Timeline where you want to insert a blank keyframe.

2 Click **Insert**.

3 Click **Blank Keyframe**.

● Flash inserts a blank keyframe.

● A hollow box precedes the blank keyframe.

in an instant

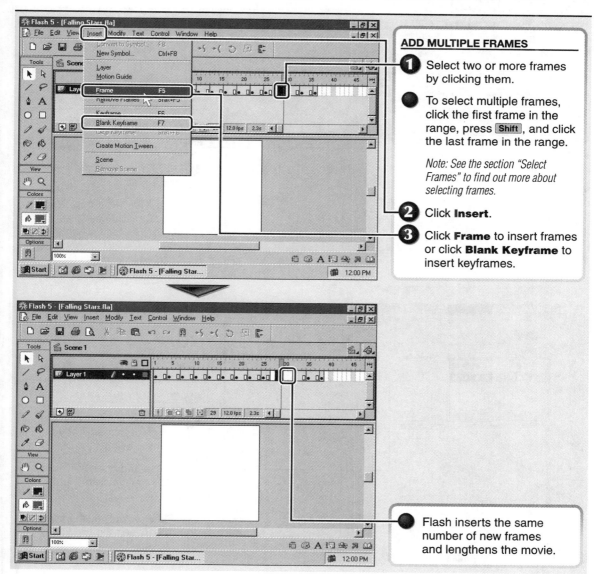

ADD MULTIPLE FRAMES

1️⃣ Select two or more frames by clicking them.

⬤ To select multiple frames, click the first frame in the range, press **Shift**, and click the last frame in the range.

Note: See the section "Select Frames" to find out more about selecting frames.

2️⃣ Click **Insert**.

3️⃣ Click **Frame** to insert frames or click **Blank Keyframe** to insert keyframes.

⬤ Flash inserts the same number of new frames and lengthens the movie.

111

SELECT FRAMES

When you work with frames in the Flash Timeline, you must select a single frame or multiple frames in order to edit them for your animation.

SELECT FRAMES

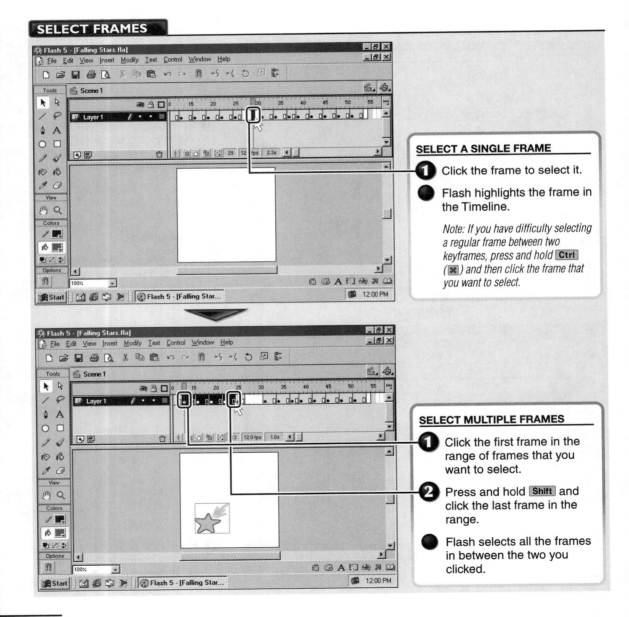

SELECT A SINGLE FRAME

1 Click the frame to select it.

● Flash highlights the frame in the Timeline.

Note: If you have difficulty selecting a regular frame between two keyframes, press and hold Ctrl (⌘) and then click the frame that you want to select.

SELECT MULTIPLE FRAMES

1 Click the first frame in the range of frames that you want to select.

2 Press and hold Shift and click the last frame in the range.

● Flash selects all the frames in between the two you clicked.

MODIFY FRAME PROPERTIES

You can use the Frame panel to help organize frames with labels, assign actions, or even add sound clips.

MODIFY FRAME PROPERTIES

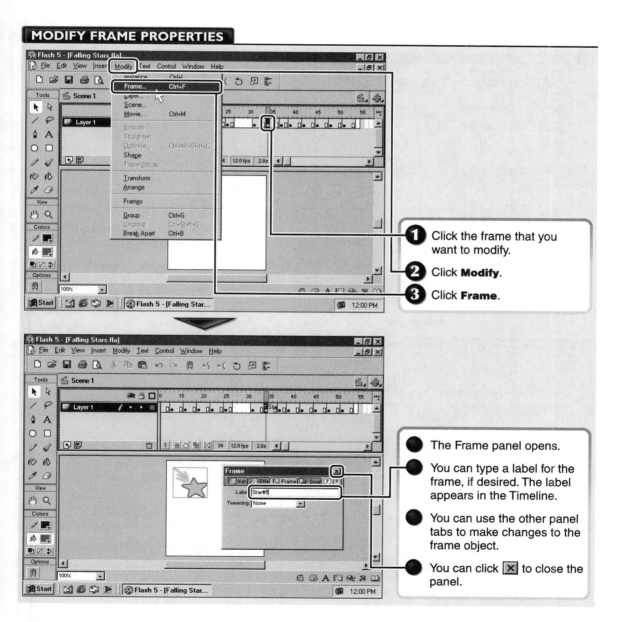

1 Click the frame that you want to modify.

2 Click **Modify**.

3 Click **Frame**.

● The Frame panel opens.

● You can type a label for the frame, if desired. The label appears in the Timeline.

● You can use the other panel tabs to make changes to the frame object.

● You can click ☒ to close the panel.

MOVE AND COPY FRAMES

One way that you can edit your movie is to move or copy frames in the animation sequence. You cannot copy frames like you copy other objects in Flash; you must use the Copy Frames and Paste Frames commands found in the Edit menu.

MOVE A FRAME

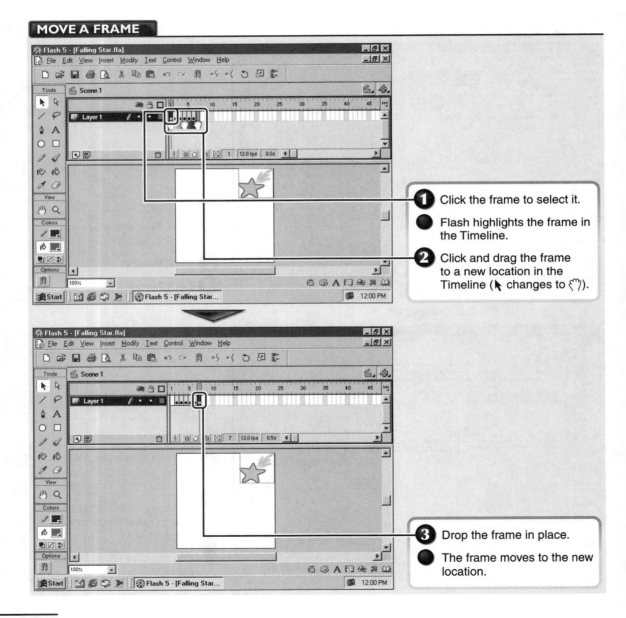

① Click the frame to select it.

● Flash highlights the frame in the Timeline.

② Click and drag the frame to a new location in the Timeline (k changes to ⊰ᵐ⊱).

③ Drop the frame in place.

● The frame moves to the new location.

in an *instant*

COPY A FRAME

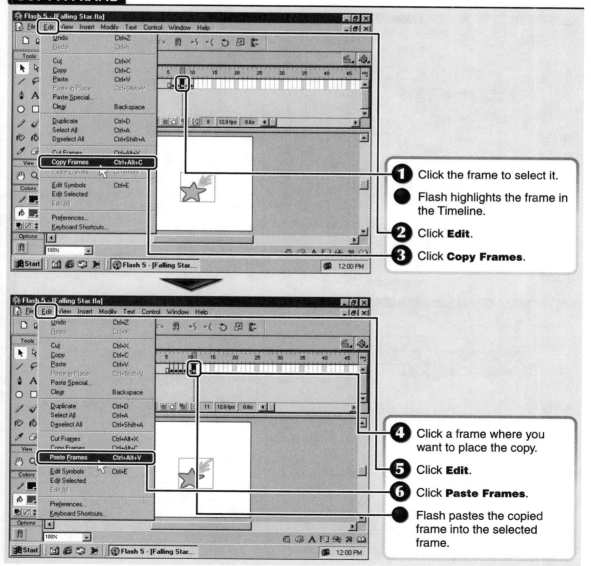

1 Click the frame to select it.

● Flash highlights the frame in the Timeline.

2 Click **Edit**.

3 Click **Copy Frames**.

4 Click a frame where you want to place the copy.

5 Click **Edit**.

6 Click **Paste Frames**.

● Flash pastes the copied frame into the selected frame.

115

DELETE FRAMES

You can remove frames that you no longer need. To delete frames from the Timeline, you use the Remove Frames command.

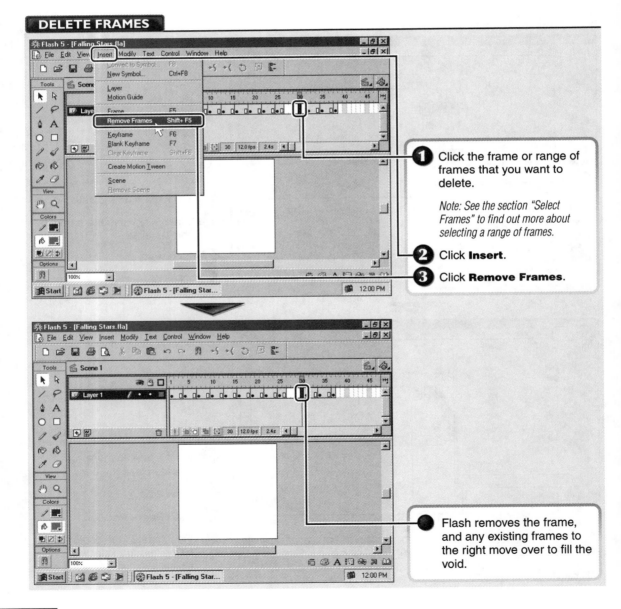

1 Click the frame or range of frames that you want to delete.

Note: See the section "Select Frames" to find out more about selecting a range of frames.

2 Click **Insert**.

3 Click **Remove Frames**.

● Flash removes the frame, and any existing frames to the right move over to fill the void.

REMOVE KEYFRAME STATUS

When you remove a frame's keyframe status, you demote it
to a regular frame. If you change a keyframe's status, all the
in-between frames associated with it are altered as well.

REMOVE KEYFRAME STATUS

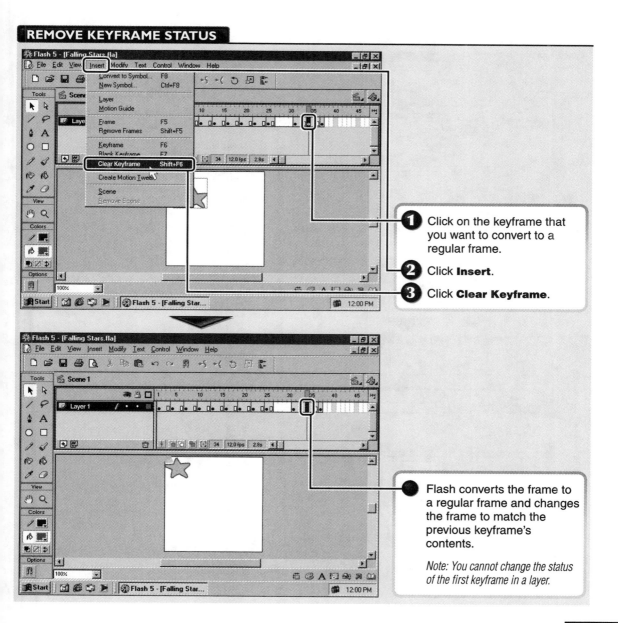

1 Click on the keyframe that
you want to convert to a
regular frame.

2 Click **Insert**.

3 Click **Clear Keyframe**.

● Flash converts the frame to
a regular frame and changes
the frame to match the
previous keyframe's
contents.

*Note: You cannot change the status
of the first keyframe in a layer.*

117

CREATE FRAME-BY-FRAME ANIMATION

You can create the illusion of movement by changing the placement or appearance of the Stage content from keyframe to keyframe in the Flash Timeline. This type of animation is called *frame-by-frame animation*.

CREATE FRAME-BY-FRAME ANIMATION

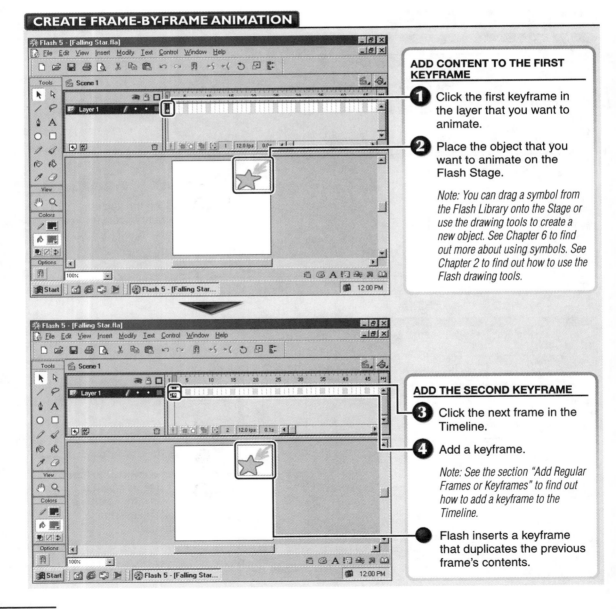

ADD CONTENT TO THE FIRST KEYFRAME

1 Click the first keyframe in the layer that you want to animate.

2 Place the object that you want to animate on the Flash Stage.

Note: You can drag a symbol from the Flash Library onto the Stage or use the drawing tools to create a new object. See Chapter 6 to find out more about using symbols. See Chapter 2 to find out how to use the Flash drawing tools.

ADD THE SECOND KEYFRAME

3 Click the next frame in the Timeline.

4 Add a keyframe.

Note: See the section "Add Regular Frames or Keyframes" to find out how to add a keyframe to the Timeline.

● Flash inserts a keyframe that duplicates the previous frame's contents.

in an *instant*

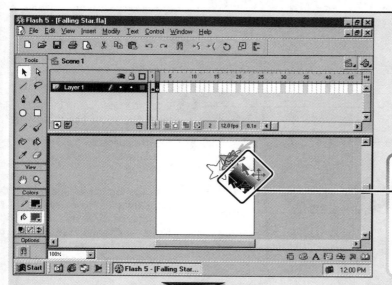

CHANGE THE OBJECT SLIGHTLY

5 Change the object slightly to animate it. For example, move the object a bit on the Stage or change the object's appearance (such as a different color or size).

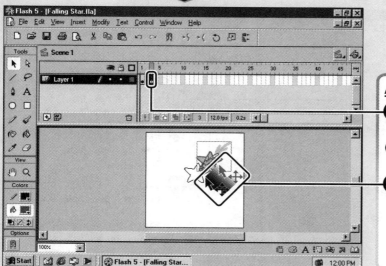

ADD THE THIRD KEYFRAME

6 Click the next frame in the layer and add a keyframe.

⬤ Flash duplicates the previous keyframe's contents.

7 Change the object slightly again. For example, move the object a bit more on the Stage or change the object's appearance (such as a different color or size).

CONTINUED

CREATE FRAME-BY-FRAME ANIMATION

You can learn animation principles by creating a simple sequence, such as moving an object across the Stage. In this section, the sample animation has a star that appears to drop from the top right to the bottom left.

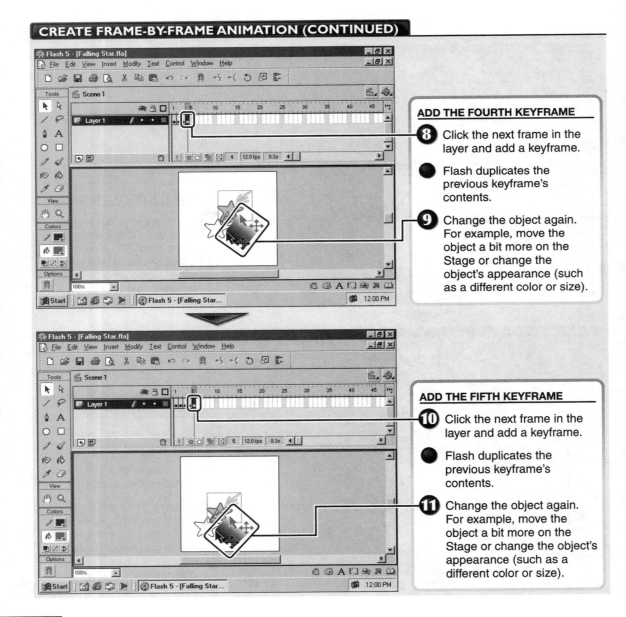

ADD THE FOURTH KEYFRAME

8 Click the next frame in the layer and add a keyframe.

● Flash duplicates the previous keyframe's contents.

9 Change the object again. For example, move the object a bit more on the Stage or change the object's appearance (such as a different color or size).

ADD THE FIFTH KEYFRAME

10 Click the next frame in the layer and add a keyframe.

● Flash duplicates the previous keyframe's contents.

11 Change the object again. For example, move the object a bit more on the Stage or change the object's appearance (such as a different color or size).

in an *instant*

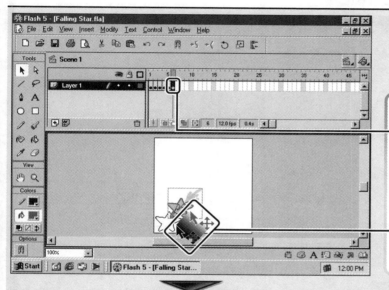

ADD THE SIXTH KEYFRAME

12 Click the next frame in the layer and add a final keyframe.

● Flash duplicates the previous keyframe's contents.

13 Change the object again for the final keyframe in the animation sequence.

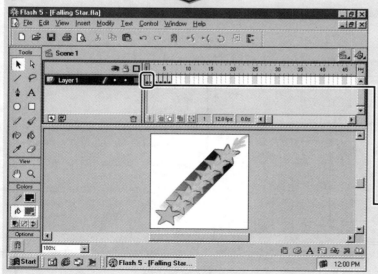

PLAY BACK THE MOVIE

14 Click the first keyframe in the layer and press **Enter**.

● Flash plays the entire animation sequence.

ONION-SKINNING AN ANIMATION

You can use Flash's onion-skinning feature to view the frames preceding and following the current frame and see how their movements relate to the current frame. The current frame's contents are fully displayed, while objects in the frames surrounding the current frame are dimmed or outlined.

ONION-SKINNING AN ANIMATION

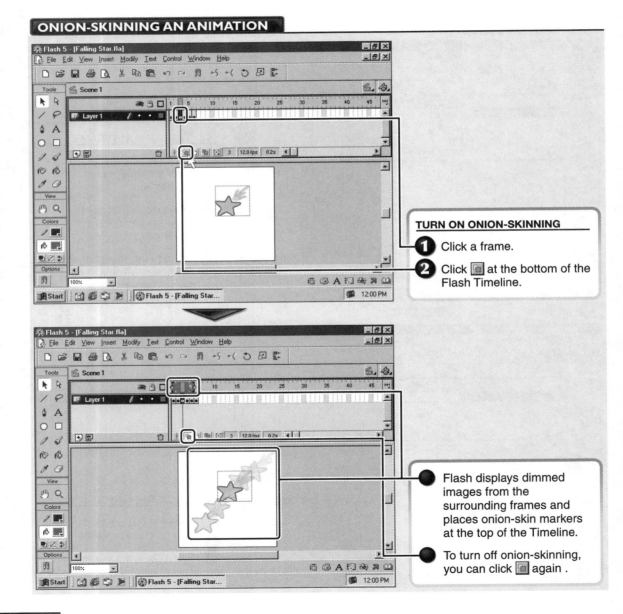

TURN ON ONION-SKINNING

1 Click a frame.

2 Click ⬛ at the bottom of the Flash Timeline.

● Flash displays dimmed images from the surrounding frames and places onion-skin markers at the top of the Timeline.

● To turn off onion-skinning, you can click ⬛ again.

in an *instant*

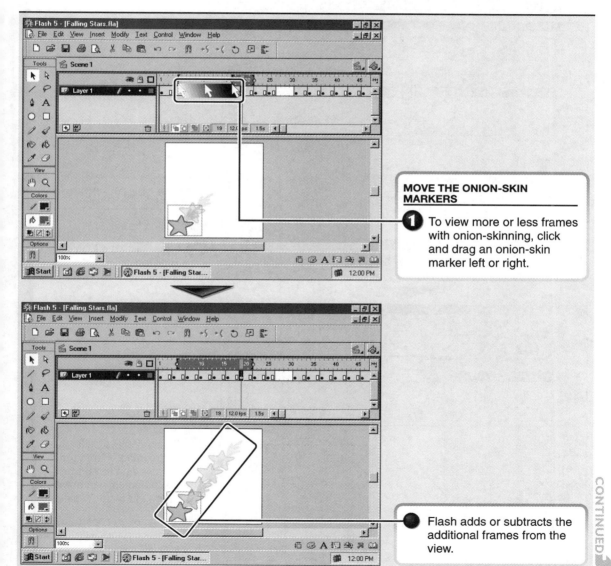

MOVE THE ONION-SKIN MARKERS

1 To view more or less frames with onion-skinning, click and drag an onion-skin marker left or right.

● Flash adds or subtracts the additional frames from the view.

CONTINUED

123

ONION-SKINNING AN ANIMATION

You can control which frames appear in onion-skin mode by using the onion-skin markers that appear on the Timeline. You can also control the markers by using the Modify Onion Markers pop-up menu.

ONION-SKINNING AN ANIMATION (CONTINUED)

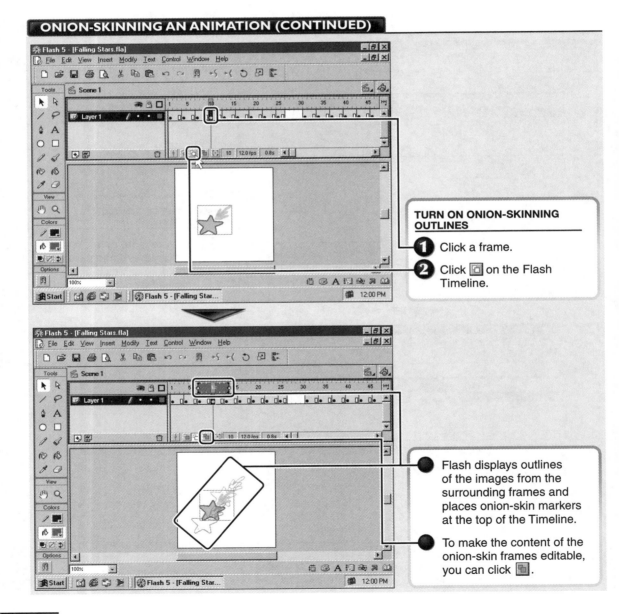

TURN ON ONION-SKINNING OUTLINES

1 Click a frame.

2 Click the icon on the Flash Timeline.

● Flash displays outlines of the images from the surrounding frames and places onion-skin markers at the top of the Timeline.

● To make the content of the onion-skin frames editable, you can click the icon.

in an *instant*

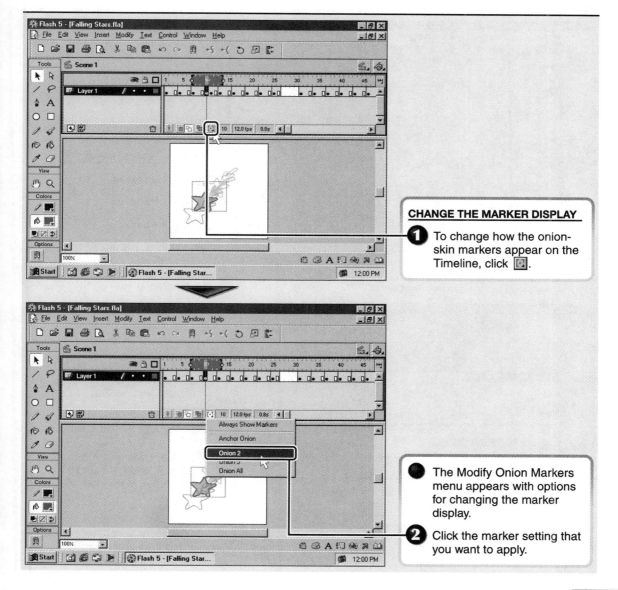

CHANGE THE MARKER DISPLAY

1 To change how the onion-skin markers appear on the Timeline, click 🔲.

● The Modify Onion Markers menu appears with options for changing the marker display.

2 Click the marker setting that you want to apply.

125

CREATE SCENES

To help you organize your movies, you can break up your movie into scenes. Scenes are subsets of the whole movie turned into their own independent Timelines.

CREATE SCENES

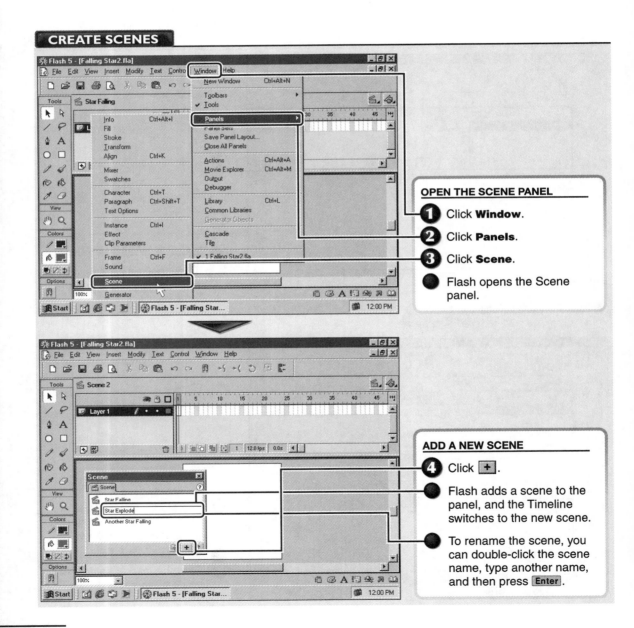

OPEN THE SCENE PANEL

1 Click **Window**.

2 Click **Panels**.

3 Click **Scene**.

● Flash opens the Scene panel.

ADD A NEW SCENE

4 Click ⊞.

● Flash adds a scene to the panel, and the Timeline switches to the new scene.

● To rename the scene, you can double-click the scene name, type another name, and then press Enter.

in an *instant*

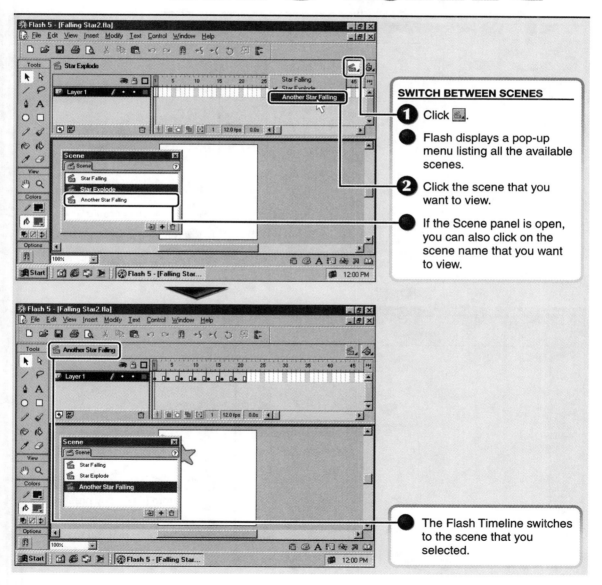

SWITCH BETWEEN SCENES

1 Click 🎬.

Flash displays a pop-up menu listing all the available scenes.

2 Click the scene that you want to view.

If the Scene panel is open, you can also click on the scene name that you want to view.

The Flash Timeline switches to the scene that you selected.

PREVIEW A FLASH ANIMATION

You can preview your animation to check the movie sequence and see how it plays. The Test Movie command plays your animation in the Flash Player window.

PREVIEW A FLASH ANIMATION

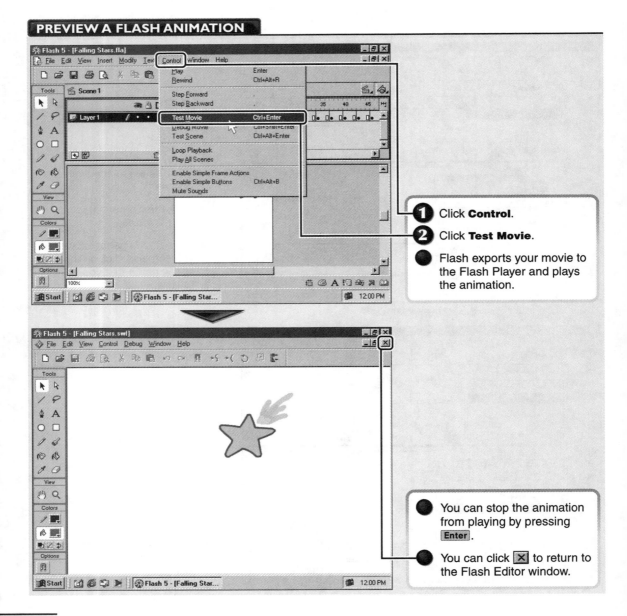

1 Click **Control**.

2 Click **Test Movie**.

● Flash exports your movie to the Flash Player and plays the animation.

● You can stop the animation from playing by pressing `Enter`.

● You can click ☒ to return to the Flash Editor window.

ADJUST THE ANIMATION SPEED

The animation frame rate is constant throughout a movie, but you can slow down or speed up an animation by adding or subtracting frames. By adding in-between frames rather than keyframes, you do not increase the movie's file size.

ADJUST THE ANIMATION SPEED

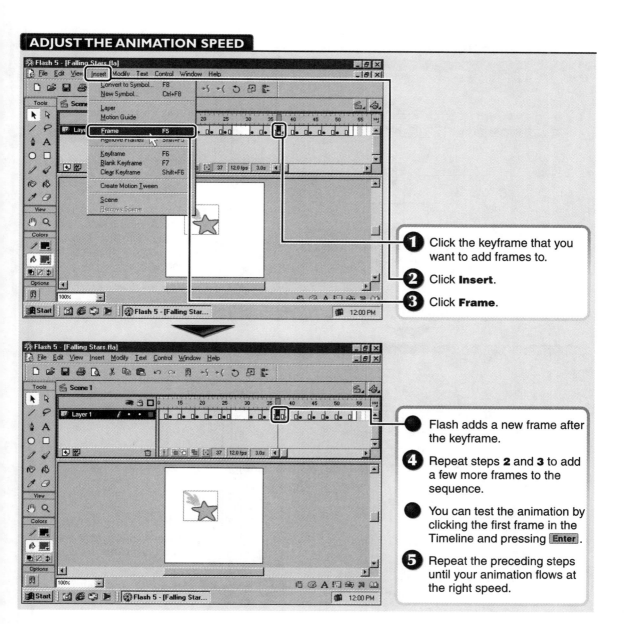

1 Click the keyframe that you want to add frames to.

2 Click **Insert**.

3 Click **Frame**.

● Flash adds a new frame after the keyframe.

4 Repeat steps **2** and **3** to add a few more frames to the sequence.

● You can test the animation by clicking the first frame in the Timeline and pressing Enter.

5 Repeat the preceding steps until your animation flows at the right speed.

129

CREATE A MOTION TWEEN

You can animate moving symbols with a motion tween. A *motion tween* is when you define two points of movement in the Timeline with two keyframes and then let Flash calculate all the frames needed between the two points. You can motion tween only symbols or grouped objects, and you can tween only one symbol per layer.

CREATE A MOTION TWEEN

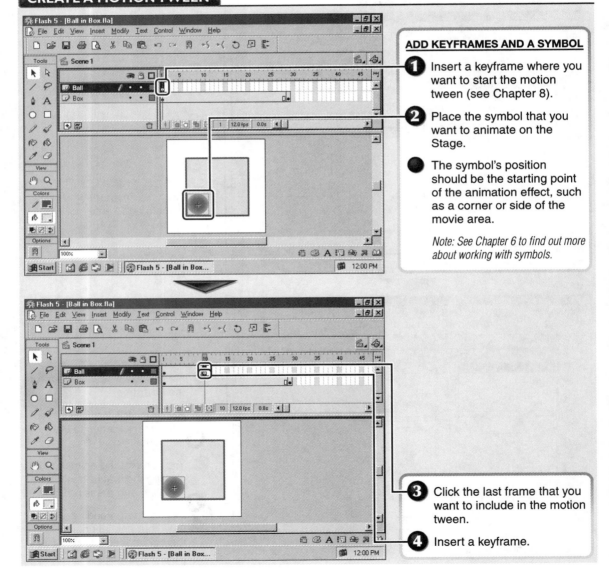

ADD KEYFRAMES AND A SYMBOL

1 Insert a keyframe where you want to start the motion tween (see Chapter 8).

2 Place the symbol that you want to animate on the Stage.

● The symbol's position should be the starting point of the animation effect, such as a corner or side of the movie area.

Note: See Chapter 6 to find out more about working with symbols.

3 Click the last frame that you want to include in the motion tween.

4 Insert a keyframe.

in an *instant*

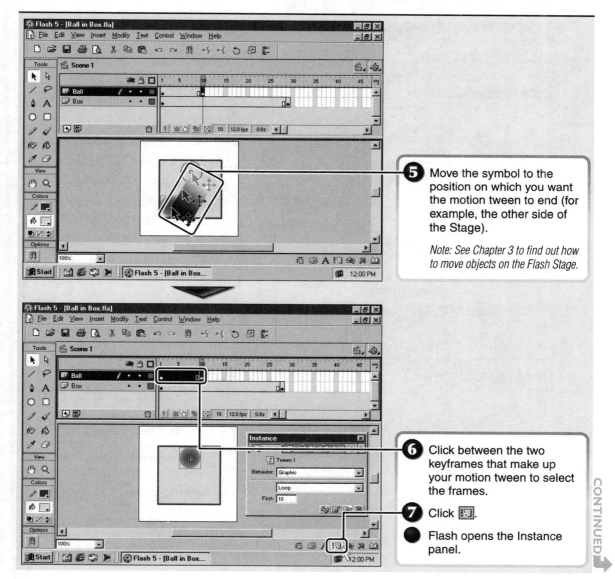

5 Move the symbol to the position on which you want the motion tween to end (for example, the other side of the Stage).

Note: See Chapter 3 to find out how to move objects on the Flash Stage.

6 Click between the two keyframes that make up your motion tween to select the frames.

7 Click 🖳.

● Flash opens the Instance panel.

CONTINUED

CREATE A MOTION TWEEN

You can assign as many motion tween segments as you like throughout your movie, or you can make your animation one long motion tween.

CREATE A MOTION TWEEN (CONTINUED)

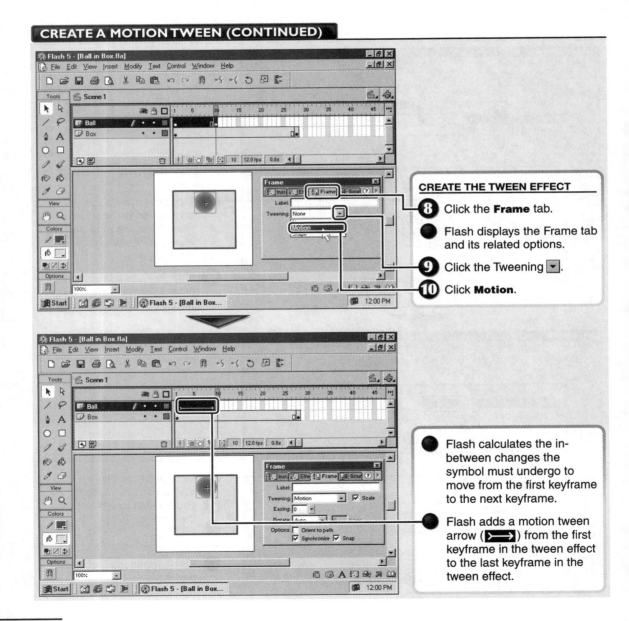

CREATE THE TWEEN EFFECT

8 Click the **Frame** tab.

● Flash displays the Frame tab and its related options.

9 Click the Tweening ▼.

10 Click **Motion**.

● Flash calculates the in-between changes the symbol must undergo to move from the first keyframe to the next keyframe.

● Flash adds a motion tween arrow (▶━━▶) from the first keyframe in the tween effect to the last keyframe in the tween effect.

in an *instant*

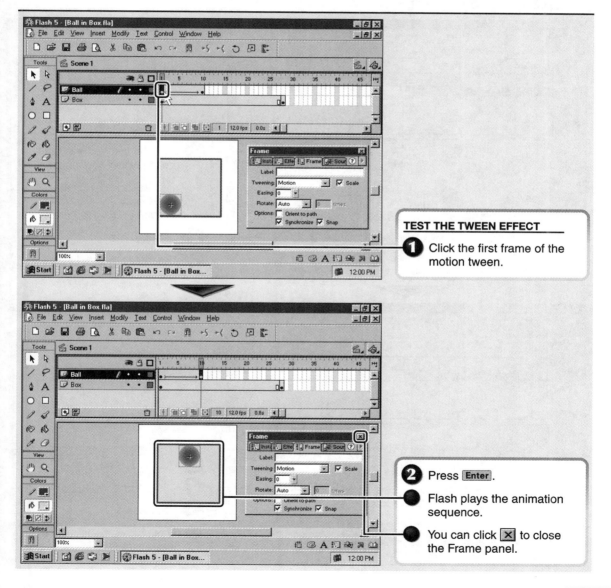

TEST THE TWEEN EFFECT

1 Click the first frame of the motion tween.

2 Press Enter.

● Flash plays the animation sequence.

● You can click ✕ to close the Frame panel.

STOP A MOTION TWEEN

If your movie uses a motion tween, the tween is in effect until you tell it to stop. If you add additional frames to the end of the movie, Flash tries to create more motion tween effects, unless you turn off the motion tween property.

STOP A MOTION TWEEN

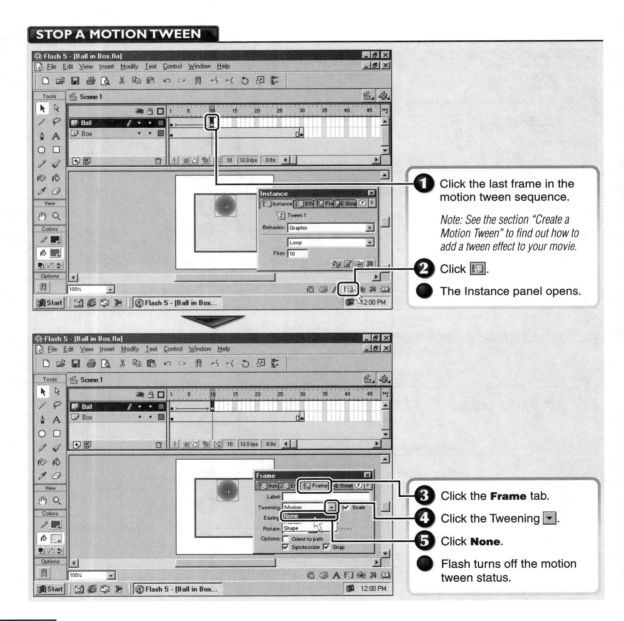

① Click the last frame in the motion tween sequence.

Note: See the section "Create a Motion Tween" to find out how to add a tween effect to your movie.

② Click 🔳.

● The Instance panel opens.

③ Click the **Frame** tab.

④ Click the Tweening 🔽.

⑤ Click **None**.

● Flash turns off the motion tween status.

ADD A KEYFRAME TO A MOTION TWEEN

You can make changes to a motion tween by adding keyframes to the animation sequence. For example, you may want to change the direction the object is moving in a motion tween animation. If you add a keyframe to change the direction, Flash reconfigures the in-between frames to reflect changes in the new keyframe.

ADD A KEYFRAME TO A MOTION TWEEN

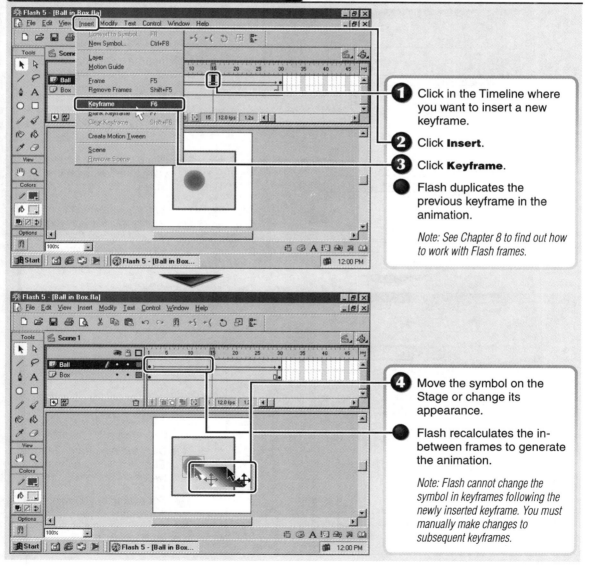

① Click in the Timeline where you want to insert a new keyframe.

② Click **Insert**.

③ Click **Keyframe**.

● Flash duplicates the previous keyframe in the animation.

Note: See Chapter 8 to find out how to work with Flash frames.

④ Move the symbol on the Stage or change its appearance.

● Flash recalculates the in-between frames to generate the animation.

Note: Flash cannot change the symbol in keyframes following the newly inserted keyframe. You must manually make changes to subsequent keyframes.

135

ANIMATE BY ROTATING A SYMBOL

You can turn a regular symbol from your Flash Library into an animated object that rotates. This method requires a series of keyframes in which you control how much rotation occurs in each keyframe. When you assign the sequence motion tween status, Flash calculates the in-between frames to create the rotation effect.

ANIMATE BY ROTATING A SYMBOL

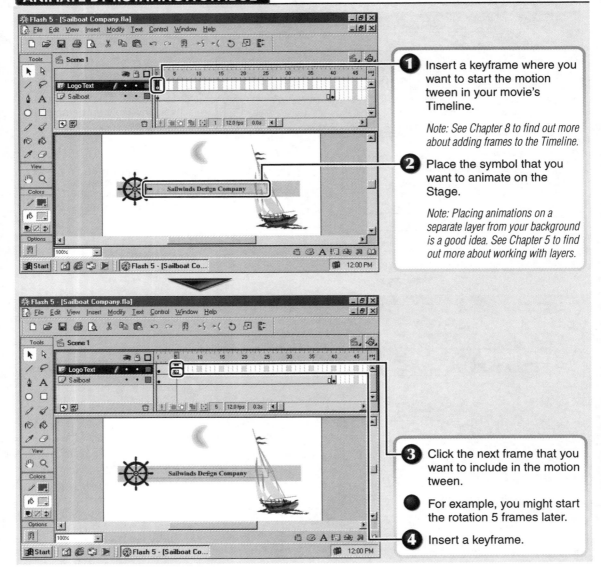

① Insert a keyframe where you want to start the motion tween in your movie's Timeline.

Note: See Chapter 8 to find out more about adding frames to the Timeline.

② Place the symbol that you want to animate on the Stage.

Note: Placing animations on a separate layer from your background is a good idea. See Chapter 5 to find out more about working with layers.

③ Click the next frame that you want to include in the motion tween.

● For example, you might start the rotation 5 frames later.

④ Insert a keyframe.

in an *instant*

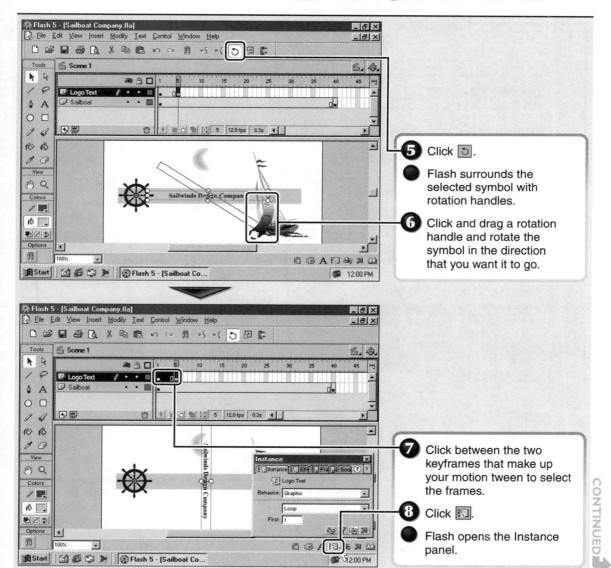

5 Click 🔄.

● Flash surrounds the selected symbol with rotation handles.

6 Click and drag a rotation handle and rotate the symbol in the direction that you want it to go.

7 Click between the two keyframes that make up your motion tween to select the frames.

8 Click 🖼.

● Flash opens the Instance panel.

CONTINUED

137

You can create keyframes at key points of the animation Timeline to rotate your symbol. For example, you may change the rotation's progress by stretching it out over four keyframes, rotating the symbol 90 degrees each time. Then add regular frames between the keyframes to lengthen the animation time.

ANIMATE BY ROTATING A SYMBOL (CONTINUED)

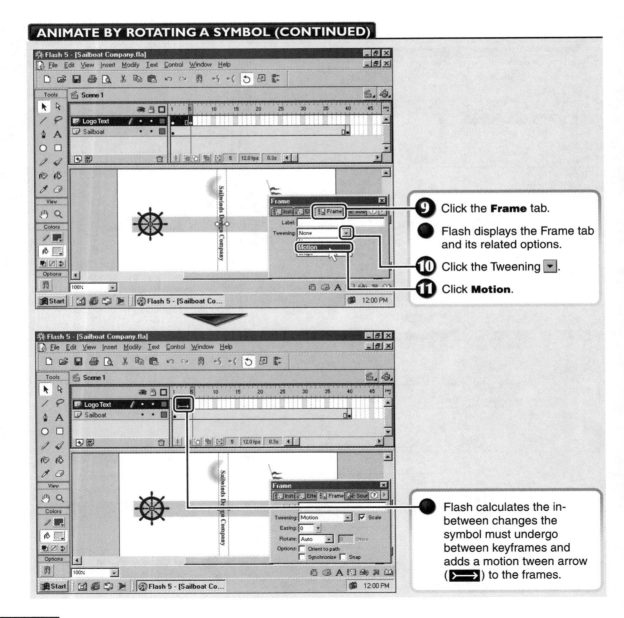

9 Click the **Frame** tab.

● Flash displays the Frame tab and its related options.

10 Click the Tweening ▼.

11 Click **Motion**.

● Flash calculates the in-between changes the symbol must undergo between keyframes and adds a motion tween arrow (▶━▶) to the frames.

in an instant

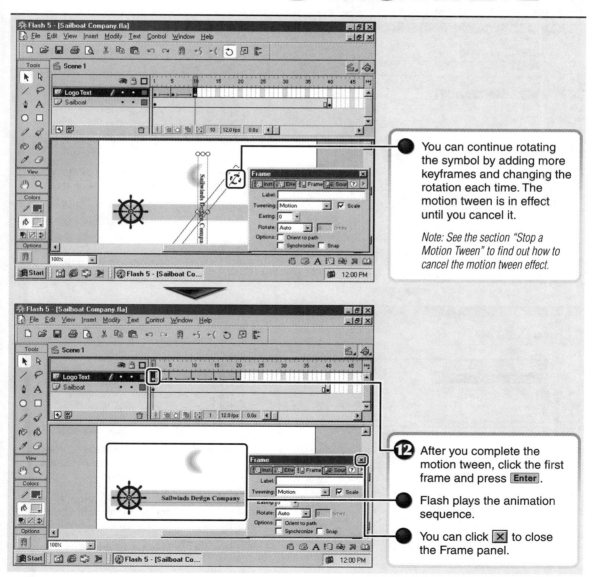

You can continue rotating the symbol by adding more keyframes and changing the rotation each time. The motion tween is in effect until you cancel it.

Note: See the section "Stop a Motion Tween" to find out how to cancel the motion tween effect.

After you complete the motion tween, click the first frame and press **Enter**.

Flash plays the animation sequence.

You can click ⊠ to close the Frame panel.

ANIMATE BY SPINNING A SYMBOL

You can create an animation effect that makes a symbol appear to spin. Using two identical keyframes, you can tell Flash to rotate the symbol in the in-between frames to create a spinning effect. Because a spin is a 360 degree rotation, you do not have to alter the keyframe content.

ANIMATE BY SPINNING A SYMBOL

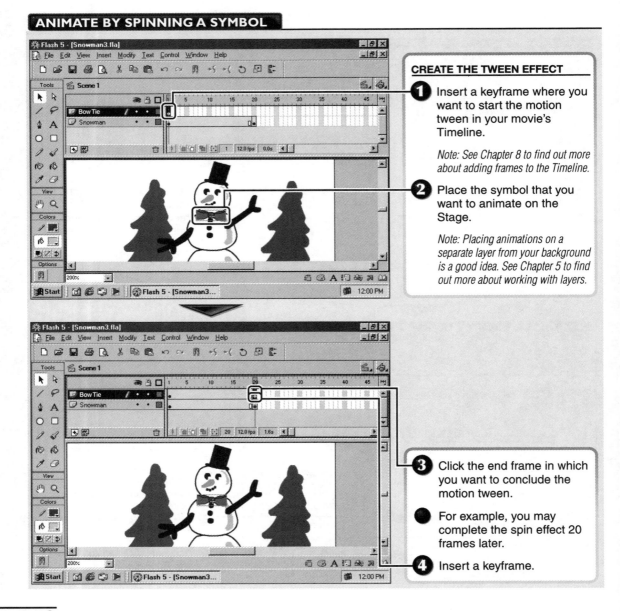

CREATE THE TWEEN EFFECT

1 Insert a keyframe where you want to start the motion tween in your movie's Timeline.

Note: See Chapter 8 to find out more about adding frames to the Timeline.

2 Place the symbol that you want to animate on the Stage.

Note: Placing animations on a separate layer from your background is a good idea. See Chapter 5 to find out more about working with layers.

3 Click the end frame in which you want to conclude the motion tween.

● For example, you may complete the spin effect 20 frames later.

4 Insert a keyframe.

in an *instant*

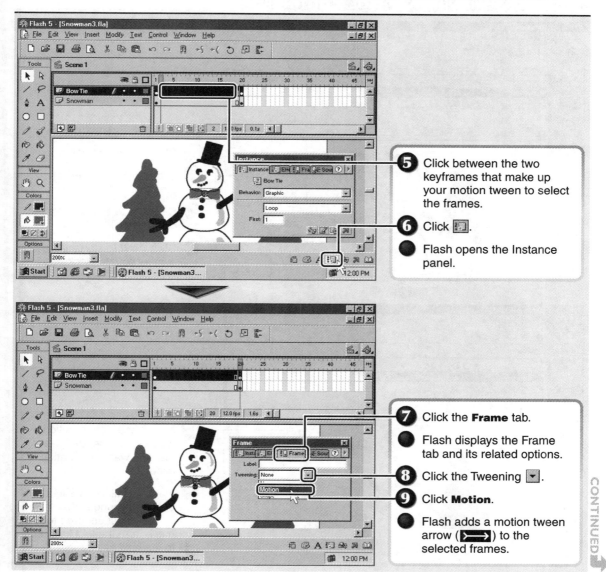

5 Click between the two keyframes that make up your motion tween to select the frames.

6 Click ▦.

● Flash opens the Instance panel.

7 Click the **Frame** tab.

● Flash displays the Frame tab and its related options.

8 Click the Tweening ▼.

9 Click **Motion**.

● Flash adds a motion tween arrow (▶━━▶) to the selected frames.

CONTINUED▶

141

ANIMATE BY SPINNING A SYMBOL

You can use the Rotation controls to spin items such as corporate logos or text blocks. Flash takes care of differing each frame in the sequence for you. You can specify how many times the symbol rotates and exactly which direction it goes.

ANIMATE BY SPINNING A SYMBOL (CONTINUED)

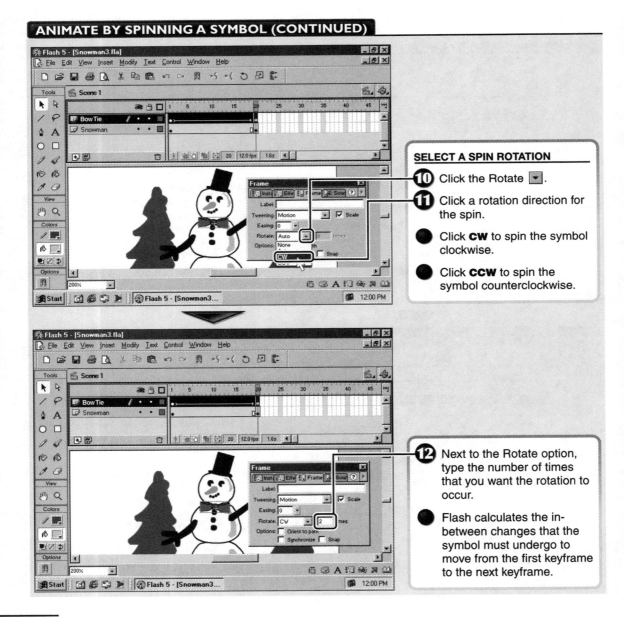

SELECT A SPIN ROTATION

🔟 Click the Rotate ▾.

1️⃣1️⃣ Click a rotation direction for the spin.

⬤ Click **CW** to spin the symbol clockwise.

⬤ Click **CCW** to spin the symbol counterclockwise.

1️⃣2️⃣ Next to the Rotate option, type the number of times that you want the rotation to occur.

⬤ Flash calculates the in-between changes that the symbol must undergo to move from the first keyframe to the next keyframe.

in an *instant*

1 Click the first frame of the
motion tween.

2 Press Enter.

● Flash plays the animation
sequence.

● You can click X to close
the Frame panel.

ANIMATE BY CHANGING A SYMBOL'S SIZE

You can use the motion tween technique to create an animation that changes size. You define two keyframes, one of which includes a symbol scaled to a new size. With the motion tween effect applied, Flash fills in all the in-between frames to create the illusion of growth or shrinkage.

ANIMATE BY CHANGING A SYMBOL'S SIZE

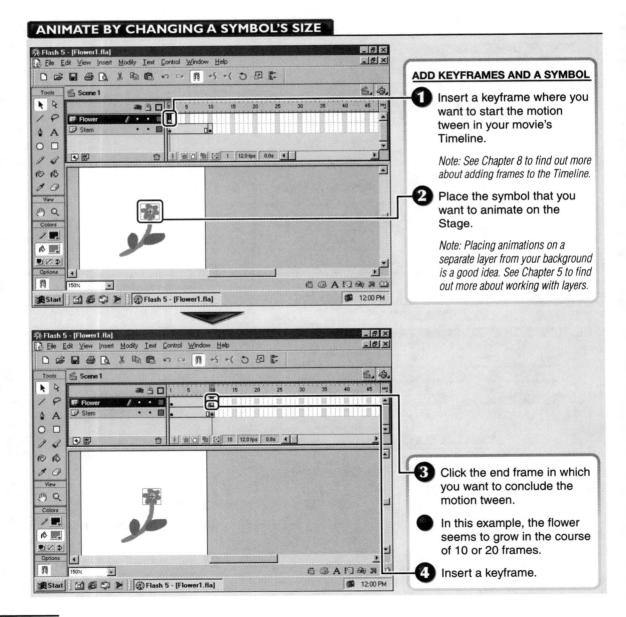

ADD KEYFRAMES AND A SYMBOL

1 Insert a keyframe where you want to start the motion tween in your movie's Timeline.

Note: See Chapter 8 to find out more about adding frames to the Timeline.

2 Place the symbol that you want to animate on the Stage.

Note: Placing animations on a separate layer from your background is a good idea. See Chapter 5 to find out more about working with layers.

3 Click the end frame in which you want to conclude the motion tween.

● In this example, the flower seems to grow in the course of 10 or 20 frames.

4 Insert a keyframe.

in an *instant*

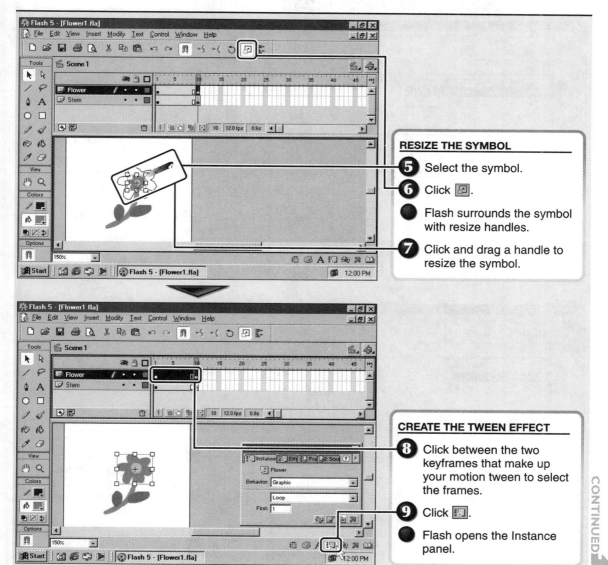

RESIZE THE SYMBOL

5 Select the symbol.

6 Click 🖽.

● Flash surrounds the symbol with resize handles.

7 Click and drag a handle to resize the symbol.

CREATE THE TWEEN EFFECT

8 Click between the two keyframes that make up your motion tween to select the frames.

9 Click 🖾.

● Flash opens the Instance panel.

CONTINUED

145

ANIMATE BY CHANGING A SYMBOL'S SIZE

You can use the Scale option in the Frame panel to make symbols grow or shrink. The speed at which this occurs depends on how many frames you insert between the two defining keyframes. You can experiment with the number of regular frames to create just the right animation speed.

ANIMATE BY CHANGING A SYMBOL'S SIZE (CONTINUED)

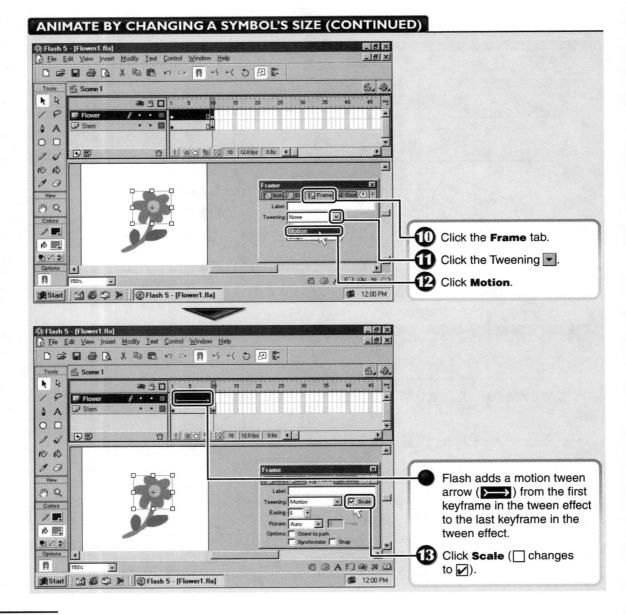

🔟 Click the **Frame** tab.

⓫ Click the Tweening 🔽.

⓬ Click **Motion**.

● Flash adds a motion tween arrow (▶━▶) from the first keyframe in the tween effect to the last keyframe in the tween effect.

⓭ Click **Scale** (☐ changes to ☑).

in an *instant*

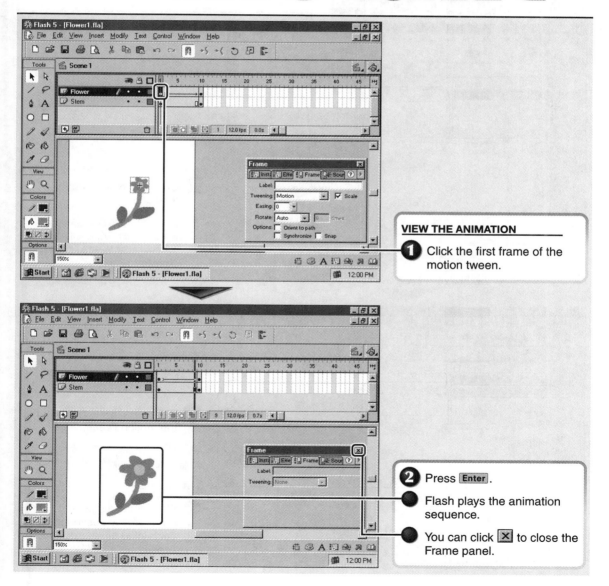

VIEW THE ANIMATION

1 Click the first frame of the motion tween.

2 Press Enter.

Flash plays the animation sequence.

You can click ☒ to close the Frame panel.

147

ANIMATE SYMBOLS ALONG A PATH

You can make a symbol follow a path in your movie. Using the motion tween technique and a motion guide layer, you define two points in the sequence and draw a line that tells Flash exactly where you want the symbol to move. Flash calculates all the in-between frames for you.

ANIMATE SYMBOLS ALONG A PATH

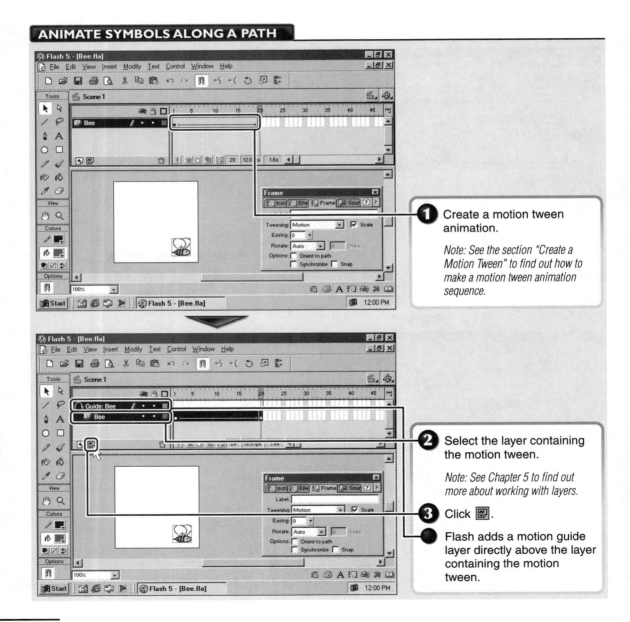

1 Create a motion tween animation.

Note: See the section "Create a Motion Tween" to find out how to make a motion tween animation sequence.

2 Select the layer containing the motion tween.

Note: See Chapter 5 to find out more about working with layers.

3 Click [image].

■ Flash adds a motion guide layer directly above the layer containing the motion tween.

in an *instant*

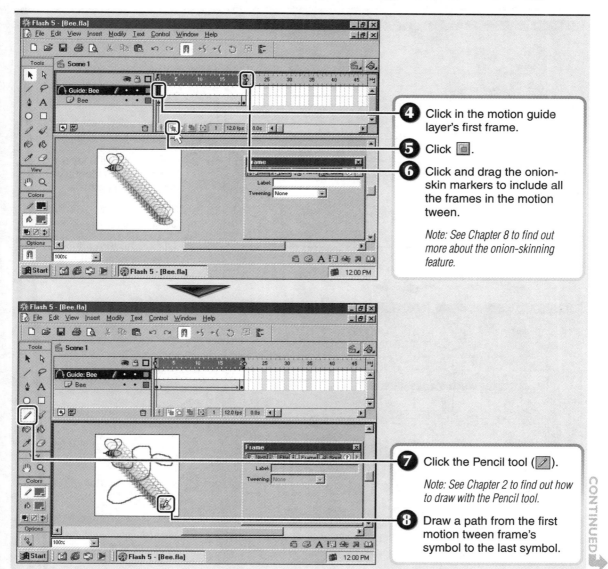

4 Click in the motion guide layer's first frame.

5 Click 🗐.

6 Click and drag the onion-skin markers to include all the frames in the motion tween.

Note: See Chapter 8 to find out more about the onion-skinning feature.

7 Click the Pencil tool (✎).

Note: See Chapter 2 to find out how to draw with the Pencil tool.

8 Draw a path from the first motion tween frame's symbol to the last symbol.

CONTINUED

ANIMATE SYMBOLS ALONG A PATH

Your motion tween can follow any path, whether it is
extremely curvy, loops back on itself, or falls out of
the movie area's boundaries.

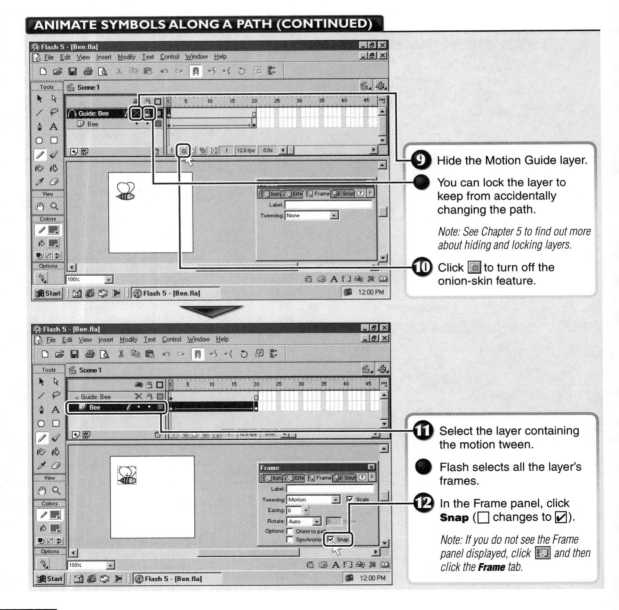

9 Hide the Motion Guide layer.

● You can lock the layer to
keep from accidentally
changing the path.

*Note: See Chapter 5 to find out more
about hiding and locking layers.*

10 Click █ to turn off the
onion-skin feature.

11 Select the layer containing
the motion tween.

● Flash selects all the layer's
frames.

12 In the Frame panel, click
Snap (☐ changes to ☑).

*Note: If you do not see the Frame
panel displayed, click 🔲 and then
click the **Frame** tab.*

in an *instant*

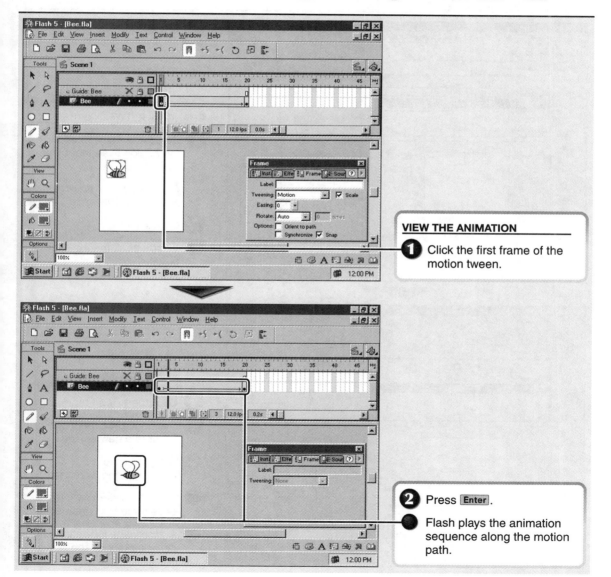

VIEW THE ANIMATION

1 Click the first frame of the motion tween.

2 Press Enter.

Flash plays the animation sequence along the motion path.

SET TWEEN SPEED

You can control a tweened animation's speed by using the Easing control. The Easing control is found in the Frame panel and enables you to speed up or slow down the tween effect.

SET TWEEN SPEED

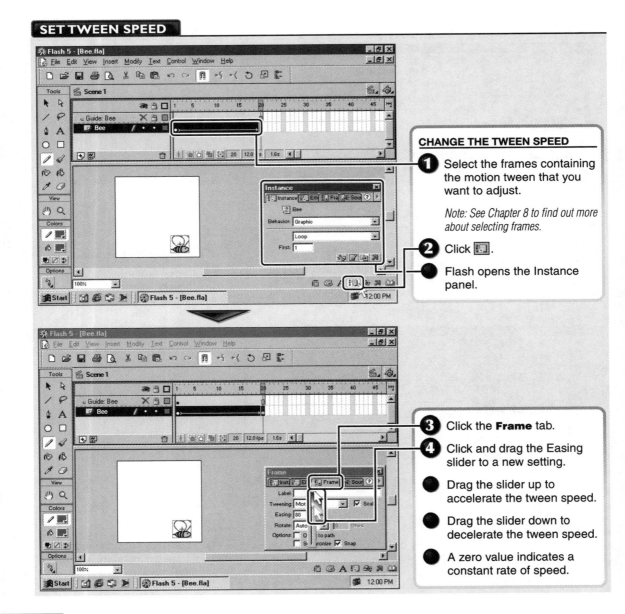

CHANGE THE TWEEN SPEED

1 Select the frames containing the motion tween that you want to adjust.

Note: See Chapter 8 to find out more about selecting frames.

2 Click ▦.

● Flash opens the Instance panel.

3 Click the **Frame** tab.

4 Click and drag the Easing slider to a new setting.

● Drag the slider up to accelerate the tween speed.

● Drag the slider down to decelerate the tween speed.

● A zero value indicates a constant rate of speed.

in an *instant*

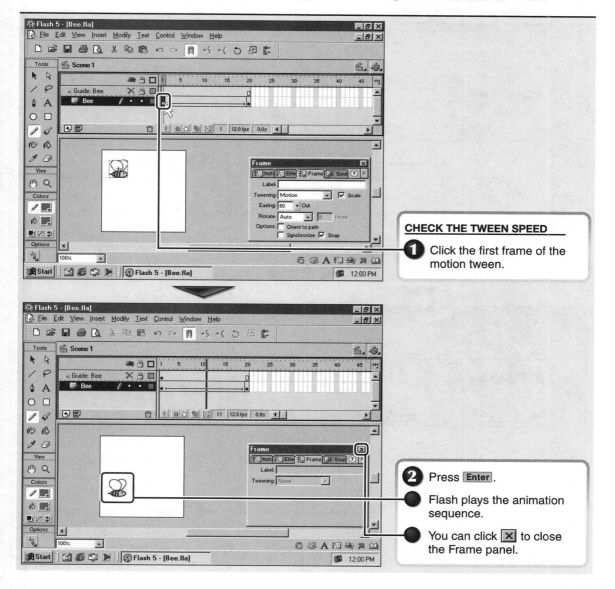

CHECK THE TWEEN SPEED

1 Click the first frame of the motion tween.

2 Press Enter.

Flash plays the animation sequence.

You can click ✕ to close the Frame panel.

CREATE A SHAPE TWEEN

You can morph objects that you draw on the Stage by using a shape tween effect. Shape tweening does not require the use of symbols or groups. You can animate any object drawn with the drawing tools by using a shape tween.

CREATE A SHAPE TWEEN

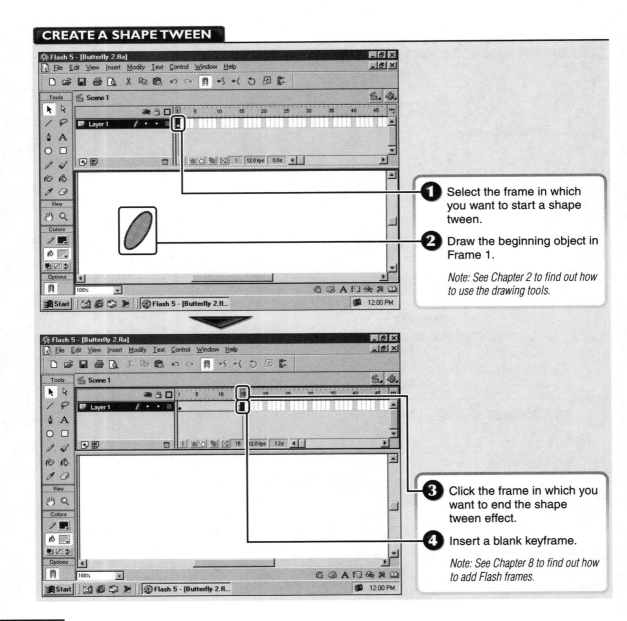

1 Select the frame in which you want to start a shape tween.

2 Draw the beginning object in Frame 1.

Note: See Chapter 2 to find out how to use the drawing tools.

3 Click the frame in which you want to end the shape tween effect.

4 Insert a blank keyframe.

Note: See Chapter 8 to find out how to add Flash frames.

in an  instant

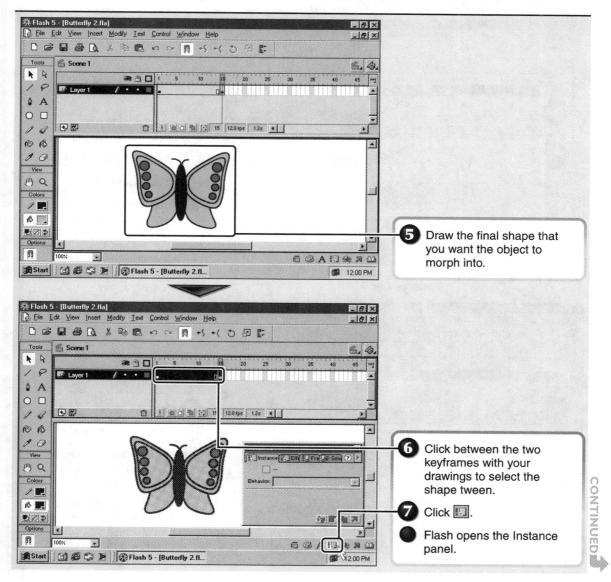

5 Draw the final shape that you want the object to morph into.

6 Click between the two keyframes with your drawings to select the shape tween.

7 Click 🔲.

● Flash opens the Instance panel.

CONTINUED

155

CREATE A SHAPE TWEEN

You can use shape tweens to morph between all kinds of objects, including text that you turn into an object. You can use as many shape tweens as you like in an animation, and you can start one right after the other in the Timeline.

CREATE A SHAPE TWEEN (CONTINUED)

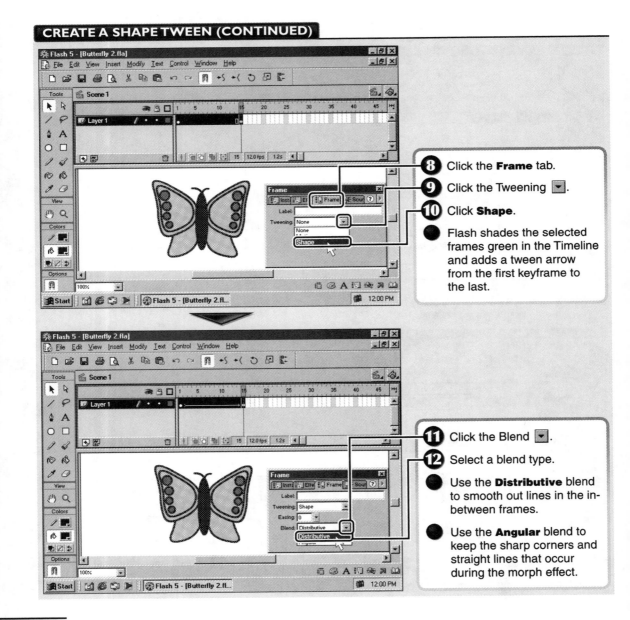

⑧ Click the **Frame** tab.

⑨ Click the Tweening 🔽.

⑩ Click **Shape**.

⬤ Flash shades the selected frames green in the Timeline and adds a tween arrow from the first keyframe to the last.

⑪ Click the Blend 🔽.

⑫ Select a blend type.

⬤ Use the **Distributive** blend to smooth out lines in the in-between frames.

⬤ Use the **Angular** blend to keep the sharp corners and straight lines that occur during the morph effect.

in an *instant*

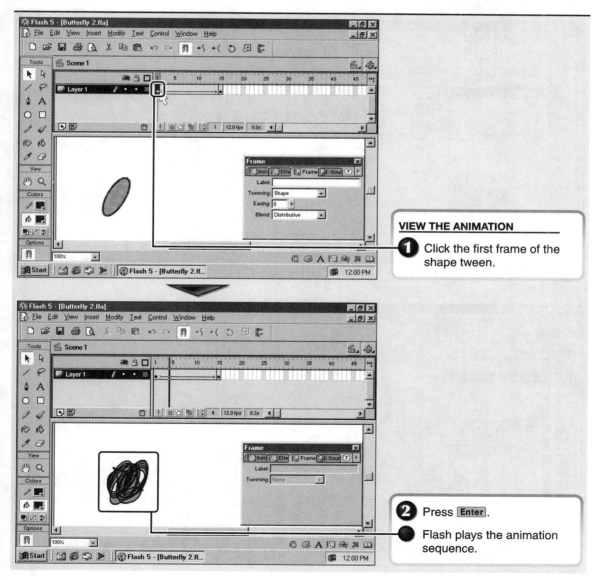

VIEW THE ANIMATION

1 Click the first frame of the shape tween.

2 Press **Enter**.

● Flash plays the animation sequence.

USING SHAPE HINTS

You can determine how to morph shapes during a shape tween by adding shape hints. A shape hint is a marker that identifies areas on the original shape that match up with areas on the final shape and mark crucial points of change.

USING SHAPE HINTS

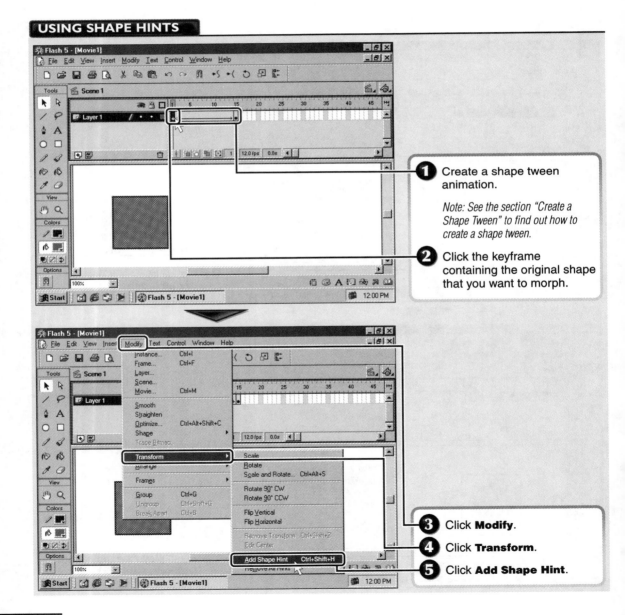

1 Create a shape tween animation.

Note: See the section "Create a Shape Tween" to find out how to create a shape tween.

2 Click the keyframe containing the original shape that you want to morph.

3 Click **Modify**.

4 Click **Transform**.

5 Click **Add Shape Hint**.

in an *instant*

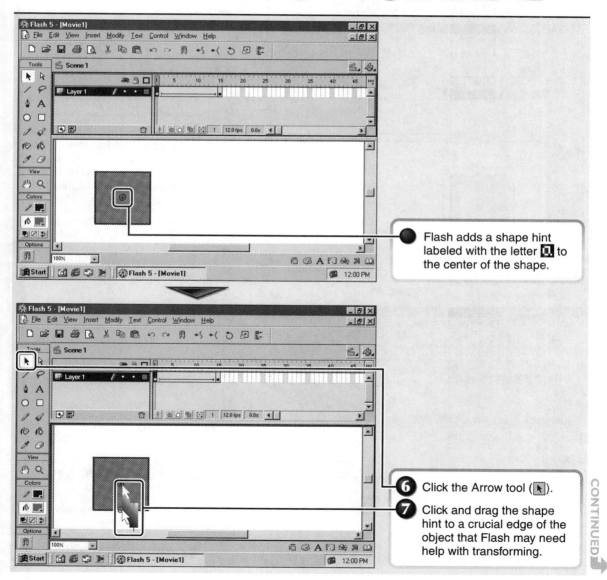

Flash adds a shape hint labeled with the letter **a** to the center of the shape.

6 Click the Arrow tool (▮).

7 Click and drag the shape hint to a crucial edge of the object that Flash may need help with transforming.

CONTINUED

The more shape hints that you add to the shape tween, the smoother the morphing transformation will be. Use the onion-skin feature (see Chapter 8) to help you view the shape changes in your animation.

USING SHAPE HINTS (CONTINUED)

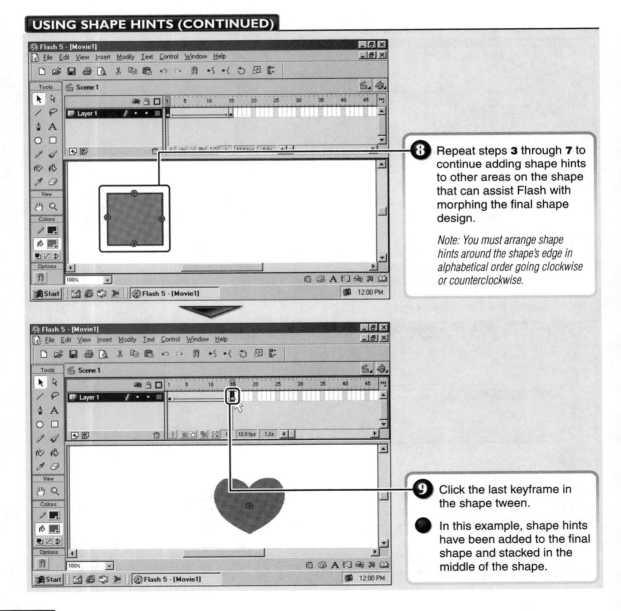

8 Repeat steps **3** through **7** to continue adding shape hints to other areas on the shape that can assist Flash with morphing the final shape design.

Note: You must arrange shape hints around the shape's edge in alphabetical order going clockwise or counterclockwise.

9 Click the last keyframe in the shape tween.

● In this example, shape hints have been added to the final shape and stacked in the middle of the shape.

in an *instant*

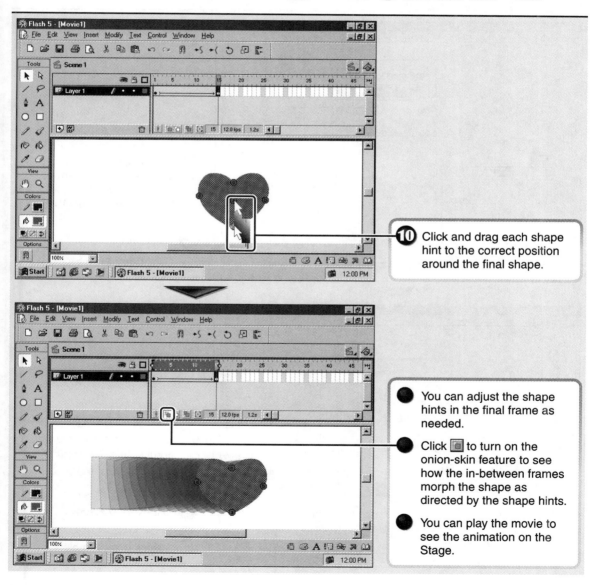

10 Click and drag each shape hint to the correct position around the final shape.

● You can adjust the shape hints in the final frame as needed.

● Click 🔳 to turn on the onion-skin feature to see how the in-between frames morph the shape as directed by the shape hints.

● You can play the movie to see the animation on the Stage.

USING REVERSE FRAMES

You can save some animating time by reversing frames in your movie. For example, if you create a motion tween that makes a symbol grow in size, you can reverse the frame sequence to create the opposite effect in the second half of the animation.

USING REVERSE FRAMES

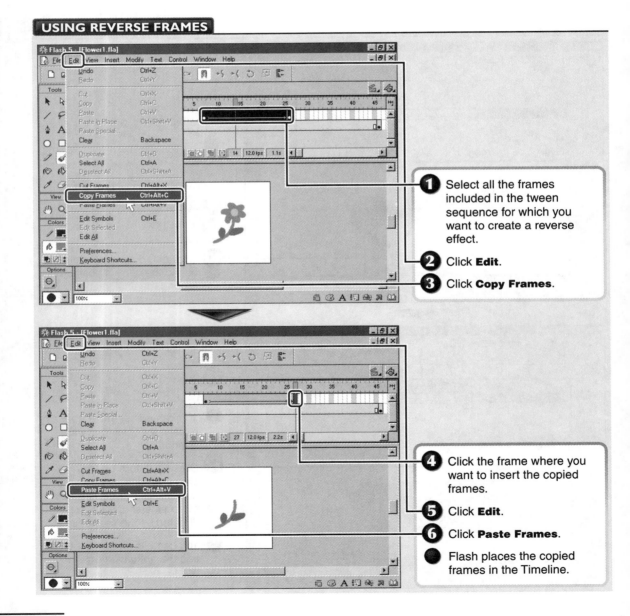

1 Select all the frames included in the tween sequence for which you want to create a reverse effect.

2 Click **Edit**.

3 Click **Copy Frames**.

4 Click the frame where you want to insert the copied frames.

5 Click **Edit**.

6 Click **Paste Frames**.

● Flash places the copied frames in the Timeline.

in an

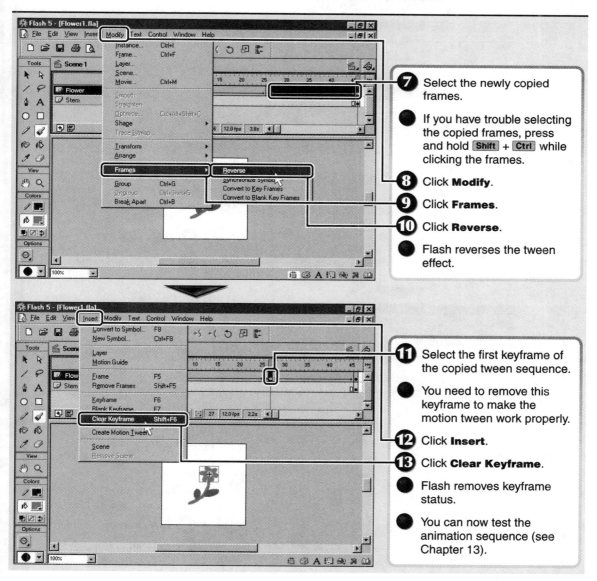

7 Select the newly copied frames.

● If you have trouble selecting the copied frames, press and hold **Shift** + **Ctrl** while clicking the frames.

8 Click **Modify**.

9 Click **Frames**.

10 Click **Reverse**.

● Flash reverses the tween effect.

11 Select the first keyframe of the copied tween sequence.

● You need to remove this keyframe to make the motion tween work properly.

12 Click **Insert**.

13 Click **Clear Keyframe**.

● Flash removes keyframe status.

● You can now test the animation sequence (see Chapter 13).

You can save an animation sequence as a movie clip that you can use again elsewhere in your movie.

SAVE AN ANIMATION AS A MOVIE CLIP

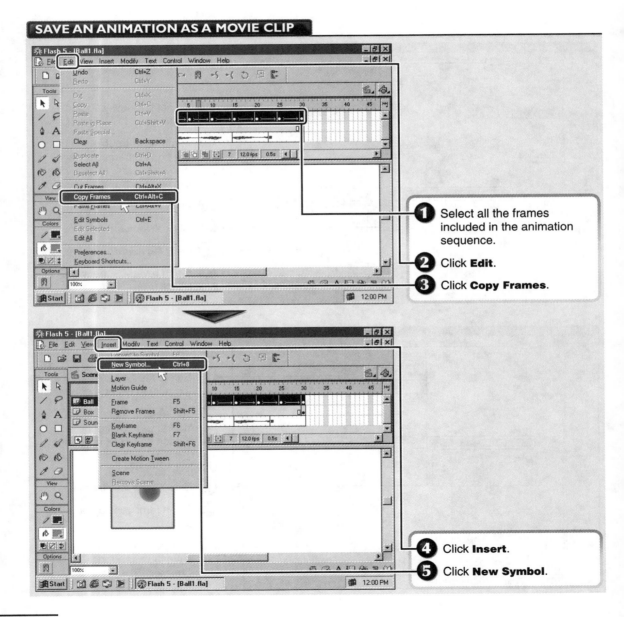

1 Select all the frames included in the animation sequence.

2 Click **Edit**.

3 Click **Copy Frames**.

4 Click **Insert**.

5 Click **New Symbol**.

in an *instant*

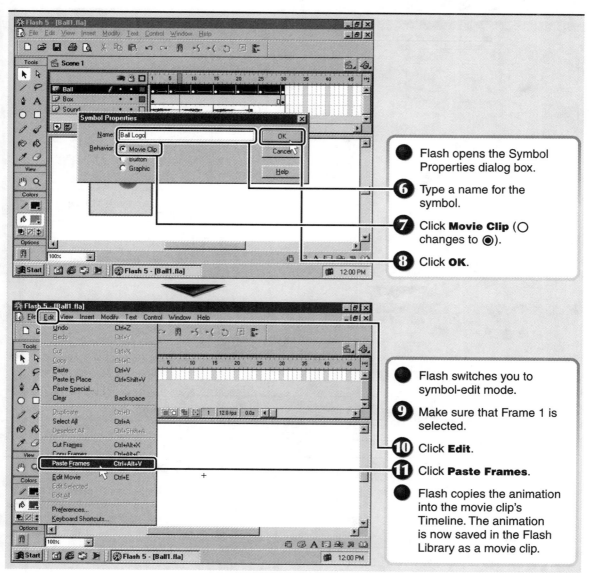

Flash opens the Symbol Properties dialog box.

6 Type a name for the symbol.

7 Click **Movie Clip** (○ changes to ◉).

8 Click **OK**.

Flash switches you to symbol-edit mode.

9 Make sure that Frame 1 is selected.

10 Click **Edit**.

11 Click **Paste Frames**.

Flash copies the animation into the movie clip's Timeline. The animation is now saved in the Flash Library as a movie clip.

CREATE A BUTTON SYMBOL

A button can be any object or drawing, such as a simple geometric shape. You can draw a new object with the Flash drawing tools, or you can use an imported graphic as a button. A button includes a Timeline with four frames: Up, Over, Down, and Hit. You must assign an image or action to each of the four button states.

CREATE A BUTTON SYMBOL

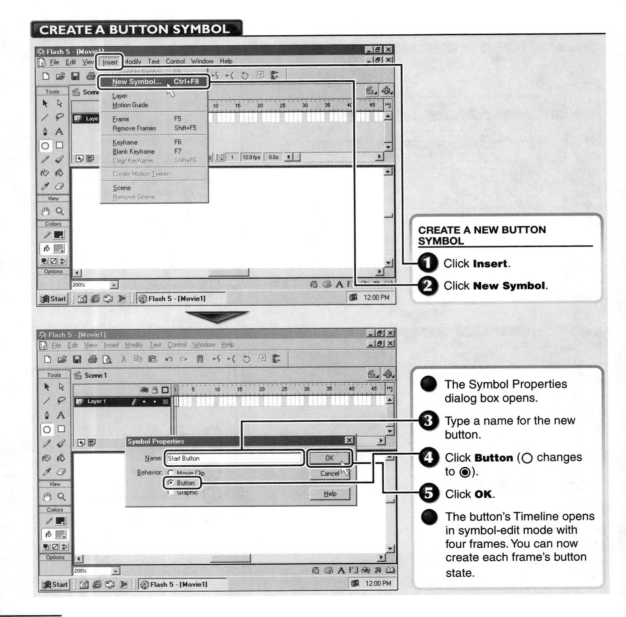

CREATE A NEW BUTTON SYMBOL

1 Click **Insert**.

2 Click **New Symbol**.

● The Symbol Properties dialog box opens.

3 Type a name for the new button.

4 Click **Button** (○ changes to ◉).

5 Click **OK**.

● The button's Timeline opens in symbol-edit mode with four frames. You can now create each frame's button state.

in an instant

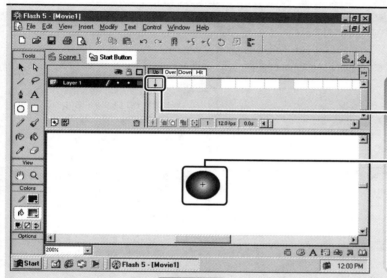

CREATE THE UP STATE

By default, Flash selects the Up frame and inserts a keyframe.

6 Create a new object to be used as the button or place an existing object on the Stage.

Note: See Chapter 2 to find out more about using the Flash drawing tools.

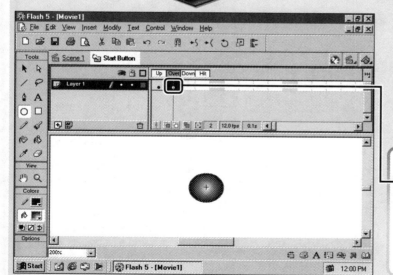

CREATE THE OVER STATE

7 Click the Over frame.

8 Press F6 to insert a keyframe into the frame.

Note: See Chapter 8 to find out more about frames.

CONTINUED

If you duplicate the same object in each button frame, you can make minor changes to make the button differ in each state. For example, you can change the color, scale, or shape for each keyframe.

CREATE A BUTTON SYMBOL (CONTINUED)

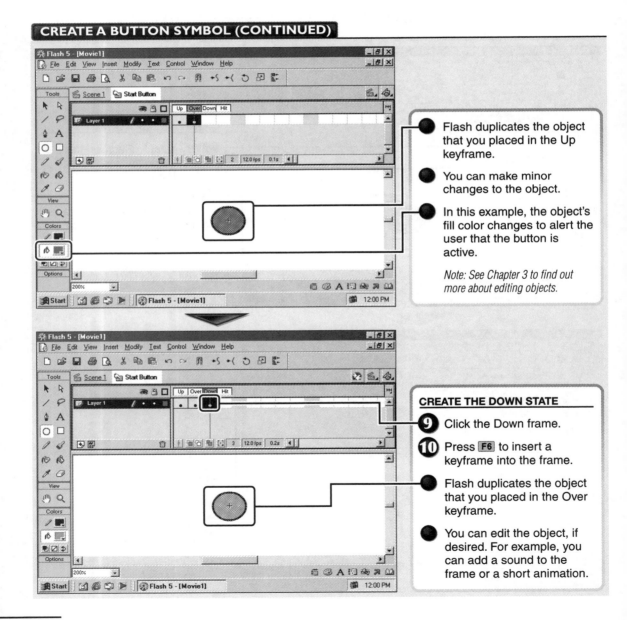

● Flash duplicates the object that you placed in the Up keyframe.

● You can make minor changes to the object.

● In this example, the object's fill color changes to alert the user that the button is active.

Note: See Chapter 3 to find out more about editing objects.

CREATE THE DOWN STATE

⑨ Click the Down frame.

⑩ Press **F6** to insert a keyframe into the frame.

● Flash duplicates the object that you placed in the Over keyframe.

● You can edit the object, if desired. For example, you can add a sound to the frame or a short animation.

in an *instant*

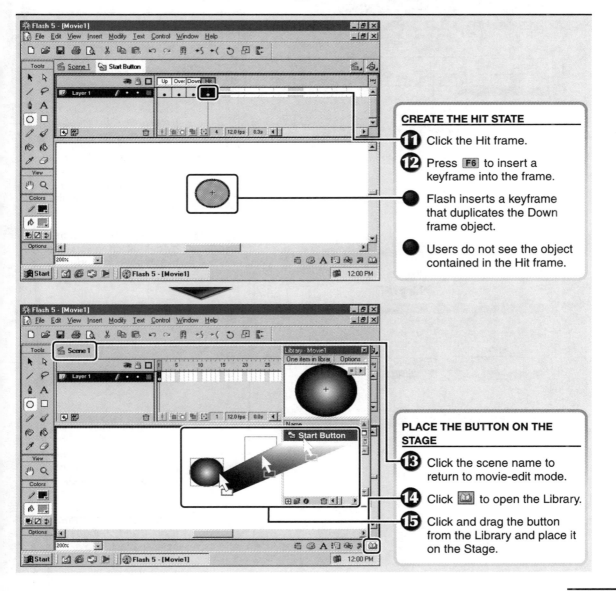

CREATE THE HIT STATE

11 Click the Hit frame.

12 Press **F6** to insert a keyframe into the frame.

● Flash inserts a keyframe that duplicates the Down frame object.

● Users do not see the object contained in the Hit frame.

PLACE THE BUTTON ON THE STAGE

13 Click the scene name to return to movie-edit mode.

14 Click 🔲 to open the Library.

15 Click and drag the button from the Library and place it on the Stage.

CREATE SHAPE-CHANGING BUTTONS

Although simple geometric shapes make good buttons, you may want something a bit more exciting. You can change the object used for each button state. For example, an ordinary circle shape button can become a flower when the user rolls the cursor over it.

CREATE SHAPE-CHANGING BUTTONS

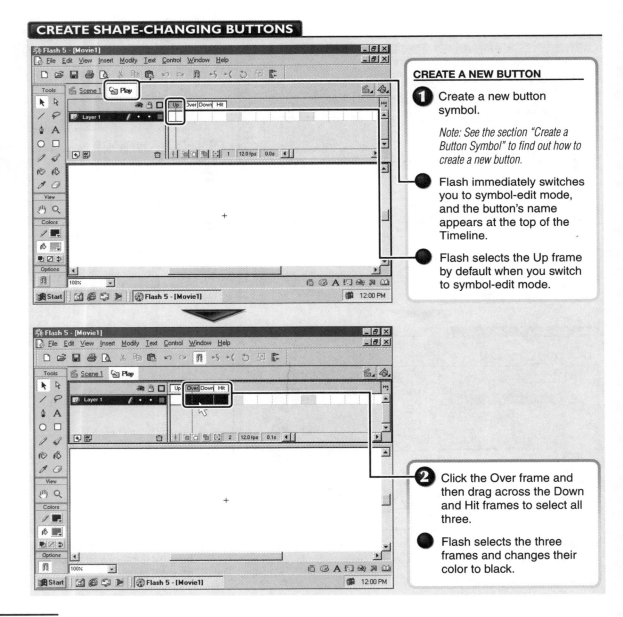

CREATE A NEW BUTTON

1 Create a new button symbol.

Note: See the section "Create a Button Symbol" to find out how to create a new button.

■ Flash immediately switches you to symbol-edit mode, and the button's name appears at the top of the Timeline.

■ Flash selects the Up frame by default when you switch to symbol-edit mode.

2 Click the Over frame and then drag across the Down and Hit frames to select all three.

■ Flash selects the three frames and changes their color to black.

in an *instant*

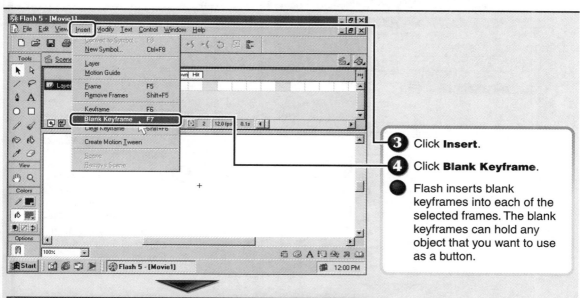

3 Click **Insert**.

4 Click **Blank Keyframe**.

● Flash inserts blank keyframes into each of the selected frames. The blank keyframes can hold any object that you want to use as a button.

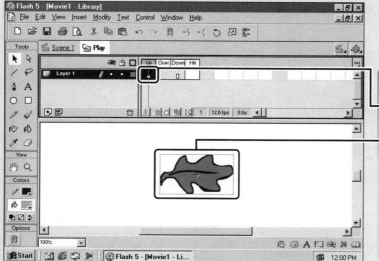

CREATE THE UP STATE

5 Click the Up frame to select it.

6 Create a new object or place an existing object on the Stage to be used as the inactive button state.

Note: See Chapter 2 to find out more about using the Flash drawing tools or see Chapter 6 to find out how to use symbols and instances.

CONTINUED

171

CREATE SHAPE-CHANGING BUTTONS

If a button's image stays the same for all four frames in the button Timeline, users cannot distinguish between its active and inactive states. Changing the button's image for each state gives users some idea of the button's status.

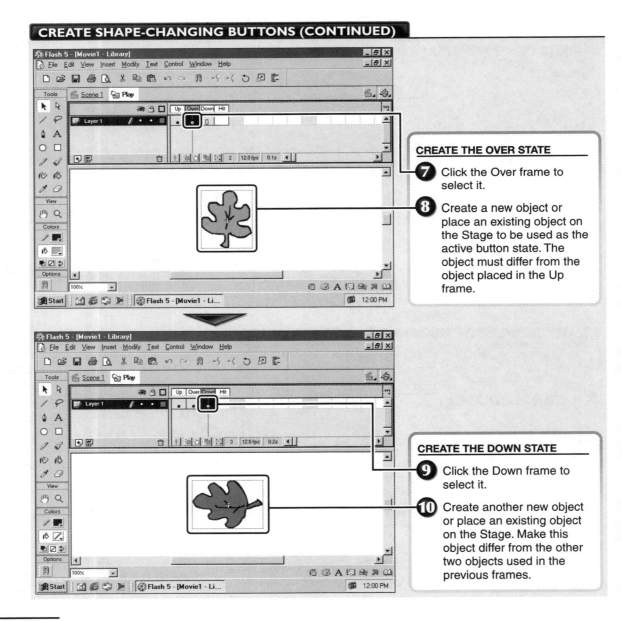

CREATE THE OVER STATE

7 Click the Over frame to select it.

8 Create a new object or place an existing object on the Stage to be used as the active button state. The object must differ from the object placed in the Up frame.

CREATE THE DOWN STATE

9 Click the Down frame to select it.

10 Create another new object or place an existing object on the Stage. Make this object differ from the other two objects used in the previous frames.

in an *instant*

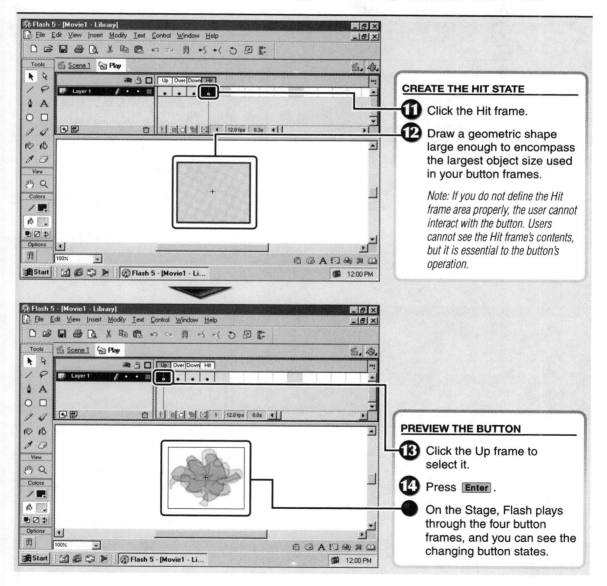

CREATE THE HIT STATE

⓫ Click the Hit frame.

⓬ Draw a geometric shape large enough to encompass the largest object size used in your button frames.

Note: If you do not define the Hit frame area properly, the user cannot interact with the button. Users cannot see the Hit frame's contents, but it is essential to the button's operation.

PREVIEW THE BUTTON

⓭ Click the Up frame to select it.

⓮ Press `Enter`.

● On the Stage, Flash plays through the four button frames, and you can see the changing button states.

173

CREATE AN ANIMATED BUTTON

You can create impressive button animation effects. For example, you can animate a button with a cartoon that includes sound. Flash makes it easy to place movie clips into your button frames.

CREATE AN ANIMATED BUTTON

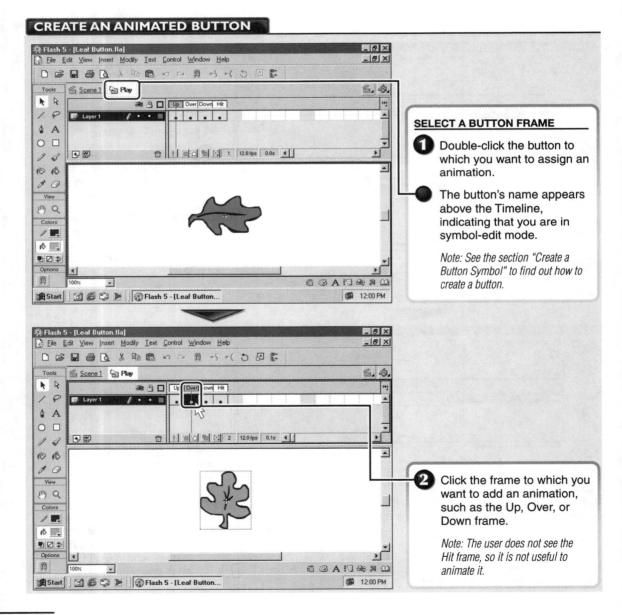

SELECT A BUTTON FRAME

1 Double-click the button to which you want to assign an animation.

■ The button's name appears above the Timeline, indicating that you are in symbol-edit mode.

Note: See the section "Create a Button Symbol" to find out how to create a button.

2 Click the frame to which you want to add an animation, such as the Up, Over, or Down frame.

Note: The user does not see the Hit frame, so it is not useful to animate it.

in an *instant*

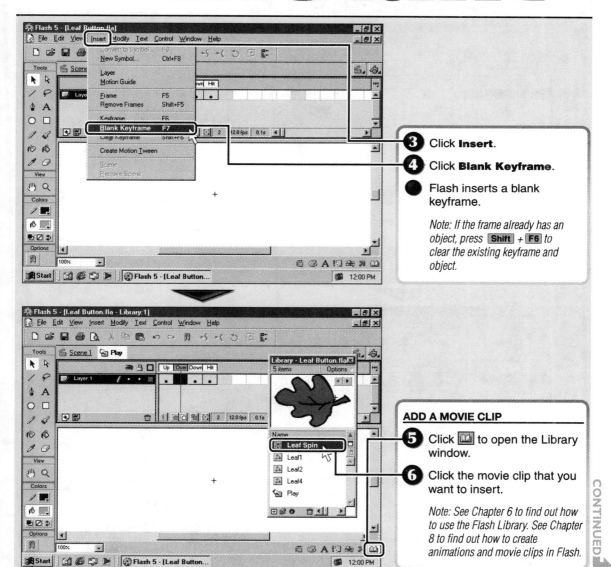

③ Click **Insert**.

④ Click **Blank Keyframe**.

● Flash inserts a blank keyframe.

Note: If the frame already has an object, press **Shift** + **F6** *to clear the existing keyframe and object.*

ADD A MOVIE CLIP

⑤ Click 📖 to open the Library window.

⑥ Click the movie clip that you want to insert.

Note: See Chapter 6 to find out how to use the Flash Library. See Chapter 8 to find out how to create animations and movie clips in Flash.

CONTINUED

CREATE AN ANIMATED BUTTON

You can add animation to any button state except the Hit frame, which is not seen by the user. For example, you may want the user to see a spinning leaf when the button is inactive, or you may want the leaf object to spin only when the user rolls the cursor over the button.

CREATE AN ANIMATED BUTTON (CONTINUED)

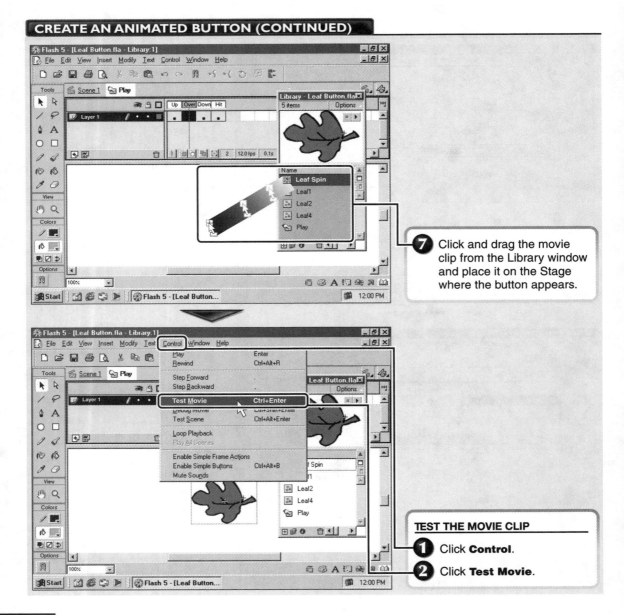

7 Click and drag the movie clip from the Library window and place it on the Stage where the button appears.

TEST THE MOVIE CLIP

1 Click **Control**.

2 Click **Test Movie**.

in an *instant*

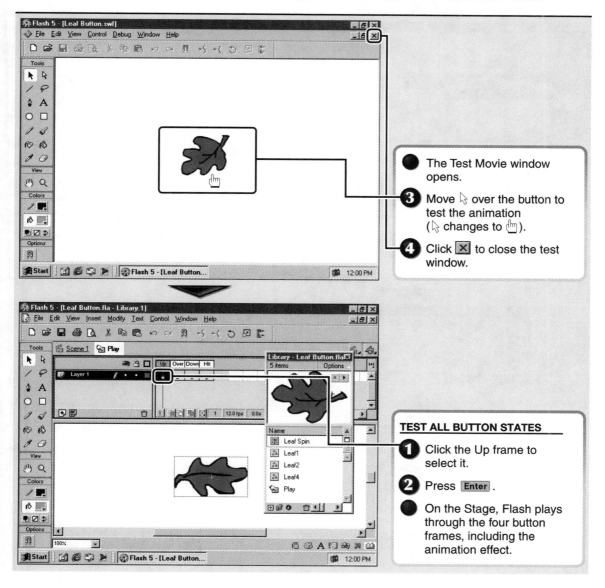

● The Test Movie window opens.

3 Move ⌖ over the button to test the animation (⌖ changes to 🖑).

4 Click ✕ to close the test window.

TEST ALL BUTTON STATES

1 Click the Up frame to select it.

2 Press Enter.

● On the Stage, Flash plays through the four button frames, including the animation effect.

ADD BUTTON ACTIONS

Buttons contain built-in actions, such as moving to the Down frame when a user clicks the button. You can add other Flash actions to your buttons. For example, you can add a Play action to a button so that a movie clip starts playing when the user clicks the button.

ADD BUTTON ACTIONS

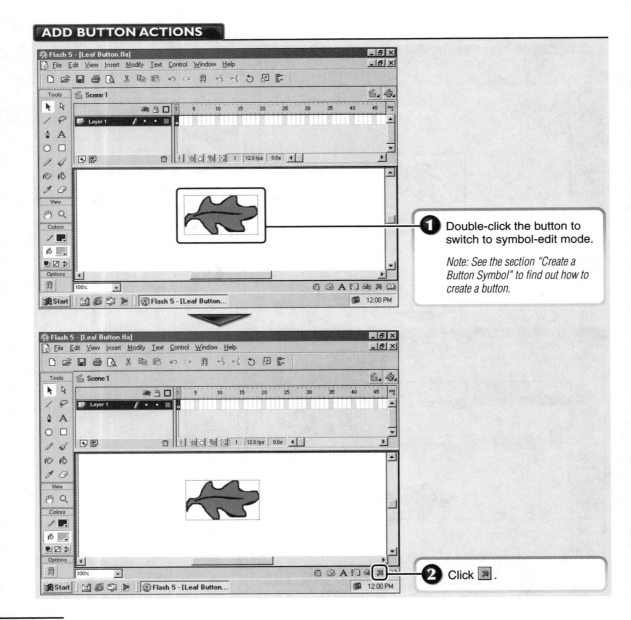

1 Double-click the button to switch to symbol-edit mode.

Note: See the section "Create a Button Symbol" to find out how to create a button.

2 Click 📄 .

178

in an *instant*

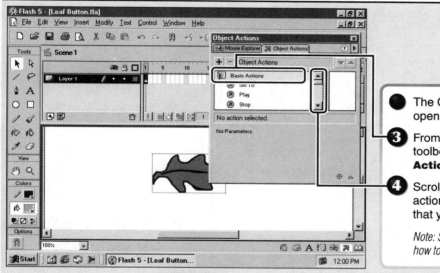

● The Object Actions box
opens.

3 From the Object Actions
toolbox list, click **Basic
Actions**.

4 Scroll through the list of
actions and locate the one
that you want to apply.

*Note: See Chapter 12 to find out
how to work with Flash actions.*

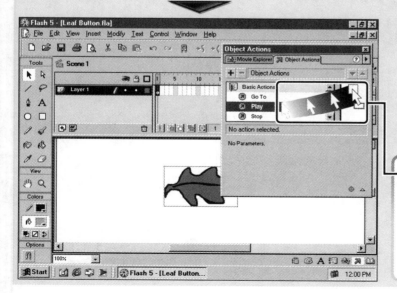

5 Click and drag the action
from the list and drop it in the
Actions list box.

● You can also double-click the
action name to immediately
place it in the Actions list
box.

CONTINUED

ADD BUTTON ACTIONS

Flash actions are simplified programming scripts that instruct Flash how to perform a certain task, such as loading a movie or stopping a sound clip. Actions include command strings to spell out exactly what action Flash must perform. You do not have to know programming to use Flash actions.

ADD BUTTON ACTIONS (CONTINUED)

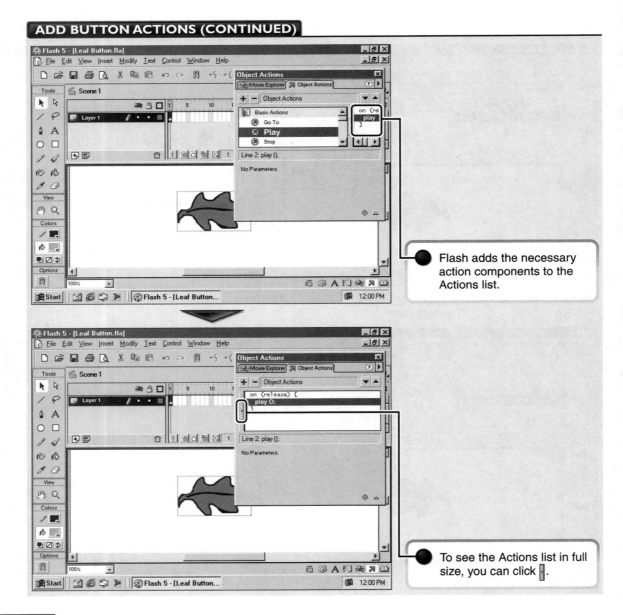

● Flash adds the necessary action components to the Actions list.

● To see the Actions list in full size, you can click .

in an *instant*

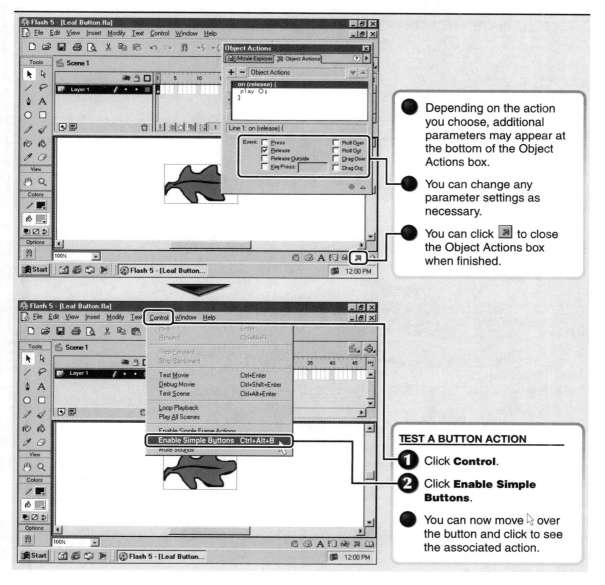

Depending on the action you choose, additional parameters may appear at the bottom of the Object Actions box.

You can change any parameter settings as necessary.

You can click 🔊 to close the Object Actions box when finished.

TEST A BUTTON ACTION

1 Click **Control**.

2 Click **Enable Simple Buttons**.

You can now move ⓡ over the button and click to see the associated action.

IMPORT A SOUND CLIP

You can import sounds from other sources for use with Flash movies and other projects. Flash supports popular sound file formats, such as WAV and AIF.

IMPORT A SOUND CLIP

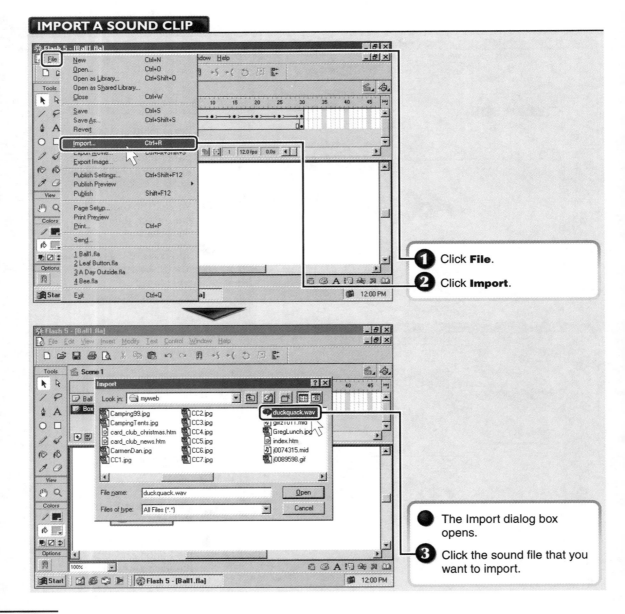

1 Click **File**.

2 Click **Import**.

● The Import dialog box opens.

3 Click the sound file that you want to import.

in an *instant*

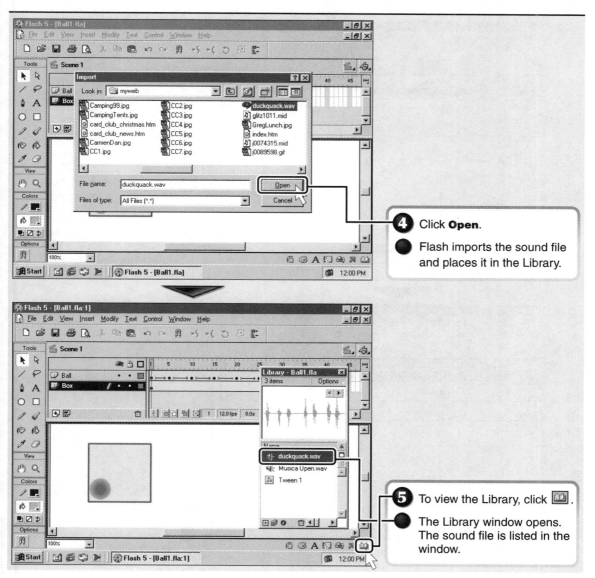

4 Click **Open**.

● Flash imports the sound file and places it in the Library.

5 To view the Library, click 📖.

● The Library window opens. The sound file is listed in the window.

ADD A SOUND LAYER

Flash helps organize your movie by enabling you to place sound clips in their own layer. This makes it easier to find sound files quickly and edit them as needed. Flash allows for multiple sound layers in your movie.

ADD A SOUND LAYER

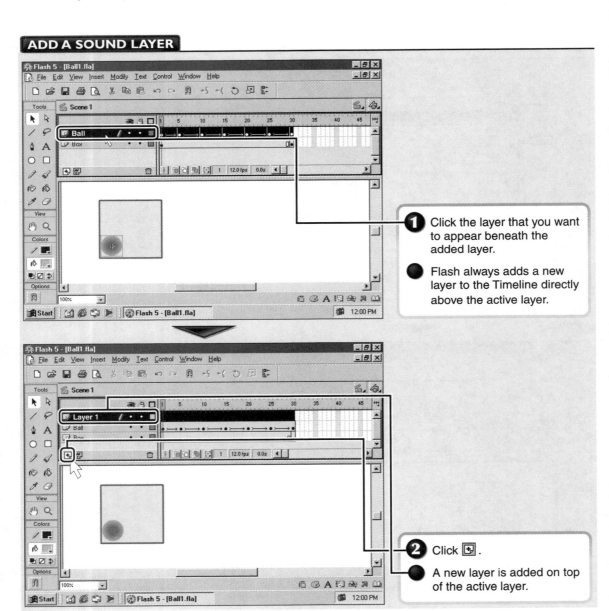

1 Click the layer that you want to appear beneath the added layer.

● Flash always adds a new layer to the Timeline directly above the active layer.

2 Click 🖿.

● A new layer is added on top of the active layer.

in an *instant*

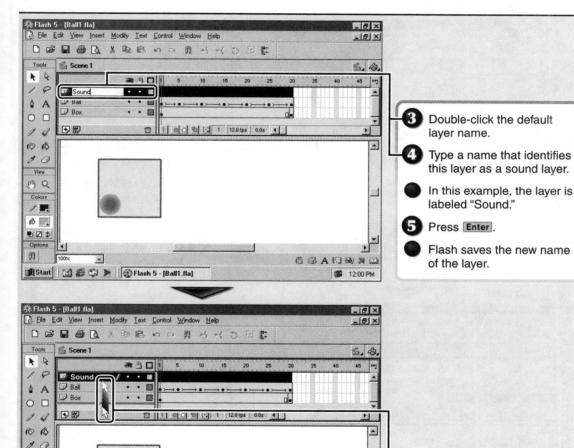

3 Double-click the default layer name.

4 Type a name that identifies this layer as a sound layer.

● In this example, the layer is labeled "Sound."

5 Press Enter.

● Flash saves the new name of the layer.

● To make the sound layer easy to find, you can drag the layer to the top or bottom of the Timeline layer stack.

ASSIGN SOUNDS TO FRAMES

You can enliven any animation sequence with a sound clip, whether you add a single sound effect or an entire sound track. Like graphics, sound files are saved as instances that can be inserted into frames on the Timeline and used throughout your movie.

ASSIGN SOUNDS TO FRAMES

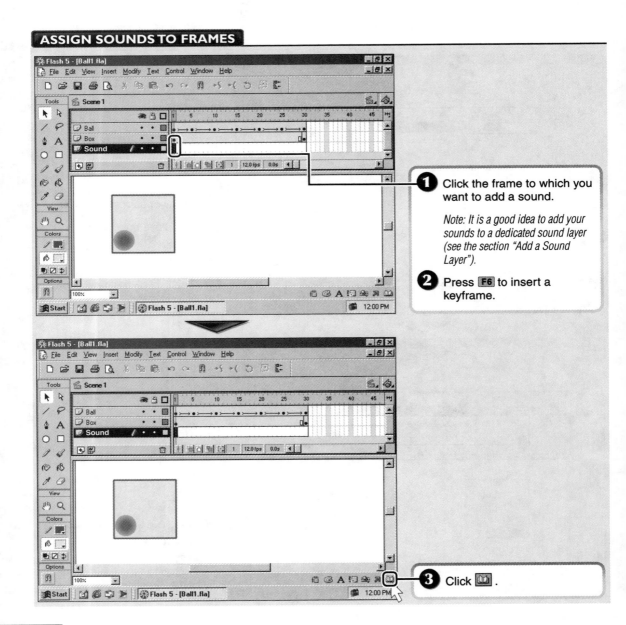

1 Click the frame to which you want to add a sound.

Note: It is a good idea to add your sounds to a dedicated sound layer (see the section "Add a Sound Layer").

2 Press F6 to insert a keyframe.

3 Click 🔲 .

in an *instant*

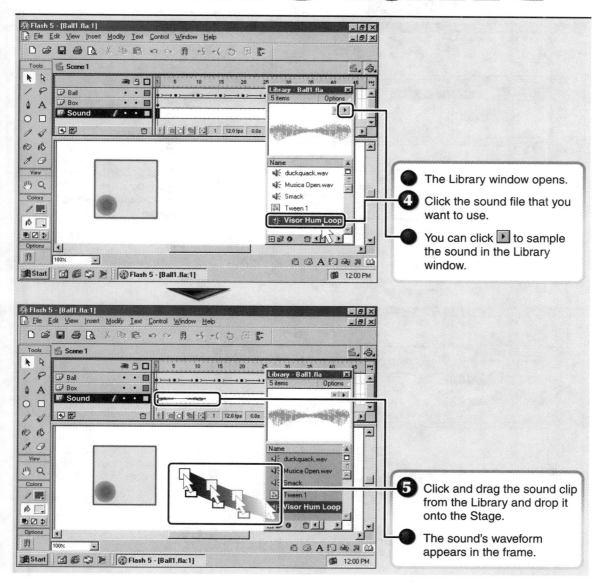

The Library window opens.

4 Click the sound file that you want to use.

You can click ▶ to sample the sound in the Library window.

5 Click and drag the sound clip from the Library and drop it onto the Stage.

The sound's waveform appears in the frame.

ASSIGN SOUNDS TO BUTTONS

You can apply sounds to buttons to help users know how to interact with the buttons or just to give the buttons added flair. For example, you may add a clicking sound that the user hears when he or she clicks the button.

ASSIGN SOUNDS TO BUTTONS

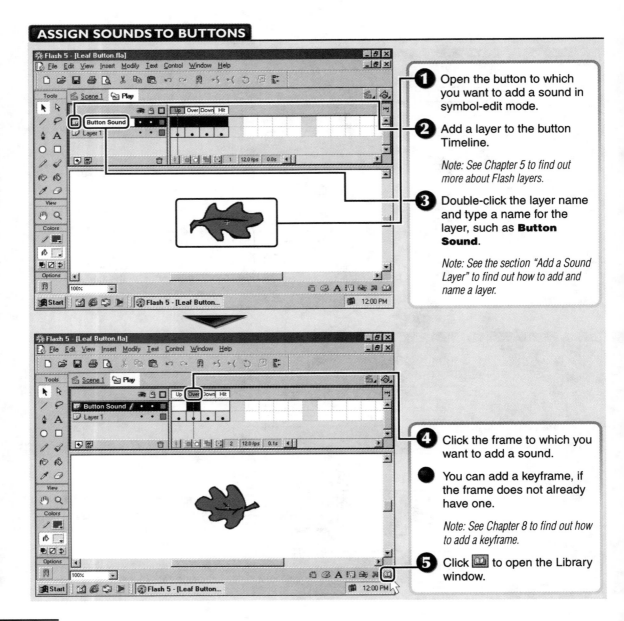

1 Open the button to which you want to add a sound in symbol-edit mode.

2 Add a layer to the button Timeline.

Note: See Chapter 5 to find out more about Flash layers.

3 Double-click the layer name and type a name for the layer, such as **Button Sound**.

Note: See the section "Add a Sound Layer" to find out how to add and name a layer.

4 Click the frame to which you want to add a sound.

● You can add a keyframe, if the frame does not already have one.

Note: See Chapter 8 to find out how to add a keyframe.

5 Click ▦ to open the Library window.

in an *instant*

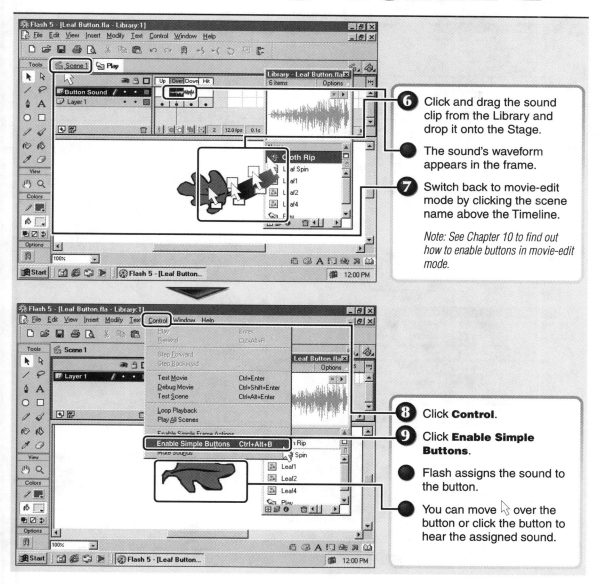

6 Click and drag the sound clip from the Library and drop it onto the Stage.

The sound's waveform appears in the frame.

7 Switch back to movie-edit mode by clicking the scene name above the Timeline.

Note: See Chapter 10 to find out how to enable buttons in movie-edit mode.

8 Click **Control**.

9 Click **Enable Simple Buttons**.

Flash assigns the sound to the button.

You can move ⓚ over the button or click the button to hear the assigned sound.

CREATE EVENT SOUNDS

You can assign event-driven sounds to be triggered by an action in your Flash project. Event sounds play in their entirety and must be completely downloaded before they begin playing. Event sounds also play in their own Timeline. By default, all sounds that you add are treated as event sounds unless you specify another type.

CREATE EVENT SOUNDS

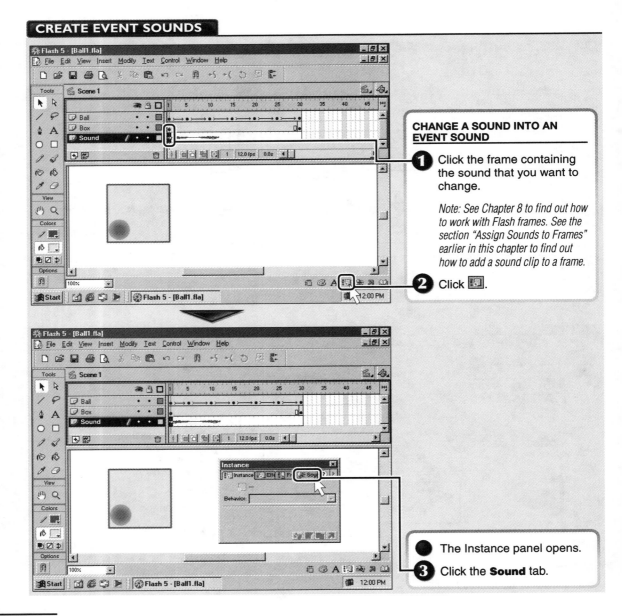

CHANGE A SOUND INTO AN EVENT SOUND

1 Click the frame containing the sound that you want to change.

Note: See Chapter 8 to find out how to work with Flash frames. See the section "Assign Sounds to Frames" earlier in this chapter to find out how to add a sound clip to a frame.

2 Click 🔲.

● The Instance panel opens.

3 Click the **Sound** tab.

in an *instant*

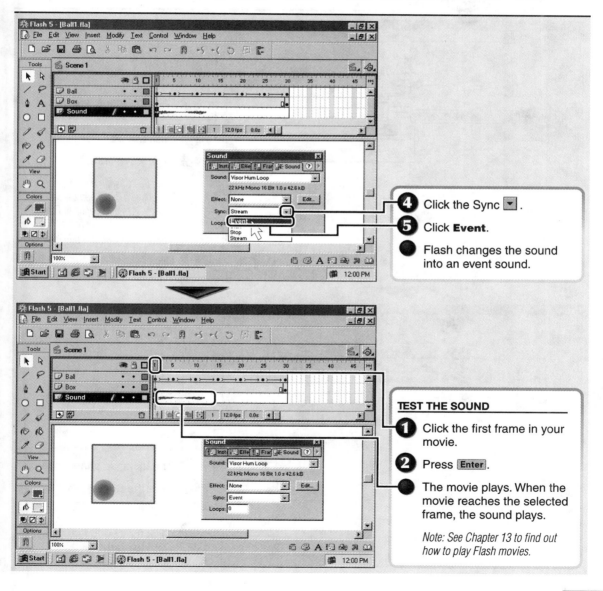

4 Click the Sync ▼.

5 Click **Event**.

● Flash changes the sound into an event sound.

TEST THE SOUND

1 Click the first frame in your movie.

2 Press Enter.

● The movie plays. When the movie reaches the selected frame, the sound plays.

Note: See Chapter 13 to find out how to play Flash movies.

191

ASSIGN START SOUNDS

You can use the Start sound control to start a
new instance of a sound even if it is already
playing from an earlier instance in your movie.
The Start sound command is handy when you
want to synchronize a sound with your animation.

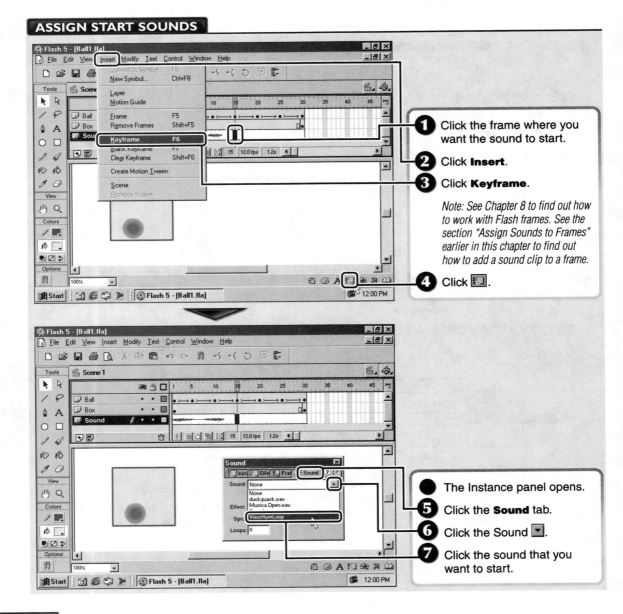

1 Click the frame where you want the sound to start.

2 Click **Insert**.

3 Click **Keyframe**.

Note: See Chapter 8 to find out how to work with Flash frames. See the section "Assign Sounds to Frames" earlier in this chapter to find out how to add a sound clip to a frame.

4 Click ⬚.

● The Instance panel opens.

5 Click the **Sound** tab.

6 Click the Sound ▾.

7 Click the sound that you want to start.

in an *instant*

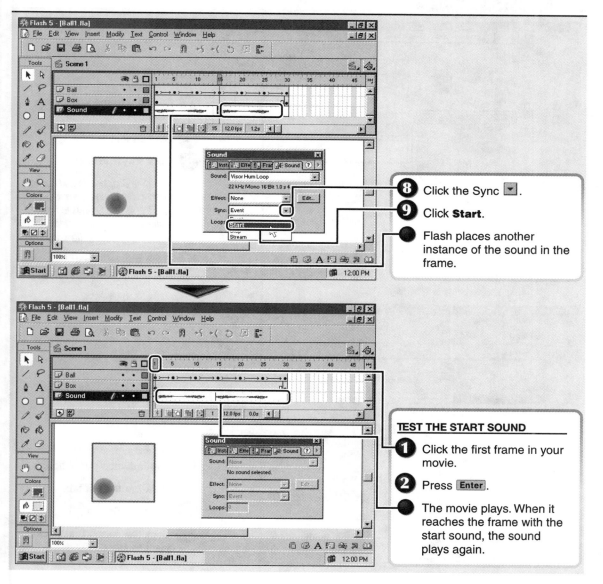

8 Click the Sync ▼.

9 Click **Start**.

● Flash places another instance of the sound in the frame.

TEST THE START SOUND

1 Click the first frame in your movie.

2 Press **Enter**.

● The movie plays. When it reaches the frame with the start sound, the sound plays again.

193

ASSIGN STOP SOUNDS

If you want to stop a sound before it reaches the end, you can insert a Stop sound command. For example, if your animation ends on a particular frame but your sound clip goes on much longer, you can put a Stop command in the frame to end the sound.

ASSIGN STOP SOUNDS

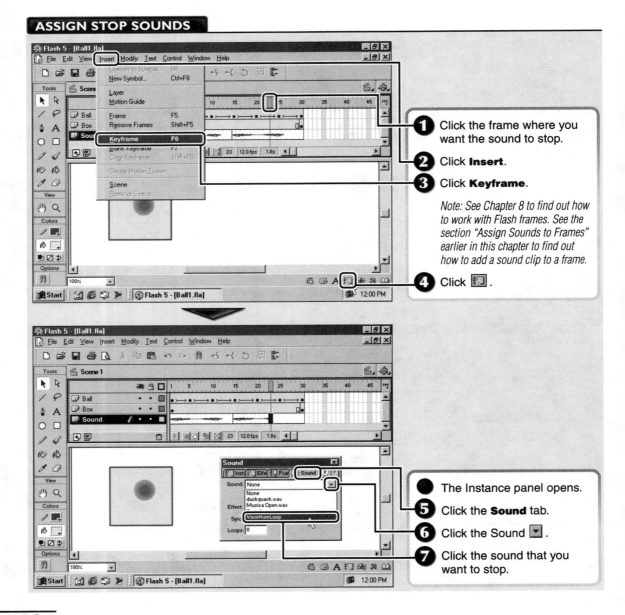

① Click the frame where you want the sound to stop.

② Click **Insert**.

③ Click **Keyframe**.

Note: See Chapter 8 to find out how to work with Flash frames. See the section "Assign Sounds to Frames" earlier in this chapter to find out how to add a sound clip to a frame.

④ Click 🔲.

● The Instance panel opens.

⑤ Click the **Sound** tab.

⑥ Click the Sound 🔽.

⑦ Click the sound that you want to stop.

in an *instant*

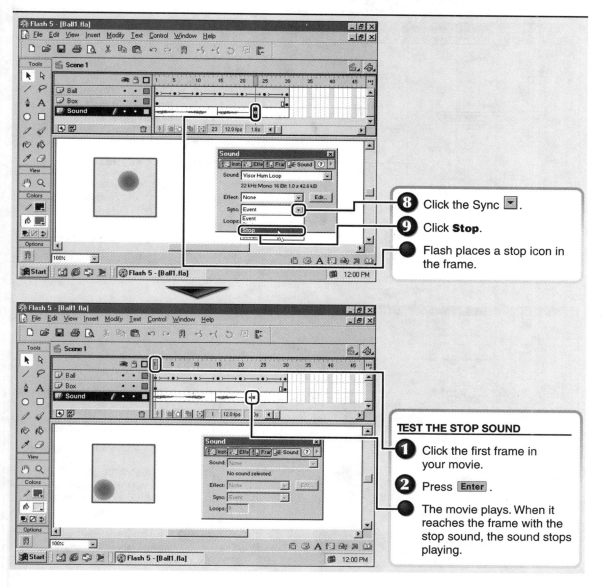

8 Click the Sync ▾.

9 Click **Stop**.

⬤ Flash places a stop icon in the frame.

TEST THE STOP SOUND

1 Click the first frame in your movie.

2 Press **Enter**.

⬤ The movie plays. When it reaches the frame with the stop sound, the sound stops playing.

195

ASSIGN STREAMING SOUNDS

You can use streaming sounds for Flash movies that you place on Web pages. The sound starts streaming as the page downloads, so the user does not have to wait for the entire file to finish downloading. Streaming sounds are good for long sound files, such as a musical sound track.

ASSIGN STREAMING SOUNDS

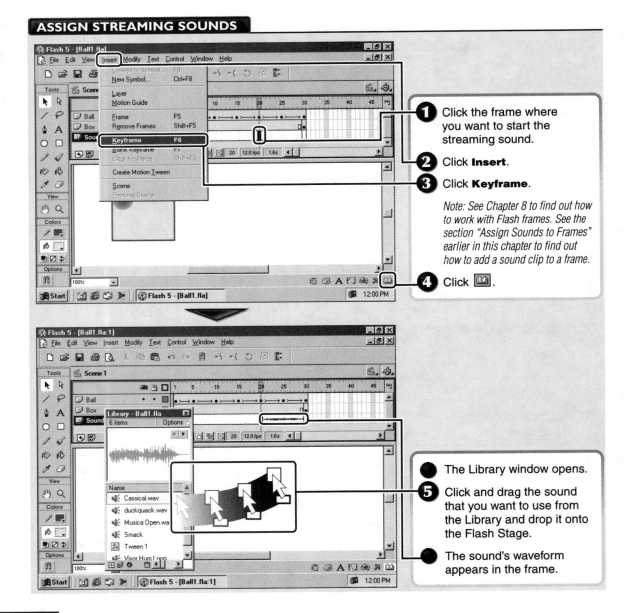

1 Click the frame where you want to start the streaming sound.

2 Click **Insert**.

3 Click **Keyframe**.

Note: See Chapter 8 to find out how to work with Flash frames. See the section "Assign Sounds to Frames" earlier in this chapter to find out how to add a sound clip to a frame.

4 Click 📖.

● The Library window opens.

5 Click and drag the sound that you want to use from the Library and drop it onto the Flash Stage.

● The sound's waveform appears in the frame.

in an instant

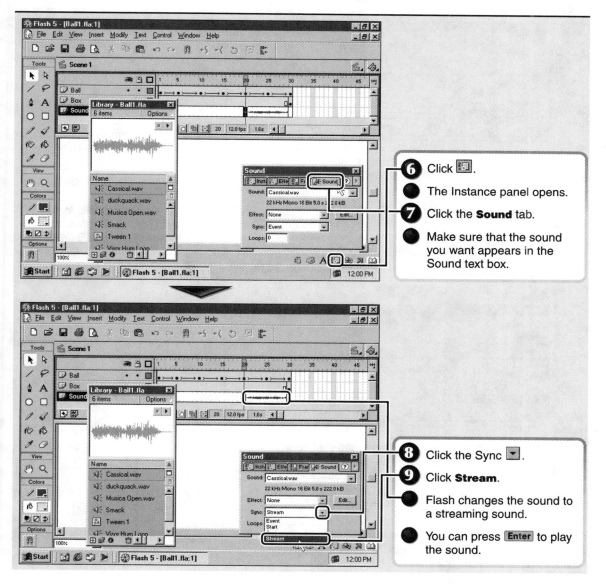

6 Click [icon].

The Instance panel opens.

7 Click the **Sound** tab.

Make sure that the sound you want appears in the Sound text box.

8 Click the Sync [▼].

9 Click **Stream**.

Flash changes the sound to a streaming sound.

You can press **Enter** to play the sound.

SET A LOOPING SOUND

You can make a sound play over and over again with the Loop command. *Looping* means to play the sound repeatedly, as many times as you like.

SET A LOOPING SOUND

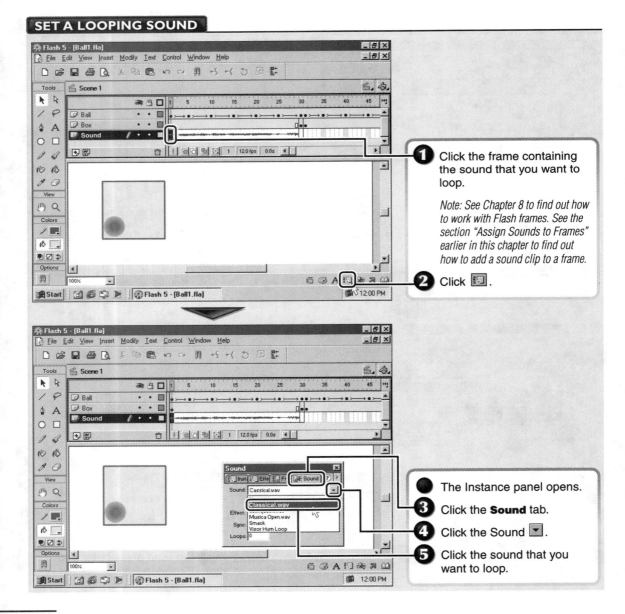

1 Click the frame containing the sound that you want to loop.

Note: See Chapter 8 to find out how to work with Flash frames. See the section "Assign Sounds to Frames" earlier in this chapter to find out how to add a sound clip to a frame.

2 Click.

● The Instance panel opens.

3 Click the **Sound** tab.

4 Click the Sound.

5 Click the sound that you want to loop.

in an instant

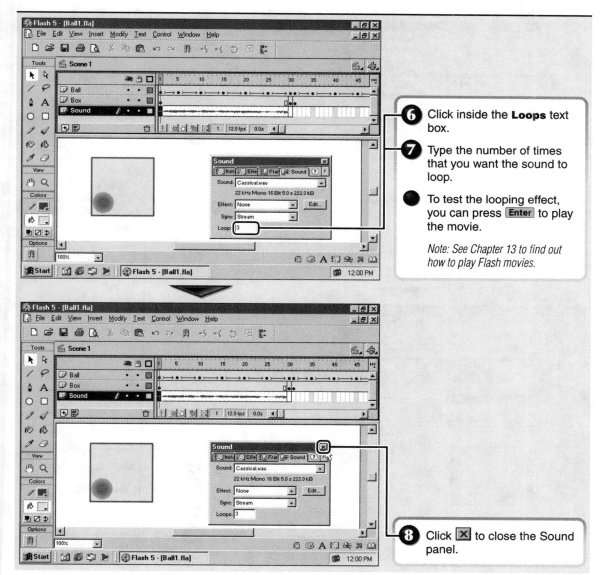

6 Click inside the **Loops** text box.

7 Type the number of times that you want the sound to loop.

● To test the looping effect, you can press **Enter** to play the movie.

Note: See Chapter 13 to find out how to play Flash movies.

8 Click ⊠ to close the Sound panel.

Flash comes with volume controls that you can use to
fade sounds in or out or to make sounds move from
one speaker to another.

EDIT SOUNDS

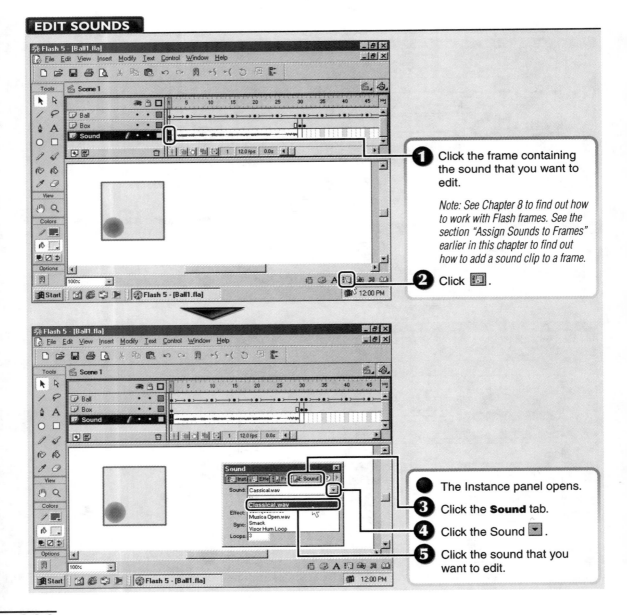

1 Click the frame containing
the sound that you want to
edit.

*Note: See Chapter 8 to find out how
to work with Flash frames. See the
section "Assign Sounds to Frames"
earlier in this chapter to find out
how to add a sound clip to a frame.*

2 Click [].

● The Instance panel opens.

3 Click the **Sound** tab.

4 Click the Sound [].

5 Click the sound that you
want to edit.

in an *instant*

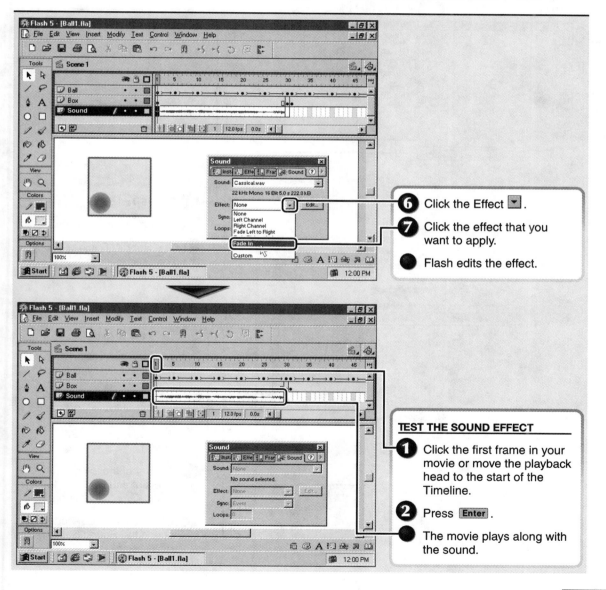

6 Click the Effect ▾.

7 Click the effect that you want to apply.

● Flash edits the effect.

TEST THE SOUND EFFECT

1 Click the first frame in your movie or move the playback head to the start of the Timeline.

2 Press Enter.

● The movie plays along with the sound.

SET AUDIO OUTPUT FOR EXPORT

You can control how sounds are exported in your Flash files. By default, Flash exports sounds in MP3 format at 16Kbps. MP3 is the emerging standard for distributing audio on the Internet.

SET AUDIO OUTPUT FOR EXPORT

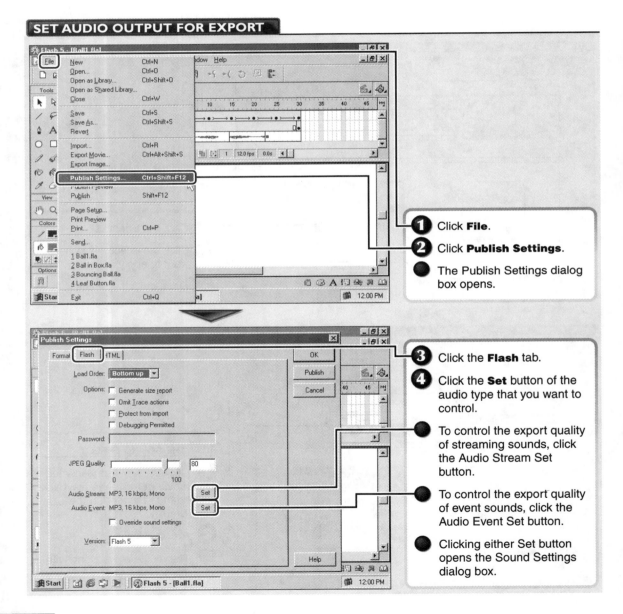

1. Click **File**.

2. Click **Publish Settings**.

● The Publish Settings dialog box opens.

3. Click the **Flash** tab.

4. Click the **Set** button of the audio type that you want to control.

● To control the export quality of streaming sounds, click the Audio Stream Set button.

● To control the export quality of event sounds, click the Audio Event Set button.

● Clicking either Set button opens the Sound Settings dialog box.

in an

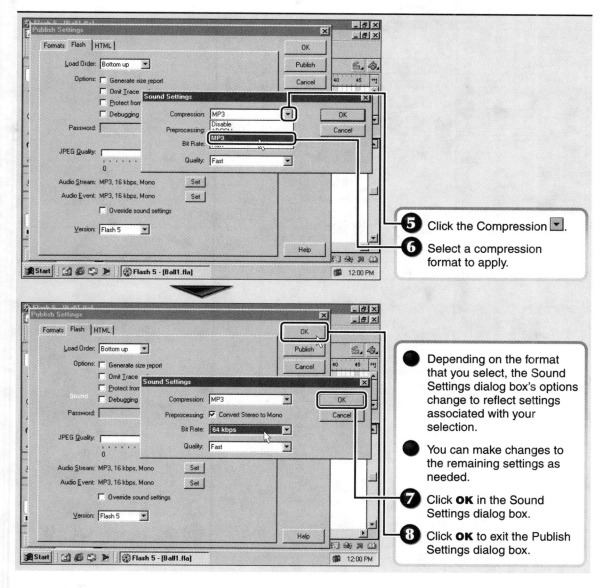

5 Click the Compression ▼.

6 Select a compression format to apply.

● Depending on the format that you select, the Sound Settings dialog box's options change to reflect settings associated with your selection.

● You can make changes to the remaining settings as needed.

7 Click **OK** in the Sound Settings dialog box.

8 Click **OK** to exit the Publish Settings dialog box.

ADD ACTIONS TO FRAMES

Frame actions trigger events that happen at certain points in your movie. You can add actions to your movie by using the Frame Actions box. Frames can include multiple actions, but you can only assign an action one frame at a time. Flash performs the actions in the order that they appear in the list.

ADD ACTIONS TO FRAMES

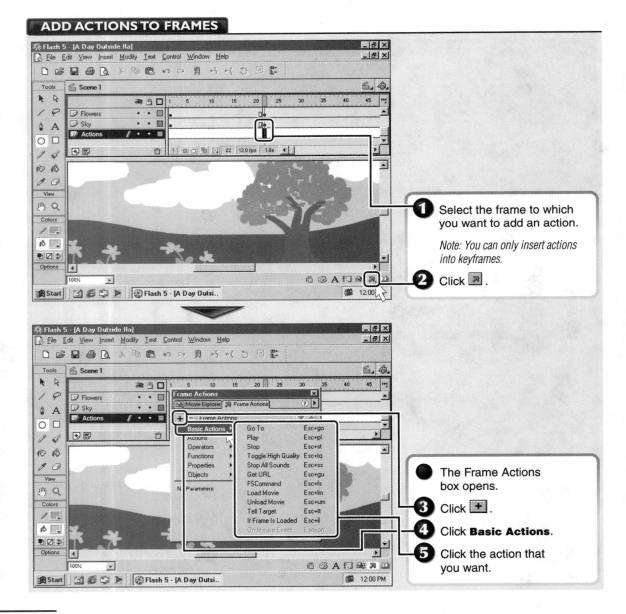

1 Select the frame to which you want to add an action.

Note: You can only insert actions into keyframes.

2 Click 🔊.

● The Frame Actions box opens.

3 Click ➕.

4 Click **Basic Actions**.

5 Click the action that you want.

in an instant

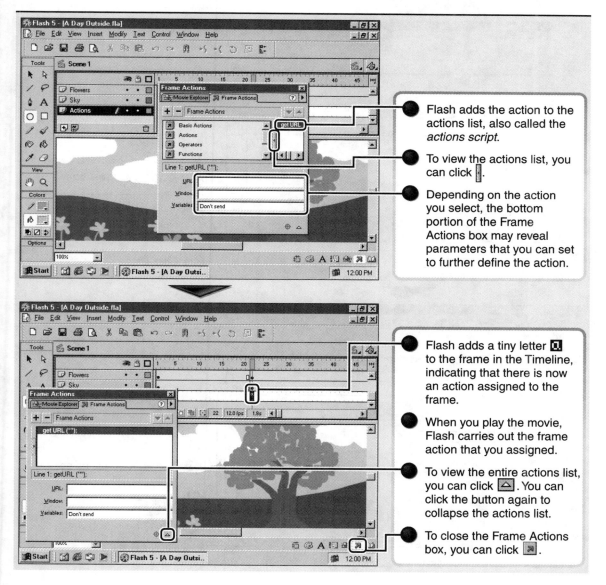

Flash adds the action to the actions list, also called the *actions script*.

To view the actions list, you can click ◄.

Depending on the action you select, the bottom portion of the Frame Actions box may reveal parameters that you can set to further define the action.

Flash adds a tiny letter **a** to the frame in the Timeline, indicating that there is now an action assigned to the frame.

When you play the movie, Flash carries out the frame action that you assigned.

To view the entire actions list, you can click △. You can click the button again to collapse the actions list.

To close the Frame Actions box, you can click ◪.

You can assign a Go To action that tells Flash
to start playing a particular frame in your movie.
The Go To action includes parameters that you
can define to play a specific frame. You can use
the Go To action with frames or buttons.

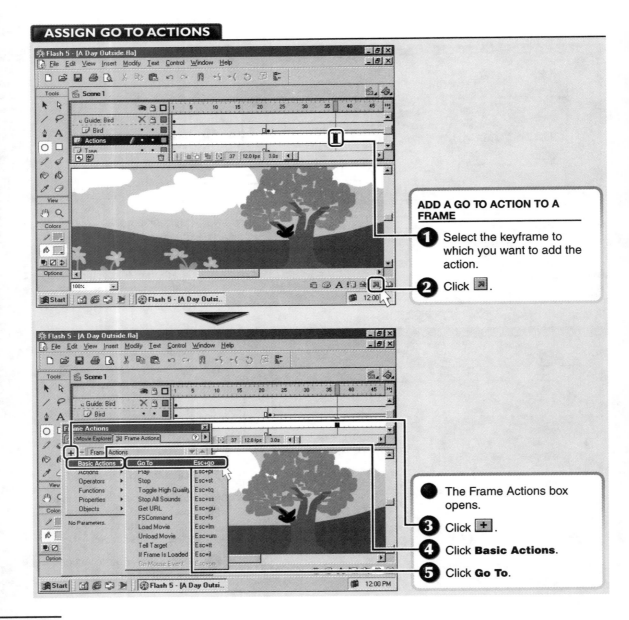

ADD A GO TO ACTION TO A FRAME

1 Select the keyframe to which you want to add the action.

2 Click ⚡.

● The Frame Actions box opens.

3 Click ➕.

4 Click **Basic Actions**.

5 Click **Go To**.

in an *instant*

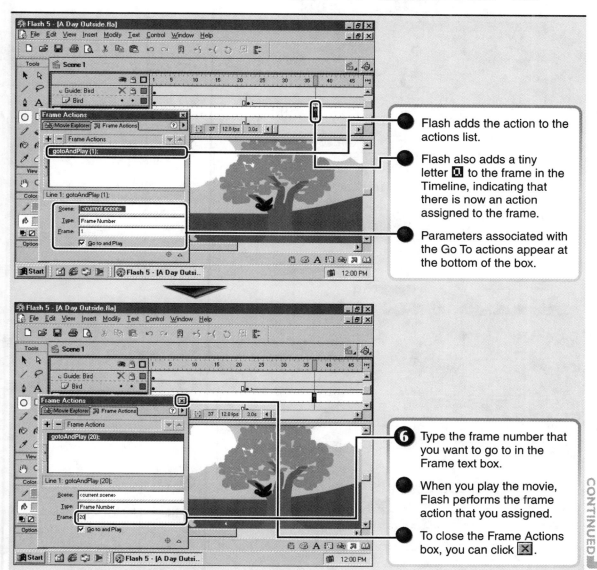

Flash adds the action to the actions list.

Flash also adds a tiny letter **a** to the frame in the Timeline, indicating that there is now an action assigned to the frame.

Parameters associated with the Go To actions appear at the bottom of the box.

6 Type the frame number that you want to go to in the Frame text box.

When you play the movie, Flash performs the frame action that you assigned.

To close the Frame Actions box, you can click ☒.

CONTINUED

ASSIGN GO TO ACTIONS

You can assign a Go To action that references a particular scene. Flash follows the instruction during the course of playing the movie and jumps to the scene that you referenced. If you edit your movie later, such as add or delete frames or entire scenes, be sure to update any Go To actions to reference the correct frames or scenes.

ASSIGN GO TO ACTIONS (CONTINUED)

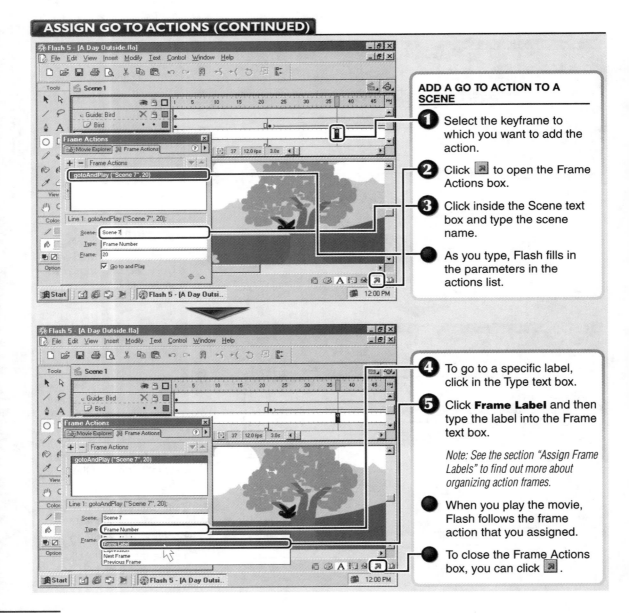

ADD A GO TO ACTION TO A SCENE

1 Select the keyframe to which you want to add the action.

2 Click 🗾 to open the Frame Actions box.

3 Click inside the Scene text box and type the scene name.

● As you type, Flash fills in the parameters in the actions list.

4 To go to a specific label, click in the Type text box.

5 Click **Frame Label** and then type the label into the Frame text box.

Note: See the section "Assign Frame Labels" to find out more about organizing action frames.

● When you play the movie, Flash follows the frame action that you assigned.

● To close the Frame Actions box, you can click 🗾.

in an *instant*

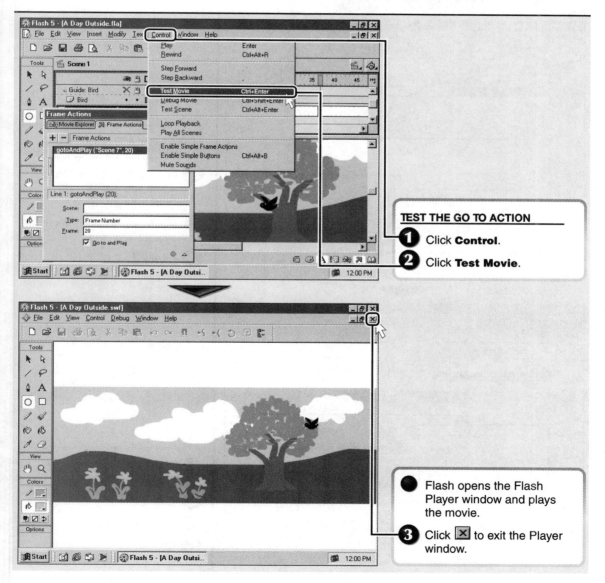

TEST THE GO TO ACTION

1 Click **Control**.

2 Click **Test Movie**.

● Flash opens the Flash Player window and plays the movie.

3 Click ☒ to exit the Player window.

ASSIGN STOP AND PLAY ACTIONS

Stop and Play are two of the most commonly used actions. You can use them for both button actions and frame actions. The Stop and Play actions act much like the Stop and Play controls found on a VCR or CD player.

ASSIGN STOP AND PLAY ACTIONS

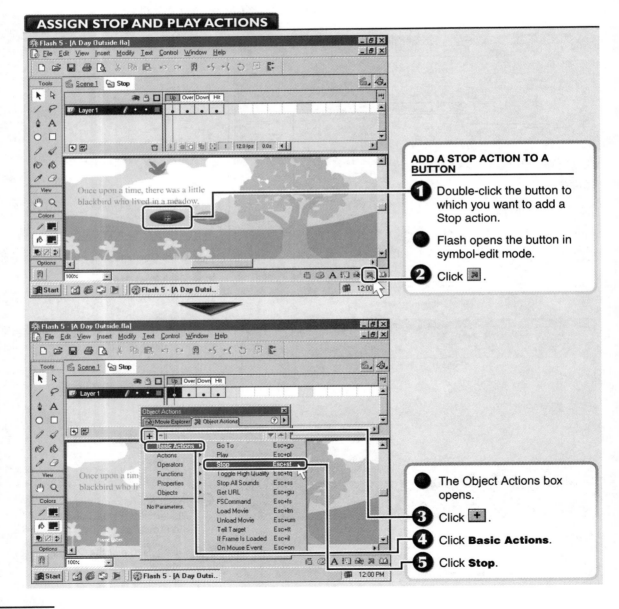

ADD A STOP ACTION TO A BUTTON

1 Double-click the button to which you want to add a Stop action.

● Flash opens the button in symbol-edit mode.

2 Click 🖹.

● The Object Actions box opens.

3 Click ➕.

4 Click **Basic Actions**.

5 Click **Stop**.

in an *instant*

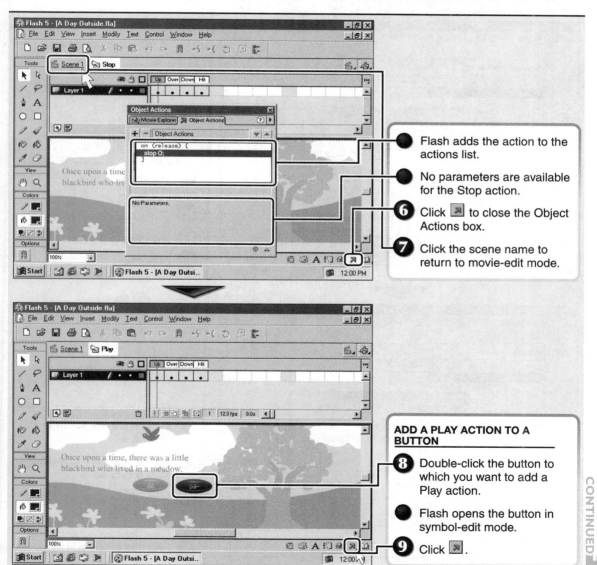

Flash adds the action to the actions list.

No parameters are available for the Stop action.

6 Click 🗿 to close the Object Actions box.

7 Click the scene name to return to movie-edit mode.

ADD A PLAY ACTION TO A BUTTON

8 Double-click the button to which you want to add a Play action.

Flash opens the button in symbol-edit mode.

9 Click 🗿.

CONTINUED

You can assign a Stop action to stop a movie from playing, or you can assign a Play action to play it again.

ASSIGN STOP AND PLAY ACTIONS (CONTINUED)

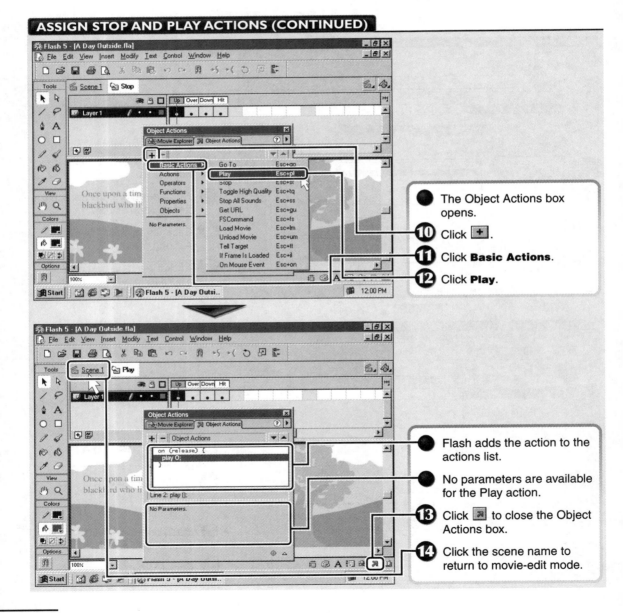

The Object Actions box opens.

⑩ Click ➕.

⑪ Click **Basic Actions**.

⑫ Click **Play**.

Flash adds the action to the actions list.

No parameters are available for the Play action.

⑬ Click 🗗 to close the Object Actions box.

⑭ Click the scene name to return to movie-edit mode.

in an *instant*

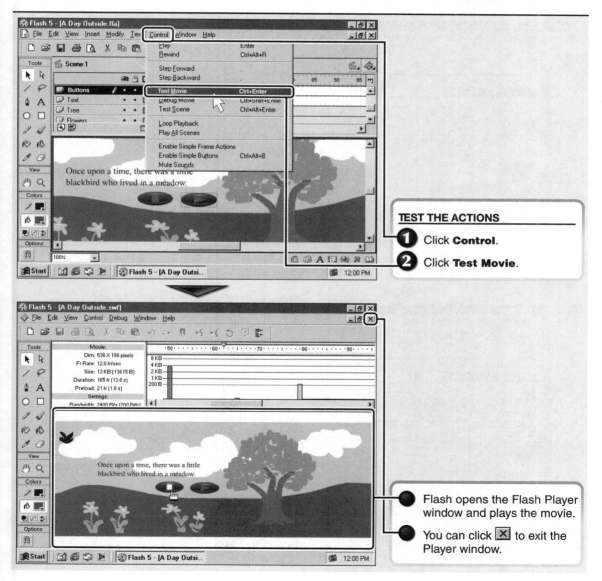

TEST THE ACTIONS

1 Click **Control**.

2 Click **Test Movie**.

● Flash opens the Flash Player window and plays the movie.

● You can click ☒ to exit the Player window.

LOAD A NEW MOVIE

You can use the Load Movie action to start a
movie file within your current movie. The Load
Movie action can replace the current movie with
another that you have previously created or play
the loaded movie on top of the current movie
as if it were another layer.

LOAD A NEW MOVIE

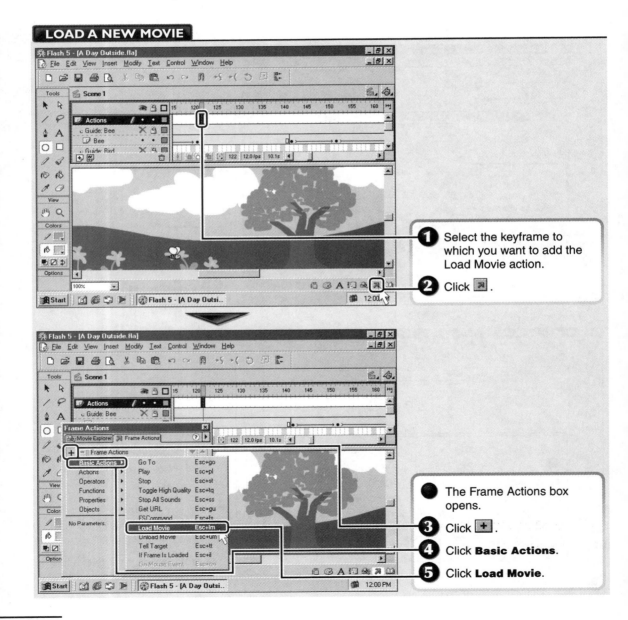

1 Select the keyframe to
which you want to add the
Load Movie action.

2 Click 🗐 .

● The Frame Actions box
opens.

3 Click ➕ .

4 Click **Basic Actions**.

5 Click **Load Movie**.

in an *instant*

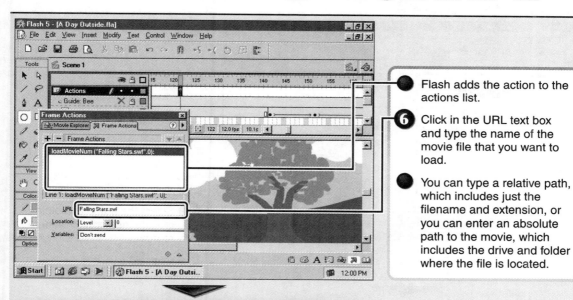

● Flash adds the action to the actions list.

6 Click in the URL text box and type the name of the movie file that you want to load.

● You can type a relative path, which includes just the filename and extension, or you can enter an absolute path to the movie, which includes the drive and folder where the file is located.

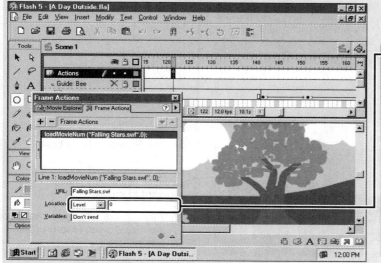

7 Select a location parameter for your movie.

● If you want the new movie to replace the current movie, leave the Location level set to 0.

● To make the new movie play on top of the current movie, type **1** or higher in the Location level text box.

● You can test the action by playing the movie in the Flash Player window.

215

CHANGE ACTION ORDER

When you add more than one action to a frame, Flash executes the actions in the order that they appear in the actions list. You can change the actions list order to reorder the actions as necessary.

CHANGE ACTION ORDER

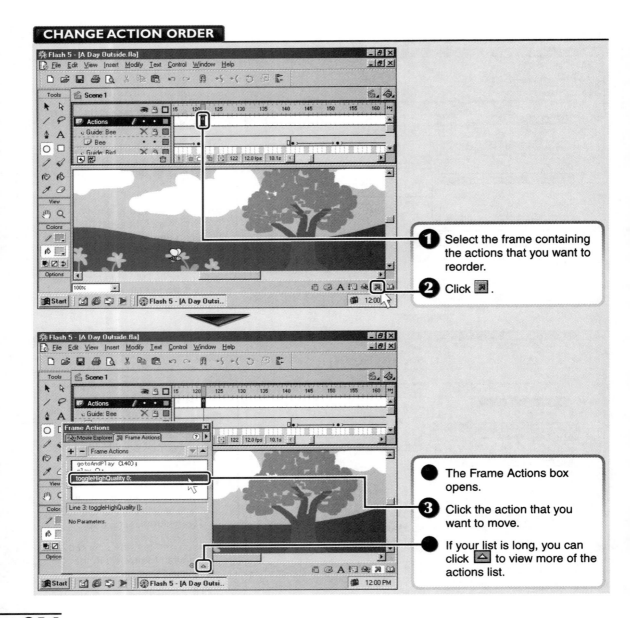

1 Select the frame containing the actions that you want to reorder.

2 Click ⑂.

● The Frame Actions box opens.

3 Click the action that you want to move.

● If your list is long, you can click ▲ to view more of the actions list.

in an *instant*

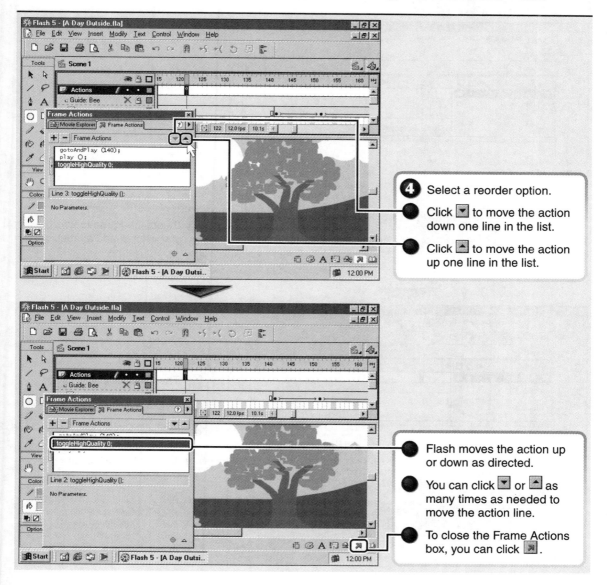

4 Select a reorder option.

● Click ▼ to move the action down one line in the list.

● Click ▲ to move the action up one line in the list.

● Flash moves the action up or down as directed.

● You can click ▼ or ▲ as many times as needed to move the action line.

● To close the Frame Actions box, you can click ▦.

217

ASSIGN FRAME LABELS

You should assign frame labels to keep your frames and actions organized. If you assign a label to a keyframe, the label appears when you move the mouse pointer over the label flag. You can also use the label name in action parameters, such as the Go To action.

ASSIGN FRAME LABELS

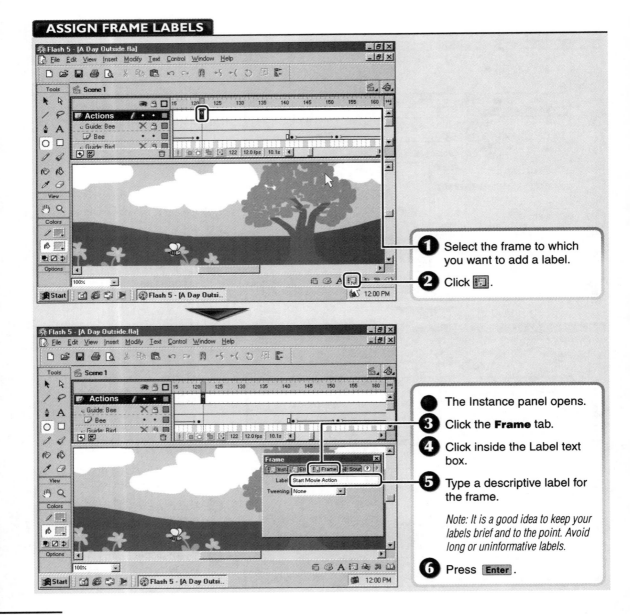

1 Select the frame to which you want to add a label.

2 Click 🔲.

■ The Instance panel opens.

3 Click the **Frame** tab.

4 Click inside the Label text box.

5 Type a descriptive label for the frame.

Note: It is a good idea to keep your labels brief and to the point. Avoid long or uninformative labels.

6 Press Enter.

in an instant

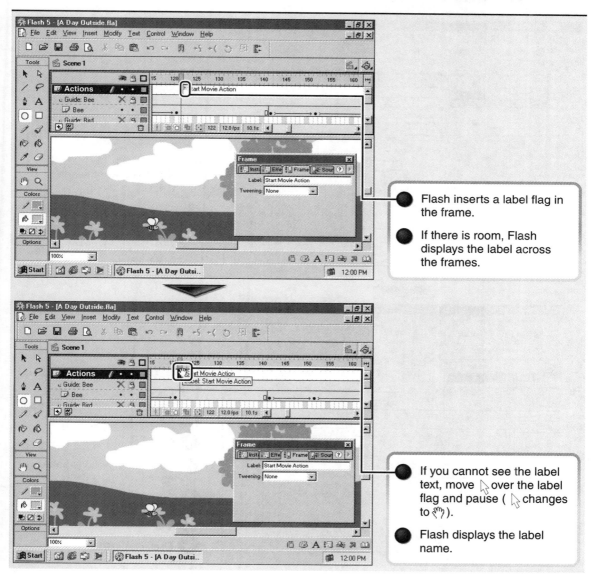

Flash inserts a label flag in
the frame.

If there is room, Flash
displays the label across
the frames.

If you cannot see the label
text, move ⬚ over the label
flag and pause (⬚ changes
to ⟨ᵐᵗ⟩).

Flash displays the label
name.

ASSIGN THE GET URL ACTION

You can use the Get URL action to take users to other files or Web pages. You can also use this action to open a file or movie in a new browser window. For example, you may insert a Get URL action in a standalone Flash Player projector movie, which, when activated, opens a browser window and downloads the specified HTML page.

ASSIGN THE GET URL ACTION

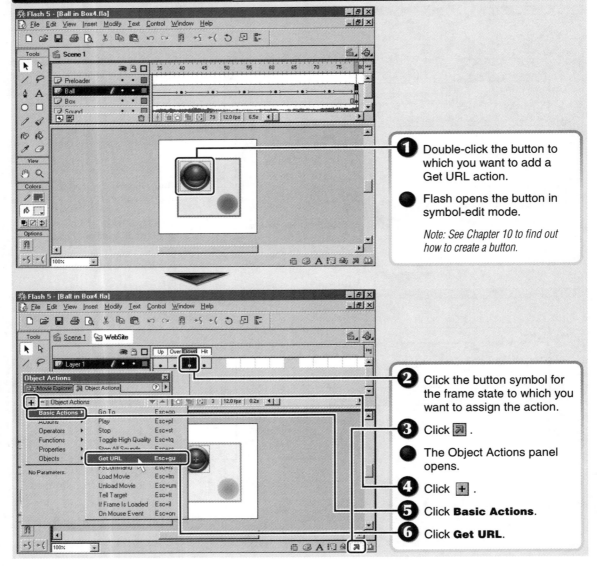

1 Double-click the button to which you want to add a Get URL action.

● Flash opens the button in symbol-edit mode.

Note: See Chapter 10 to find out how to create a button.

2 Click the button symbol for the frame state to which you want to assign the action.

3 Click 🗾 .

● The Object Actions panel opens.

4 Click 🛨 .

5 Click **Basic Actions**.

6 Click **Get URL**.

in an *instant*

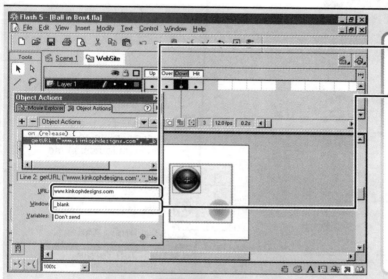

7 Type the name or path of the file that you want to open.

8 Type one of the four targets: `_self`, `_blank`, `_parent`, or `_top`.

Note: `_self` opens the page in the current frame of the current browser window. `_blank` opens the file in a completely new browser window. `_parent` opens the page in the parent of the current browser, and `_top` opens the page in the top-level frame of the current window.

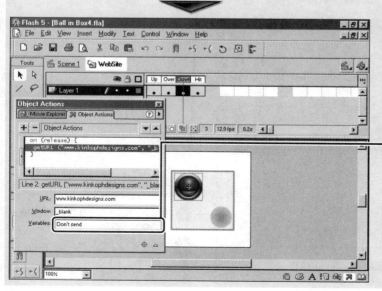

9 Click in the Variables box and select **Don't Send** from the drop-down list if you do not want to pass any variables to the target.

● You can now test the action. When you click the button, Flash loads the URL that you specified.

ASSIGN THE TELL TARGET ACTION

You can use the Tell Target action to control and manipulate the individual Timelines of your movie clips. In other words, you can control the Timelines of movies within your movie without having to assign the action to a specific Timeline. You just have to target the Timeline that you want to control.

ASSIGN THE TELL TARGET ACTION

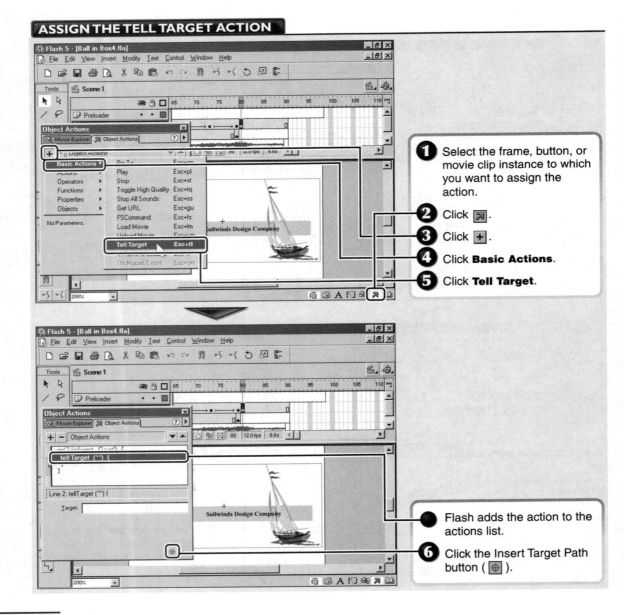

1 Select the frame, button, or movie clip instance to which you want to assign the action.

2 Click ➔.

3 Click ➕.

4 Click **Basic Actions**.

5 Click **Tell Target**.

■ Flash adds the action to the actions list.

6 Click the Insert Target Path button (⊕).

in an *instant*

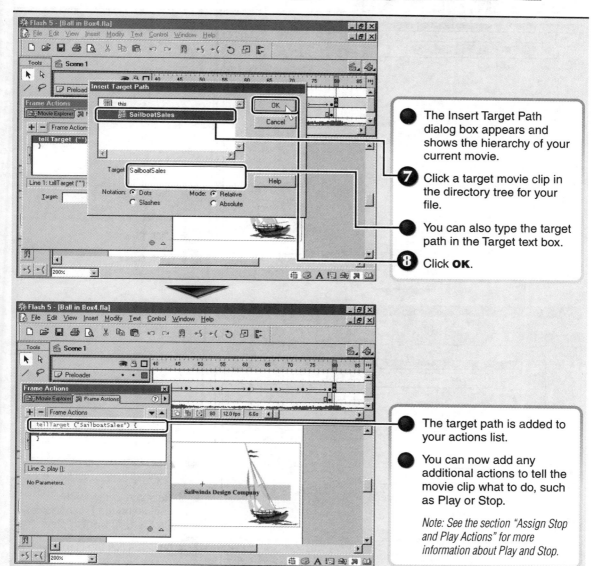

The Insert Target Path dialog box appears and shows the hierarchy of your current movie.

⑦ Click a target movie clip in the directory tree for your file.

You can also type the target path in the Target text box.

⑧ Click **OK**.

The target path is added to your actions list.

You can now add any additional actions to tell the movie clip what to do, such as Play or Stop.

Note: See the section "Assign Stop and Play Actions" for more information about Play and Stop.

PLAY A FLASH MOVIE IN FLASH

You can use the Flash Player to play your Flash movies.
The Flash Player is installed when you install Flash 5
onto your computer.

PLAY A FLASH MOVIE IN FLASH

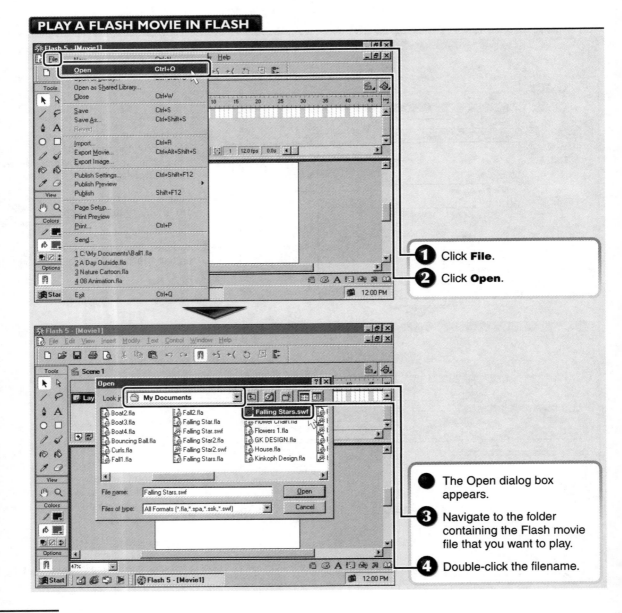

1 Click **File**.

2 Click **Open**.

● The Open dialog box appears.

3 Navigate to the folder containing the Flash movie file that you want to play.

4 Double-click the filename.

in an *instant*

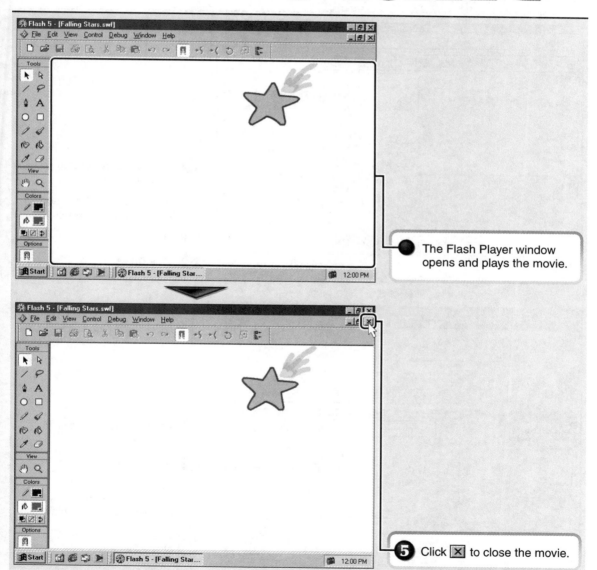

● The Flash Player window opens and plays the movie.

5 Click ✕ to close the movie.

PLAY A FLASH MOVIE IN A BROWSER

You can play a Flash movie using a brower's Flash plug-in. Most browsers, such as Microsoft Internet Explorer and Netscape Navigator, include the Flash Player plug-in program for playing SWF files.

PLAY A FLASH MOVIE IN A BROWSER

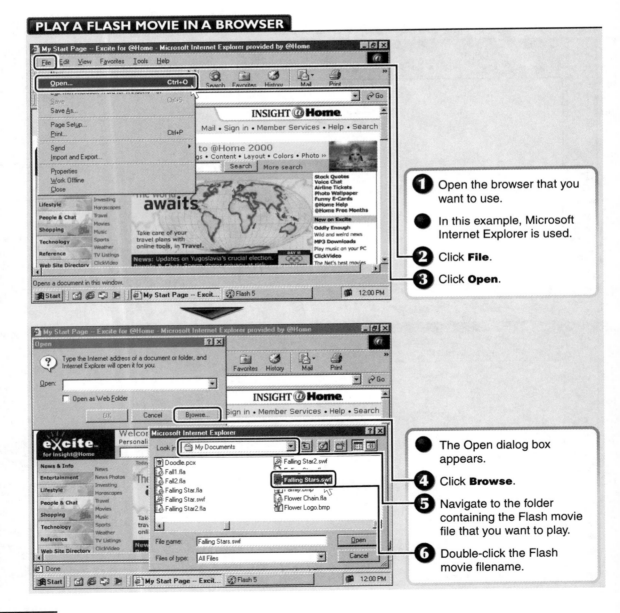

1 Open the browser that you want to use.

■ In this example, Microsoft Internet Explorer is used.

2 Click **File**.

3 Click **Open**.

■ The Open dialog box appears.

4 Click **Browse**.

5 Navigate to the folder containing the Flash movie file that you want to play.

6 Double-click the Flash movie filename.

in an *instant*

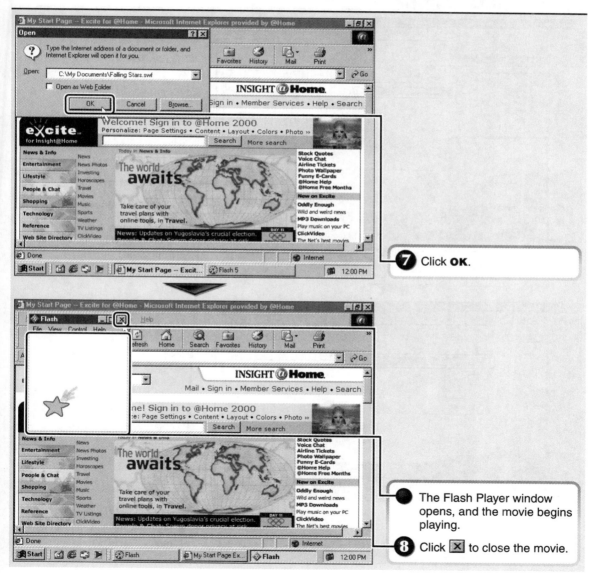

7 Click **OK**.

The Flash Player window opens, and the movie begins playing.

8 Click ☒ to close the movie.

TEST MOVIE BANDWIDTH

You can use the Bandwidth Profiler to help you determine which movie frames may cause problems during playback on the Web. You can test six different modem speeds and gauge which frames use the most bytes to see exactly where your movie may slow down during playback.

TEST MOVIE BANDWIDTH

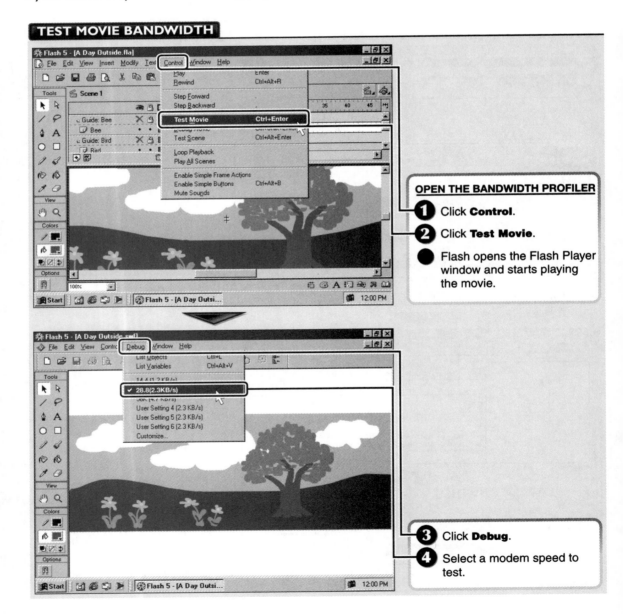

OPEN THE BANDWIDTH PROFILER

1 Click **Control**.

2 Click **Test Movie**.

● Flash opens the Flash Player window and starts playing the movie.

3 Click **Debug**.

4 Select a modem speed to test.

in an instant

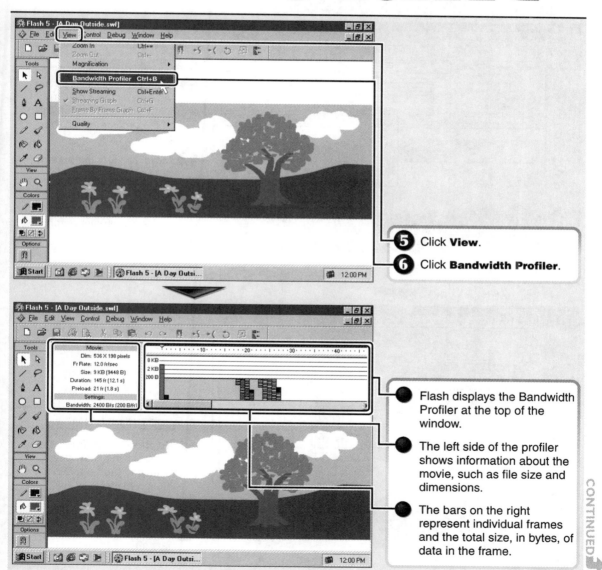

5 Click **View**.

6 Click **Bandwidth Profiler**.

● Flash displays the Bandwidth Profiler at the top of the window.

● The left side of the profiler shows information about the movie, such as file size and dimensions.

● The bars on the right represent individual frames and the total size, in bytes, of data in the frame.

CONTINUED

TEST MOVIE BANDWIDTH

You can use a Streaming Graph or Frame by Frame Graph to see how your frames play. In Streaming Graph mode, the width of each bar shows how long it takes the frame to download. In Frame by Frame Graph mode, when the frame bar extends above the red graph line, the movie will pause to download the frame.

TEST MOVIE BANDWIDTH (CONTINUED)

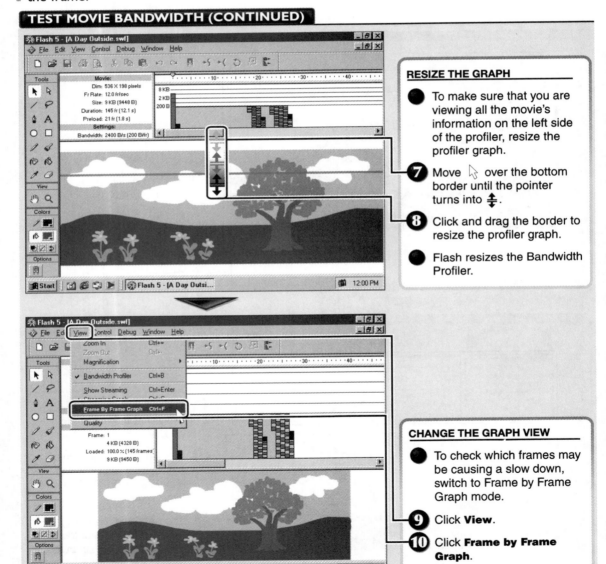

RESIZE THE GRAPH

To make sure that you are viewing all the movie's information on the left side of the profiler, resize the profiler graph.

7 Move ⬉ over the bottom border until the pointer turns into ⬍.

8 Click and drag the border to resize the profiler graph.

Flash resizes the Bandwidth Profiler.

CHANGE THE GRAPH VIEW

To check which frames may be causing a slow down, switch to Frame by Frame Graph mode.

9 Click **View**.

10 Click **Frame by Frame Graph**.

in an *instant*

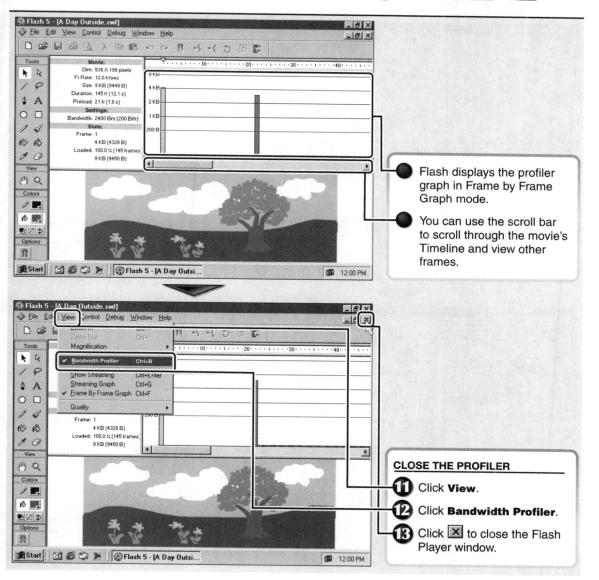

Flash displays the profiler graph in Frame by Frame Graph mode.

You can use the scroll bar to scroll through the movie's Timeline and view other frames.

CLOSE THE PROFILER

⑪ Click **View**.

⑫ Click **Bandwidth Profiler**.

⑬ Click ☒ to close the Flash Player window.

PUBLISH A MOVIE

You use two phases to publish your Flash movie.
First, you prepare the files for publishing by using
the Publish Settings dialog box. Then, you publish
the movie by using the Publish command. By
default, Flash is set up to publish your movie as
an SWF file for the Web.

PUBLISH A MOVIE

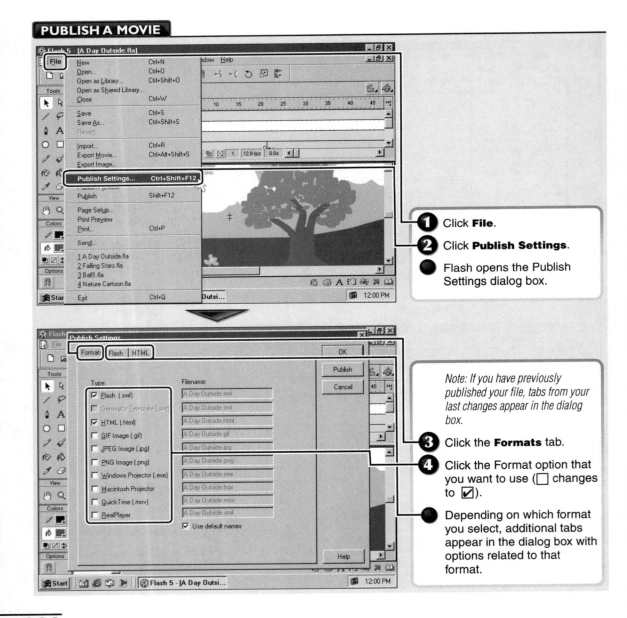

1 Click **File**.

2 Click **Publish Settings**.

● Flash opens the Publish Settings dialog box.

Note: If you have previously published your file, tabs from your last changes appear in the dialog box.

3 Click the **Formats** tab.

4 Click the Format option that you want to use (☐ changes to ☑).

● Depending on which format you select, additional tabs appear in the dialog box with options related to that format.

in an *instant*

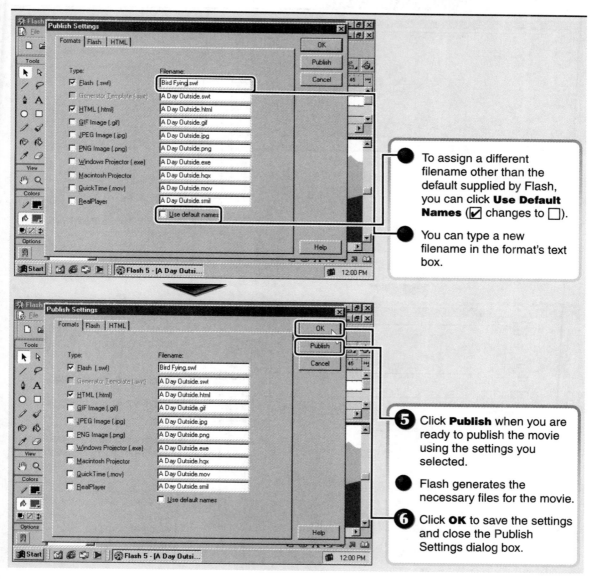

To assign a different filename other than the default supplied by Flash, you can click **Use Default Names** (☑ changes to ☐).

You can type a new filename in the format's text box.

5 Click **Publish** when you are ready to publish the movie using the settings you selected.

Flash generates the necessary files for the movie.

6 Click **OK** to save the settings and close the Publish Settings dialog box.

PUBLISH A MOVIE IN HTML FORMAT

You can save a movie in HTML format. Flash generates all
the necessary HTML code for you, including the tags needed
to view your page in both Microsoft Internet Explorer and
Netscape Navigator. You can then upload the HTML document
to your Web server.

PUBLISH A MOVIE IN HTML FORMAT

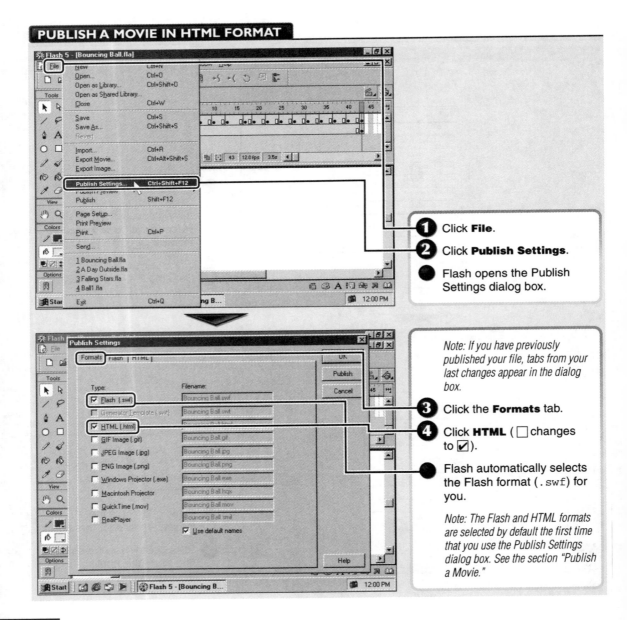

1 Click **File**.

2 Click **Publish Settings**.

● Flash opens the Publish Settings dialog box.

Note: If you have previously published your file, tabs from your last changes appear in the dialog box.

3 Click the **Formats** tab.

4 Click **HTML** (☐ changes to ☑).

● Flash automatically selects the Flash format (`.swf`) for you.

Note: The Flash and HTML formats are selected by default the first time that you use the Publish Settings dialog box. See the section "Publish a Movie."

in an *instant*

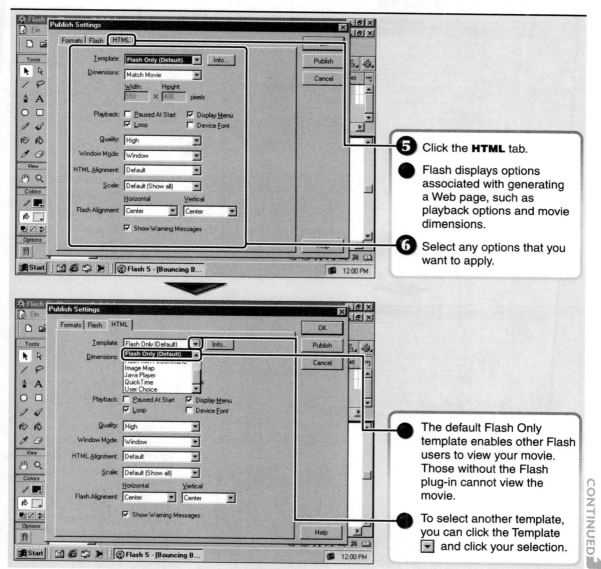

5 Click the **HTML** tab.

● Flash displays options associated with generating a Web page, such as playback options and movie dimensions.

6 Select any options that you want to apply.

● The default Flash Only template enables other Flash users to view your movie. Those without the Flash plug-in cannot view the movie.

● To select another template, you can click the Template ▾ and click your selection.

CONTINUED

You can use the options in the Publish Settings dialog box to specify exactly how you want your movie to appear in a browser. You can set alignment, dimensions, and playback options. Any changes that you make to the settings will override any previous settings for the file.

PUBLISH A MOVIE IN HTML FORMAT (CONTINUED)

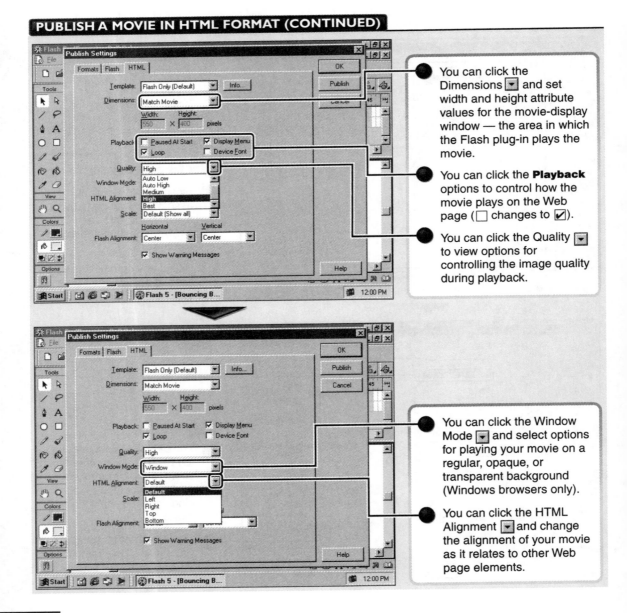

You can click the Dimensions ▼ and set width and height attribute values for the movie-display window — the area in which the Flash plug-in plays the movie.

You can click the **Playback** options to control how the movie plays on the Web page (☐ changes to ☑).

You can click the Quality ▼ to view options for controlling the image quality during playback.

You can click the Window Mode ▼ and select options for playing your movie on a regular, opaque, or transparent background (Windows browsers only).

You can click the HTML Alignment ▼ and change the alignment of your movie as it relates to other Web page elements.

in an *instant*

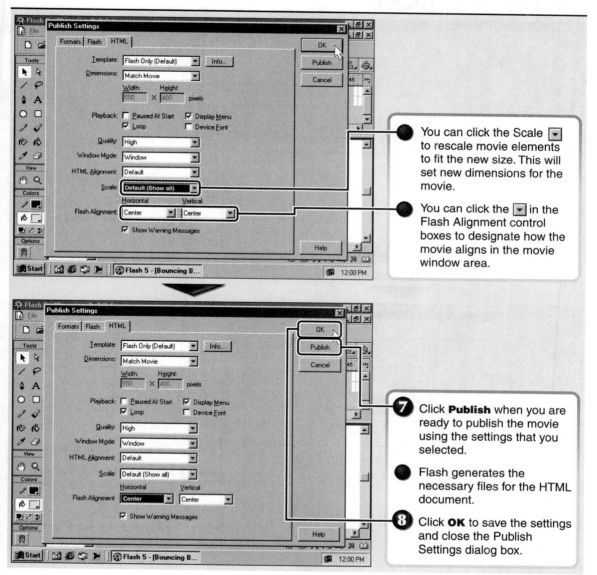

You can click the Scale ▼ to rescale movie elements to fit the new size. This will set new dimensions for the movie.

You can click the ▼ in the Flash Alignment control boxes to designate how the movie aligns in the movie window area.

7 Click **Publish** when you are ready to publish the movie using the settings that you selected.

Flash generates the necessary files for the HTML document.

8 Click **OK** to save the settings and close the Publish Settings dialog box.

CREATE A FLASH PROJECTOR

You can create a Flash movie that plays in its own Flash Player window without requiring anyone to install the Flash Player. When you publish the movie with a Windows Projector or Macintosh Projector format, Flash publishes the movie as an executable file (.exe).

CREATE A FLASH PROJECTOR

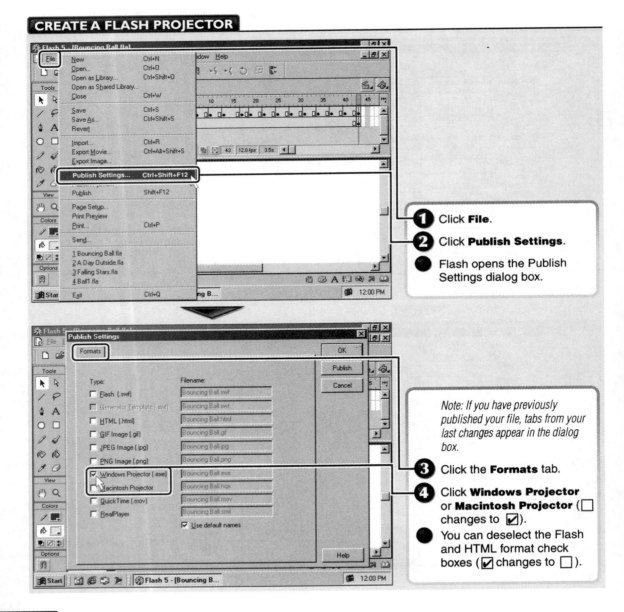

① Click **File**.

② Click **Publish Settings**.

● Flash opens the Publish Settings dialog box.

Note: If you have previously published your file, tabs from your last changes appear in the dialog box.

③ Click the **Formats** tab.

④ Click **Windows Projector** or **Macintosh Projector** (☐ changes to ☑).

● You can deselect the Flash and HTML format check boxes (☑ changes to ☐).

in an *instant*

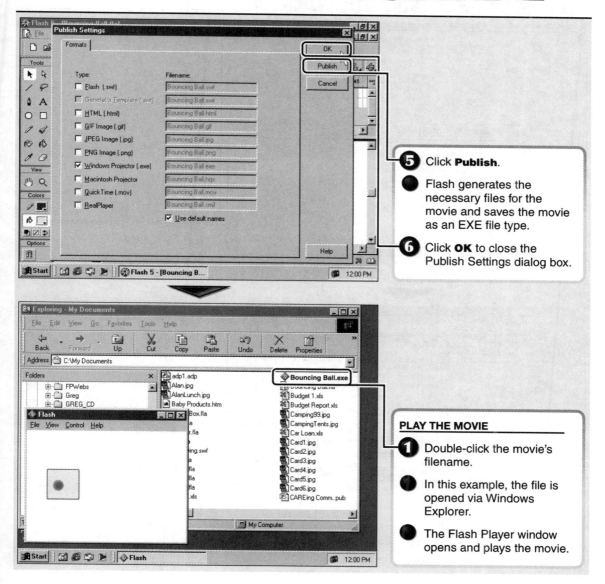

5 Click **Publish**.

● Flash generates the necessary files for the movie and saves the movie as an EXE file type.

6 Click **OK** to close the Publish Settings dialog box.

PLAY THE MOVIE

1 Double-click the movie's filename.

● In this example, the file is opened via Windows Explorer.

● The Flash Player window opens and plays the movie.

You can easily export a Flash movie to another file format
for use with other applications. For example, you may save
your movie as a Windows AVI file or as a QuickTime file.

EXPORT A FLASH MOVIE TO ANOTHER FORMAT

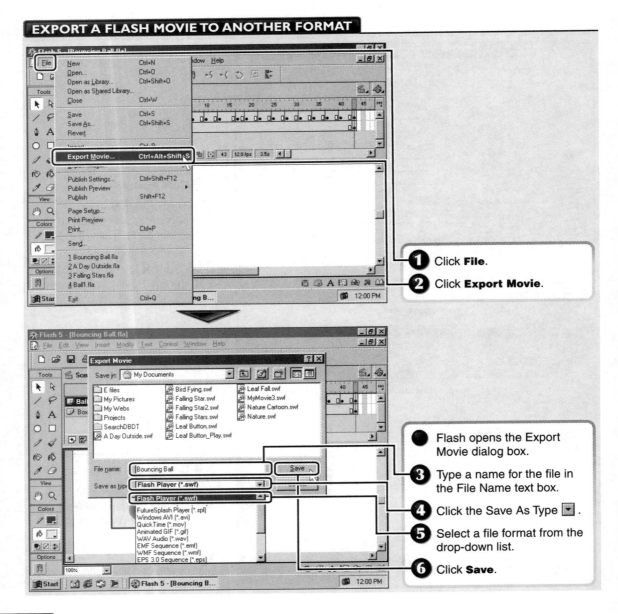

1 Click **File**.

2 Click **Export Movie**.

■ Flash opens the Export
Movie dialog box.

3 Type a name for the file in
the File Name text box.

4 Click the Save As Type ▾.

5 Select a file format from the
drop-down list.

6 Click **Save**.

in an *instant*

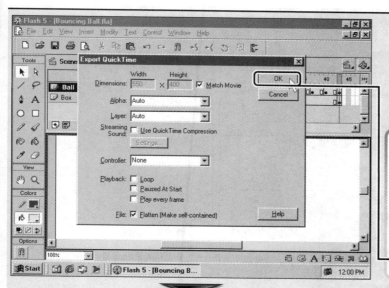

- Depending on the file type that you selected, an additional Export dialog box opens with options for size, sound, and video format.

- You can make any selections necessary.

7 Click **OK**.

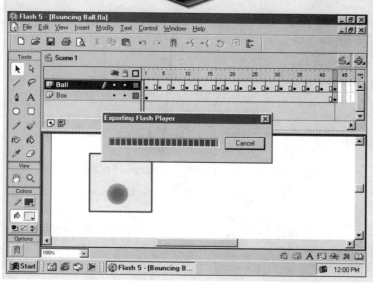

- Flash exports the movie to the designated file type.

- Depending on the file type, another dialog box, such as the Video Compression dialog box, may open first. Make any selections necessary and click **OK**.

Note: Interactive elements that you include in your Flash movies may not export to other file formats properly.

PRINT MOVIE FRAMES

Some of your Flash projects may require you to print
out a frame or series of frames. For example, you
may print out frame content to show a storyboard of
a movie. You can use the Page Setup dialog box to
specify a layout for the storyboard and then use the
Print dialog box to specify which pages to print.

PRINT MOVIE FRAMES

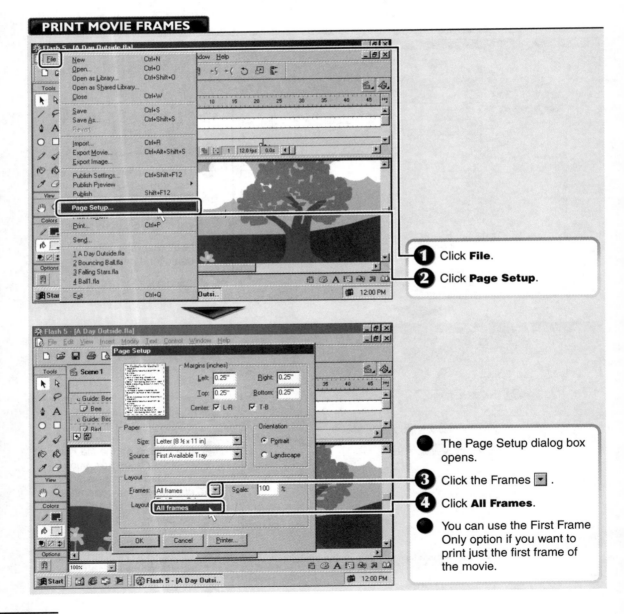

1 Click **File**.

2 Click **Page Setup**.

● The Page Setup dialog box
opens.

3 Click the Frames ▼ .

4 Click **All Frames**.

● You can use the First Frame
Only option if you want to
print just the first frame of
the movie.

in an instant

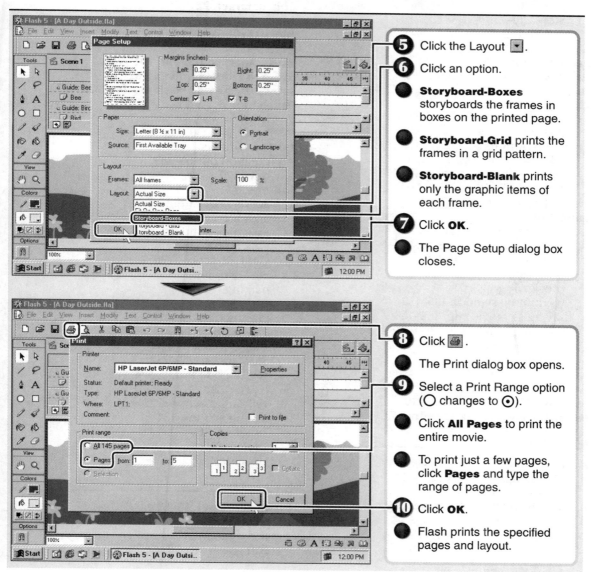

5 Click the Layout ▾.

6 Click an option.

● **Storyboard-Boxes** storyboards the frames in boxes on the printed page.

● **Storyboard-Grid** prints the frames in a grid pattern.

● **Storyboard-Blank** prints only the graphic items of each frame.

7 Click **OK**.

● The Page Setup dialog box closes.

8 Click 🖨.

● The Print dialog box opens.

9 Select a Print Range option (○ changes to ⊙).

● Click **All Pages** to print the entire movie.

● To print just a few pages, click **Pages** and type the range of pages.

10 Click **OK**.

● Flash prints the specified pages and layout.

INDEX

INDEX

INDEX

INDEX

INDEX

Other Visual Series That Help You
Read Less - Learn More™

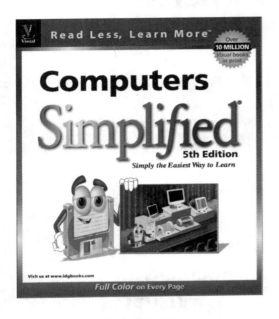

Simplified®

Teach Yourself VISUALLY™

Master VISUALLY™

Visual Blueprint

Available wherever books are sold